D0713028

Bloom's Modern Critical Interpretations

William Shakespeare's
A Midsummer Night's Dream
New Edition

Edited and with an introduction by
Harold Bloom
Sterling Professor of the Humanities
Yale University

BLOOM'S
LITERARY CRITICISM
An imprint of Infobase Publishing

Bloom's Modern Critical Interpretations: A Midsummer Night's Dream—New Edition
Copyright © 2010 by Infobase Publishing
Introduction © 2010 by Harold Bloom

Bloom's Literary Criticism
An imprint of Infobase Publishing
132 West 31st Street
New York NY 10001

Library of Congress Cataloging-in-Publication Data
William Shakespeare's A midsummer night's dream / edited and with an introduction by Harold Bloom. — New ed.
     p. cm.— (Bloom's modern critical interpretations)
  Includes bibliographical references and index.
  ISBN 978-1-60413-817-7 (alk. paper)
  1. Shakespeare, William, 1564–1616. Midsummer night's dream. I. Bloom, Harold.
  II. Title: Midsummer night's dream.
  PR2827.W54 2010
  822.3'3—dc22
                              2009043772

Bloom's Literary Criticism books are available at special discounts when purchased in bulk quantities for businesses, associations, institutions, or sales promotions. Please call our Special Sales Department in New York at (212)967-8800 or (800)322-8755.

You can find Chelsea House on the World Wide Web at
http://www.chelseahouse.com

Contributing editor: Pamela Loos
Cover design by Alicia Post
Composition by IBT Global, Troy NY
Cover printed by IBT Global, Troy NY
Book printed and bound by IBT Global, Troy NY
Date printed: March 2010
Printed in the United States of America

10 9 8 7 6 5 4 3 2 1

This book is printed on acid-free paper.

Contents

Editor's Note

My introduction takes up what I see as the work's two essential presences: the cheerfully amoral Puck and the most original figure, Bottom, who, as his name suggests, functions as the core of the play.

René Girard also examines the contributions of Bottom, a consummate actor and the play's reigning artistic temperament, while William W. E. Slights turns his attention to the changeling, the child referred to but never seen who embodies the indeterminacy of Shakespeare's text.

Jay L. Halio meditates on the play's verbal inconsistencies, followed by James L. Calderwood's exploration of *Midsummer's* anamorphic doubling, the forest setting serving as a distorted reflection of the more orderly Athenian world that lies beyond.

David Wiles views the work as an extended epithalamium, preoccupied with consummating and legitimizing the young couples' love. He is followed by Stanley Wells, who similarly regards the play in terms of translation, change, and nuptial transition.

The poet W. H. Auden sees the play as Shakespeare's first sustained engagement of the social and natural orders, while Kenneth Burke explores the play's courtly psychosis, the social stratification and divisions that would have held particular relevance to Elizabethan audiences.

The volume concludes with the fairy feminism of Regina Buccola, who assigns the power of action and resolution to the play's female characters.

HAROLD BLOOM

Introduction

On the loftiest of the world's thrones we still are sitting only
on our own Bottom.

—Montaigne, "On Experience"

I will get Peter Quince to write a ballet of this dream. It shall
be call'd "Bottom's Dream," because it hath no bottom.

I

I wish Shakespeare had given us Peter Quince's ballet (ballad), but he may
have been too wise to attempt the poem. *A Midsummer Night's Dream,* for
me, is Puck and Bottom, and I prefer Bottom. Perhaps we reduce to Puckish
individuals or Bottoms. Pucks are more charming, but Bottoms are rather
more amiable. Shakespeare's Bottom is surpassingly amiable, and I agree
with Northrop Frye that Bottom is the only mortal with experience of the
visionary center of the play. As the possible lover (however briefly) of the
Fairy Queen, Bottom remains a lasting reproach to our contemporary fashion of importing sacred violence, bestiality, and all manner of sexual antics
into Shakespeare's most fragile of visionary dramas. For who could be more
mild mannered, better natured, or sweetly humorous than the unfailingly
gentle Bottom? Titania ends up despising him, but he is simply too good
for her!

Bottom, when we first encounter him, is already a Malaprop, inaccurate
at the circumference, as it were, but sound at the core, which is what his
name means, the center of the skein on which a weaver's wool is wound. And
surely that is his function in the play; he is its core, and also he is the most

1

original figure in *A Midsummer Night's Dream*. Self-assertive, silly, ignorant, he remains a personage of absolute good will, a kind of remote ancestor to Joyce's amiable Poldy. Transformed into an outward monstrosity by Puck, he yet retains his courage, kindness, and humor and goes through his uncanny experience totally unchanged within. His initial dialogue with Titania is deliciously ironic, and he himself is in full control of the irony:

> TITANIA: I pray thee, gentle mortal, sing again.
>   Mine ear is much enamored of thy note;
>   So is mine eye enthralled to thy shape;
>   And they fair virtue's force (perforce) doth move me
>   On the first view to say, to swear, I love thee.
> BOTTOM: Methinks, mistress, you should have little reason
>   for that. And yet, to say the truth, reason and love
>   keep little company together now-a-days. The more
>   the pity that some honest neighbors will not make
>   them friends. Nay, I can gleek upon occasion.
> TITANIA: Thou art as wise as thou art beautiful.
> BOTTOM: Not so, neither; but if I had wit enough to get out
>   of this wood, I have enough to serve mine own turn.

Knowing that he lacks both beauty and wisdom, Bottom is realistic enough to see that the fairy queen is beautiful but not wise. Charmed by (and charming to) the elf foursome of Peaseblossom, Cobweb, Moth, and Mustardseed, Bottom makes us aware that they mean no more and no less to him than Titania does. Whether or not he has made love to Titania, a subject of some nasty debate among our critical contemporaries, seems to me quite irrelevant. What does matter is that he is sublimely unchanged, for worse or for better, when he wakes up from his bottomless dream:

> BOTTOM: [*Awaking.*] When my cue comes, call me, and I will
>   answer. My next is, "Most fair Pyramus." Heigh-ho!
>   Peter Quince! Flute the bellowsmender! Snout
>   the tinker! Starveling! God's my life, stol'n
>   hence, and left me asleep! I have had a most rare
>   vision. I have had a dream, past the wit of man to
>   say what dream it was. Man is but an ass, if he go
>   about t'expound this dream. Methought I was—there
>   is no man can tell what. Methought I was, and
>   methought I had,—but man is but a patch'd fool, if
>   he will offer to say what methought I had. The eye

of man hath not heard, the ear of man hath not
seen, man's hand is not able to taste, his tongue
to conceive, nor his heart to report, what my dream
was. I will get Peter Quince to write a ballet of
this dream: it shall be called "Bottom's Dream,"
because it hath no bottom; and I will sing it in the
latter end of a play, before the Duke. Peradventure, to
make it the more gracious, I shall sing it at her death.

Bottom's revision of 1 Corinthians 2:9–10 is the heart of the matter:

Eye hath not seen, nor ear heard, neither have entered into
the heart of man, the thing which God hath prepared for
them that love him.

But God hath revealed them unto us by his Spirit.

—Saint Paul

The eye of man hath not heard, the ear of man hath not
seen, man's hand is not able to taste, his tongue to conceive,
nor his heart to report, what my dream was.

—Bottom

Bottom's scrambling of the senses refuses Saint Paul's easy supernatu-
ralism, with dualistic split between flesh and spirit. Our prophet Bottom is
a monist, and so his dream urges on us a synesthetic reality, fusing flesh and
spirit. That Bottom is one for whom God has prepared the things revealed
by his spirit is made wonderfully clear in the closing dialogue between the
benign weaver and Theseus:

BOTTOM: [*Starting up.*] No, I assure you, the wall is down
          that parted their fathers. Will it please you to see the
          epilogue, or to hear a Bergomask dance between two
          of our company?
THESEUS: No epilogue, I pray you; for your play needs no excuse.

Only Bottom could assure us that the wall is down that parted all our
fathers. The weaver's common sense and natural goodness bestow on him an
aesthetic dignity, homely and humane, that is the necessary counterpoise to
the world of Puck that otherwise would ravish reality away in Shakespeare's
visionary drama.

II

Puck, being the spirit of mischief, is both a hobgoblin and "sweet Puck," not so much by turns but all at once. *A Midsummer Night's Dream* is more Puck's play than Bottom's, I would reluctantly agree, even as *The Tempest* is more Ariel's drama than it is poor Caliban's. If Puck, rather than Oberon, were in charge, then Bottom never would resume human shape and the four young lovers would continue their misadventures forever. Most of what fascinates our contemporaries about *A Midsummer Night's Dream* belongs to Puck's vision rather than to Bottom's. Amid so much of the sublime, it is difficult to prefer any single passage, but I find most unforgettable Puck's penultimate chant:

> Now the hungry lion roars,
> And the wolf behowls the moon;
> Whilst the heavy ploughman snores,
> All with weary task fordone.
> Now the wasted brands do glow,
> Whilst the screech-owl, screeching loud,
> Puts the wretch that lies in woe
> In remembrance of a shroud.
> Now it is the time of night
> That the graves all gaping wide,
> Every one lets forth his sprite,
> In the church-way paths to glide.
> And we fairies, that do run
> By the triple Hecat's team,
> From the presence of the sun,
> Following darkness like a dream,
> Now are frolic. Not a mouse
> Shall disturb this hallowed house:
> I am sent with broom before,
> To sweep the dust behind the door.

Everything problematic about Puck is summed up there; a domestic, workaday spirit, yet always uncannily *between*, between men and women, faeries and humans, nobles and mechanicals, nature and art, space and time. Puck is a spirit cheerfully amoral, free because never in love and always more amused even than amusing. The triple Hecat—heavenly moon maiden, earthly Artemis, and ruler of Hades—is more especially Puck's deity than she is the goddess worshiped by the other faeries. Hazlitt wisely contrasted Puck to Ariel by reminding us that "Ariel is a minister of retribution, who is touched with the sense of misleads." Puck just does not care; he has nothing to gain and little to lose. Only Oberon could call him "gentle," but then Oberon could see Cupid flying between moon and earth, and Puck constitutionally could not. Puck says that things please him best "that befall preposterously," where I think the last word takes on the force of the later coming earlier and the earlier later. As a kind of flying metalepsis or trope of transumption, Puck is indeed what the rhetorician Puttenham called a far-fetcher.

The midsummer night's dream, Puck tells us in his final chant, is ours, since we "but slumb'red here, / While these visions did appear." What are we dreaming when we dream Puck? "Shadows" would be his reply, in a familiar Shakespearean trope, yet Puck is no more a shadow than Bottom is. Free of love, Puck becomes an agent of the irrational element in love, its tendency to overvalue the object, as Freud grimly phrased it. A man or woman who incarnates Puck is sexually very dangerous, because he or she is endlessly mobile, invariably capable of transforming object-libido back into ego-libido again. Puckish freedom is overwhelmingly attractive, but the blow it strikes you will cause it no pain. Falling in love with a Puck is rather like turning life into a game of hockey.

Theseus, in the play's most famous speech, associated the lover with the poet and the lunatic in a perfectly Freudian conglomerate, since all forsake the reality principle, all assert the omnipotence of thought, and all thus yield themselves up to an ultimate narcissism. If Theseus is a Freudian, Bottom is not but represents an older wisdom, the amiable sapience, mixed with silliness, of the all too natural man. Puck, quicksilver and uncaring, defines the limits of the human by being so far apart from the human.

How can one play contain both Bottom and Puck? Ariel and Caliban both care, though they care on different sides and in different modes. Puck has no human feeling and so no human meaning; Bottom is one of the prime Shakespearean instances of how human meaning gets started, by a kind of immanent overflow, an ontological excess of being in excess of language. Only a dream, we might think, could contain both Bottom and Puck, but the play, however fantastic, is no fantasy but an imitation that startles the reality principle and makes it tremble rather like a guilty thing surprised.

RENÉ GIRARD

Bottom's One-Man Show

In *A Midsummer Night's Dream*, two groups of human beings spend the night in the wood. The first consists of four unhappy lovers who tear each other apart, the second of some local craftsmen who prepare a play for the celebration of Theseus's wedding.

Wretched as it is, their stage adaptation of *Pyramus and Thisby* remains beyond the capacities of these illiterate amateurs. But their passion for the theater is intense, especially in the case of Bottom, a born actor with an enormous appetite for impersonation.

At the craftsmen's first meeting—in act 1, scene 2—Quince, the director, distributes the various roles. Bottom gets asked first. He will play the leading man, Pyramus. He wishes it had been "a tyrant," but it is a lover and a lover will do. Bottom feigns indifference, but he is so eager to act, so excited by the prospect, that he will grab any role. Speaking compulsively, he announces that he will "move storms." Eager to stop this ranting, Quince turns to Flute and asks him to play Thisby.

Flute feels awkward at the thought of a woman's role. He tries to excuse himself on the ground that he has "a beard coming." Bottom begs Quince to let him have the role of Thisby. He will not give up playing Pyramus; yet he wants the other role as well, and immediately, even though he knows nothing of the story, he tries to show what he can do with it:

From *The Current in Criticism: Essays on the Present and Future of Literary Theory*, edited by Clayton Koelb and Virgil Lokke, pp. 99–122. © 1987 by Purdue Research Foundation.

And I may hide my face, let me play Thisby
too. I'll speak in a monstrous little voice. "Thisne!
Thisne! Ah, Pyramus, my love dear! thy Thisby
dear, and lady dear!"[1]

Quince disagrees. He thinks that the hero and the heroine should be
played by different actors:

"No, no, you must play Pyramus; and,
Flute, you Thisby."

In order to avoid further trouble, Quince hurriedly proceeds to assign
two more roles, Thisby's mother and Pyramus's father, with no interference
from Bottom this time, but then comes the turn of the lion. The role goes to
Snug, who complains that he is "slow of study" and requests "a written score."
You may do it "extempore," Quince replies, "for it is nothing but roaring." To
Bottom, this reluctance of the prospective lion is an irresistible temptation
and, once again, he asks for the role:

Let me play the lion too. I will roar, that I
will do any man's heart good to hear me. I will roar,
that I will make the Duke say, "Let him roar again;
let him roar again."

The role leaves little room for interpretation, but Quince is so irritated
that he challenges Bottom's understanding of it:

An you should do it too terribly, you
would fright the Duchess and the ladies, that
they would shrike; and that were enough to hang
us all.
          All. That would hang us, every mother's son.

The craftsmen hang on every word of their leader and then always mimic
him in a chorus. In the face of unanimous opposition, Bottom makes a hasty
retreat. He is too much of a mime not to give an audience what it requests:

I grant you, friends, if you should fright the
ladies out of their wits, they would have no more
discretion but to hang us; but I will aggravate my

voice so that I will roar you as gently as any suck-
ing dove; I will roar you and 'twere any nightin-gale.

As long as Bottom gets his role, whatever the populace wants, the populace will get. But even if the lion, now, sounds like a nightingale, it must retain
some features of the former beast or it would not be identifiable as such.
Bottom is turning it, therefore, into a birdlike lion, a warring conflation of
opposites, some kind of monster.

Too much mimetic adaptability is seen as unfavorable to the creative
imagination. It would seem to stifle it, but beyond a certain threshold—which
Bottom is crossing—the two tend to merge. With his most remarkable talent
for changing anything into anything else, Bottom's handling of his various
roles already resembles the process of mythological metamorphosis. Unlike
Alberich of *The Ring*, Bottom has no need of magical contraptions such as the
Tarnhelm. At the slightest signal from his public, he can transform himself,
now into a ferocious dragon, now into the sweetest little nightingale.

An exasperated Quince repeats in no uncertain terms that Bottom will
play no part but Pyramus. Next, the question arises of how the moon should
be represented, and also the dreadful wall, the famous wall that cruelly sepa-
rates the two lovers. The solution almost goes without saying. Let an actor
impersonate the wall, let an actor impersonate the moon.

Bottom would love to be that moon, Bottom would love to be that wall.
To play the beloved as well as the lover does not satisfy his appetite for acting; in addition, he wants to be the obstacle that stands between the two. He
and his fellows can passionately embrace even those objects that seem to lie
beyond the wildest dreams of impersonation, turning them into an infinite
number of theatrical parts. All of these Bottom would like to keep for himself, and even the most insignificant ones he can relinquish only with the
sense of a huge personal loss.

Try as he may, Quince will not find a role that does not suit Bottom's
talent. *Mimesis* is running wild. Even the slightest hint, now—almost any
gesture—can trigger new impersonations. The man reminds us of a suggest-
ible subject in the hands of a clever hypnotist. The only difference is that he
needs no hypnotist; he is gifted and mixed up enough to play both roles, the
hypnotizer and the hypnotized. He enters into all conceivable and inconceiv-
able roles with such passion that he is losing sight of his own personality.

The first scene with the craftsmen, as well as the first scene with the
lovers, takes place in the city, whereas the second takes place in the woods.
Each group seems to have some business out there, but the real business is the
midsummer night madness.

We can see right away that, in the interval between act 1 and act 3, the bumpkins' excitement has not abated but increased. Bottom is the first to speak, as always, and he finds a way to compel the attention of Quince:

> *Bottom.* There are things in this comedy of Pyramus
> and Thisby that will never please. First, Pyramus
> must draw a sword to kill himself; which the ladies
> cannot abide. How answer you that?

Quince was the one, earlier, who conjured up the specter of the frightened ladies *à propos* of the lion. Bottom cleverly extends this concern to the suicide of Pyramus. He mimics the argument of Quince and wraps himself up in the mantle of the *metteur en scène*. The better to manipulate Quince, he surrenders once again to his hysterical penchant for mimicry and shows us that his talent for impersonation is not limited to theatrical roles. He undermines the authority of Quince by turning himself into a second Quince and a contagious example to everybody else. Quince cannot silence him, this time, without silencing himself.

> *Snout.* By'r lakin, a parlous fear.
> *Starveling.* I believe we must leave the killing out, when all
> is done.
> *Bottom.* Not a whit! I have a device to make all well.
> Write me a prologue, and let the prologue seem to
> say we will do no harm with our swords, and that
> Pyramus is not killed indeed; and for the more bet-
> ter assurance, tell them that I Pyramus am not
> Pyramus, but Bottom the weaver. This will put
> them out of fear.

Once again, of course, the only purpose of Bottom is to monopolize the stage. He wants to be the prologue and the epilogue and everything in between.

In his desire to prevent any confusion between a simulated death and a real one, Bottom wants the fictional Pyramus—himself—to emphasize his real identity; but he devises his prologue in such a way as to suggest the opposite of what he means.

The prologue should say: "My name is Bottom and I am merely pretending to be a certain Pyramus whose suicide is feigned"; but Bottom names Pyramus first, in the first person, saying in fact: "I Pyramus" as if it were his real identity and wishing, no doubt, that it were. And then, when his real name, Bottom, finally shows up, it is treated as an actor's part in the title page of a printed play; it is followed by a mention of the man's trade. The prologue says: "Bottom the weaver," which is the way the name appears in the listing of roles at the beginning of *A Midsummer Night's Dream*.

We are listening, we feel, to an actor named Pyramus who has to play a fictional weaver named Bottom, a modest role with which he is not very pleased. Inside the play, this belief is wrong but, from the spectators' standpoint, it makes good sense. We are actually watching a play that includes a fictional weaver named Bottom. It is quite possible that the actor might be named Pyramus.

Bottom contaminates us with his own madness; we share in the general dizziness, but so mildly that not even the most timid ladies can be frightened. It feels like a few bubbles of champagne on an empty stomach.

In order to describe what is going on here, the grayish jargon of "identity crises" and "split personalities" will not do. It may be appropriate to the static condition of the contemporary neurotic, patiently rehashing his various "problems" and the interminable "analysis" of the same, until death do them part. It is ridiculously inadequate here. Bottom's crisis is more tempestuous and *critical* than the neurotic's condition but, unlike that of the psychotic, it will leave no traces. It is temporary, and it will have a resolution. It is also collective. Bottom is only the supreme exemplification of what happens to all his companions.

This crisis is an attenuated or partly ritualized version of the mimetic crisis described in *Violence and the Sacred*.[2] All words, images and gesticulations intended by the craftsmen as a preventive against the imaginary panic of the ladies are really worsening symptoms of that crisis. As they exhibit their mimetic symptoms to one another, they also mimic them, bringing them to fever pitch. The entire scene describes a mimetic contagion of lost identity that affects Bottom most spectacularly but not him alone, as we soon shall see.

The "I Pyramus" is only a portent of things to come. It represents a transitional phase on the road to a collective hallucination similar to the climax of a primitive ritual, because all rituals are the more or less ritualized reenactment of the real crisis that precedes.

Shakespeare is aware that the theater is itself a form of ritual, and—like all rituals—it can go wrong, it can revert to the real mimetic crisis in which it originates. This is what happens with the craftsmen, but only to a certain extent. The comedy will not turn into a tragedy.

A few lines down we have another clue to the rapid disintegration of Bottom's normal handling of reality. Our old friend the lion once again serves as a catalyst. We can surmise that, between the two meetings, this lion has haunted the imagination of the mechanicals. Now even the quiet ones, Snout the tinker and Starveling the tailor, begin to evince panic.

> *Snout.* Will not the ladies be afeard of the lion?
> *Starveling.* I fear it, I promise you.
> *Bottom.* Masters, you ought to consider with your-
> [selves], to bring in (God shield us!) a lion
> among ladies, is a most dreadful thing; for there is
> not a more fearful wild-fowl than your lion living;
> and we ought to look to't.
> *Snout.* Therefore another prologue must tell he is
> not a lion.
> *Bottom.* Nay; you must name his name, and half his
> face must be seen through the lion's neck, and he
> himself must speak through, saying thus, or to the
> same defect: "Ladies," or "Fair ladies, I would wish
> you," or "I would request you," or "I would
> entreat you, not to fear, not to tremble: my life
> for yours. If you think I come hither as a lion, it
> were pity of my life. No! I am no such thing; I am
> a man as other men are"; and there indeed let him
> name his name, and tell them plainly he is Snug the
> joiner.

Just as Bottom imitated Quince a little earlier, now Snout imitates Bottom. His turn has come to emulate Bottom and demand still one more reassuring prologue after the style of his hero. But Bottom does not recognize the idea as his own when he hears it from the mouth of someone else. Great artists do not like to be copied. Just as he had been interrupted by Quince, he now keeps interrupting Snout; he has a brighter idea: a speech by the dumb beast himself. As the actor will "name his name" and fasten himself solidly to his real identity, "half his face must be seen through the lion's neck."

The first metamorphosis of the lion was not scary enough. Now we have a second one. A creature half-man, half-beast is uncannier than a combination of beast and beast, uncannier, *a fortiori*, than the honest-to-goodness lion demanded by the original script. The mere invention of this improved monster sends shivers down the spine of the inventors.

This fragment of a human face surrounded by leonine features looks strikingly like the sort of primitive mask that Shakespeare had probably never seen but that his genius invents almost *ex nihilo*. The playwright's sense of timing is excellent. We have reached the moment when the participants in an orgiastic ritual would put on masks quite similar to the one imagined by Bottom: weird compositions of animal and human features. The inspiration is very much the same because the experience is the same. Bottom and his friends are going through the type of crisis after which rituals are patterned.

Bottom's compulsive impersonations resemble the possessive trance as much as the resulting images resemble primitive masks. The craftsmen live in a culture that does not encourage such phenomena. But perhaps the distant past was different. At one time, the midsummer festival may have been a ritual similar to the orgiastic rituals in ancient and primitive cultures.

Turn-of-the-century anthropologists such as Sir James George Frazer thought that they were the first to rediscover that origin, but, two and three centuries ahead of modern research, Shakespeare already thought along similar if not identical lines. The midsummer festival figures only in the title. The play itself contains one single mention of "the rites of May," and that is all. This inconsistent vagueness does not really matter. All these festivals were similar; any one of them can provide the ritual framework in which the experience of Bottom and the craftsmen can be fitted because they were all generated by the type of mythical genesis that Shakespeare describes.

The possessive trance may closely resemble playacting, but it is an error simply to equate the one with the other, as some researchers such as Michel Leiris have been inclined to do. When genuine, the trance represents a degree of involvement so great that the impersonation becomes involuntary and cannot be stopped at will. Correspondingly, it represents a high degree of self-*dispossession*, higher, no doubt, than what normally happens in the Western theater.

It all happens to Bottom. Shakespeare seems to regard the theater as a mild form of the trance, one that must derive from the "real thing" originally and can revert to it on occasion—with highly predisposed individuals such as Bottom, or when the circumstances are favorable.

All our craftsmen tacitly assume that the weaker sex in their audience—which really means the queen of the Amazons and her attendants—will be extremely prone to panic. Their principal reason for thinking so is that they themselves are on the verge of a panic. It is normal for people in that condition to project it outside of themselves. They detect a threat of imminent panic somewhere in the vicinity and devise hasty measures against it. As they try to implement these measures, they make one another believe that the panic has already arrived, which indeed it has, as soon as everybody believes that it has. Their strategy is the one an infinitely clever man would select if he had joined a group of terrorists with the express intention of triggering a mass panic.

The solicitude for the ladies is a facade behind which the craftsmen can unleash their imaginations and produce more and more horrifying monsters. As the craftsmen try to reassure the hypothetical fears of others, they only succeed in scaring themselves out of their wits, and *there is not the slightest difference between their self-induced but nevertheless objectively real panic*, which is a sociological event occurring in the real world, *and the ritual pattern to which that panic necessarily conforms*, because all ritual originates in some event of this type.

A transitional product of Bottom's "seething brain," the humanlike lion belongs to a phase more advanced than the birdlike lion of the previous phase; it corresponds to an intensification of the crisis, a greater loss of "self-identity." But the final and climactic phase is still to come.

In the second phase, we already have full-fledged monsters—creatures no longer "species-specific," as the modern specialists would say (rather redundantly and mimetically, being threatened themselves with undifferentiation). But the craftsmen do not yet quite *believe* in the reality of their own creations.

Give them one more minute and they do. This is the only difference between the ass-headed Bottom and the shenanigans that precede this not-so-mysterious apparition. To all his friends, Bottom has become a real monster. And we are apprised of the fact in a manner so strikingly suited to the force of the hallucination that we are likely to miss the point entirely.

Shakespeare treats Bottom's amazing *translation* both as if it were "the real thing" and also as if it were a prank that Puck is playing on the bumpkins. But Puck is no one but the spirit of the entire midsummer night. And the progress of its spirit can be traced both in an irrational manner by following the evolution of Puck, which pleases the light-hearted and absent-minded spectators, and in the slightly less transparent manner of our analysis, which does not uncover anything that Shakespeare has not intentionally written into his text. The anthropological genius of the playwright displays itself openly from the beginning to the end of this magnificent text.

The apparition walks upon the stage. The imaginary products of Bottom's "seething brain" have been elevated to the status of "real" characters. This shift in the dramatic handling of the theme expresses the climax of the crisis with such power that it makes it invisible to the average spectator. Even the best critics have yet to understand what their author is really up to.

If the spectator has missed the manner in which the monstrous gradually insinuates itself among the near-hysterical craftsmen, he/she will take Puck, Oberon, Titania, and their cortege of fairies at face value, mistaking them for the heroes and heroines of one more subplot that is just as independent of the other two as these two are, or rather seem to be, of one another.

From the simultaneously structural and genetic standpoint of our "neo-mimetic" criticism, the "translation" of Bottom and the intervention of the "fairies" mark the culmination of the dynamic process triggered by the collective decision to perform a play. It is not a magical irruption, a sudden and inexplicable disturbance in a static situation of bucolic peace among people going peacefully about their business of acting, it is the climax of successive structural transformations that are related to one another in such a way that, ultimately, they must be regarded as a *continuous process*. This precedence of continuity over discontinuity is not a return to a pre-structural perspective.

Out of mimetic sympathy with Bottom, mixed with a good deal of exasperation, the craftsmen all cross the threshold of hallucination simultaneously in act 3, scene 1:

> [*Enter* Puck, *and* Bottom *with an ass's head.*]
>   Bottom. "If I were fair, Thisby, I were only thine."
>   Quince. O monstrous! O strange! We are haunted.
> Pray, masters, fly, masters! Help!
> [*Exeunt* Quince, Snug, Flute, Snout, *and* Starveling.]
> . . .
>   Quince. Bless thee, Bottom, bless thee! Thou art translated.

Quince is first to tip over the brink, and he takes everybody with him; or rather, everybody follows him into the abyss of unreason because everybody imitates him. Until then, Quince had seemed the most clear-headed of the lot; the asinine interruptions of Bottom must have undermined his strength. In a sense, he does not lose his mind: he finally sees with his own eyes the ass-headed monster that keeps persecuting him.

Half the face of an ass can be seen through Bottom's neck. The body remains mostly human, being that of a great lover, but it takes more than a mere Thisby to conquer this Pyramus. It takes the queen of the fairies whom, to a large extent, Bottom himself has become. She talks as wittily as a prologue, but he retains a curious predilection for hay, as well as the immobility of a brick wall, another well-known characteristic of the ass.

If we do not see the mimetic process behind the weird metamorphosis of Bottom, we will have to believe that *someone* rather than something is responsible, and we will have to reinvent Puck, or Robin Goodfellow, the hobgoblin of English folklore, or perhaps Oberon, Titania, etc. They can all be metaphors for the entire process because they all are the products of Bottom's "seething brain."

That is why they reproduce the antics of the craftsmen and of the lovers at their own supernatural level. And since Puck is supposed to plant only a cardboard ass-head upon the real head of Bottom, even the ladies and the critics that would be most offended by any degree of mimetic undifferentiation between violence and the sacred do not have to understand anything and therefore fear nothing.

The habitual reading is that the intervention of Puck and the intersection of the three plots depend on no rationally intelligible sequence. Shakespeare is "playing" in haphazard fashion. Puck provides a welcome break with the trivial realism of the craftsmen, a delightful diversion but no more. The important thing, today, is that the play should make no sense at all. The play must be as senseless as the lovers and the craftsmen imagine their experience to be. It must be the child of a capricious and unmotivated imagination. If we tried to make sense out of it, we would spoil the pleasure of the text.

The chaotic and the discontinuous are present at the dramatic level only, for the spectators who watch the play as naively as the craftsmen and the lovers experience it. There is another rationale for the various incidents that Shakespeare has deliberately inscribed into the play, but he has done so in such a fashion that only a certain type of attention will see it.

When Bottom turns into an ass and marries Titania, the panic that had been brewing for a while reaches ebullition. The same generative force produces the entire world of the fairies that earlier had produced the still-half-believed "translations" and conflations of various beings, the monstrous mixture of a lion and of a man, and the metamorphosis of the lion into a nightingale.

If Bottom could choose one theatrical role and stick to it, he would not lose his mind. One single impersonation would have enough stability and permanence to prevent the generation of monsters. The weaver becomes drunk on a kaleidoscope of impersonations that keeps revolving faster and faster.

He resembles these clowns whose act consists in changing suits so fast that they seem to be wearing the same suit all the time, but it is made up of many colors and shapes all jumbled together. Bottom ends up with a very strange costume, indeed. Maybe it is Joseph's "coat of many colors."

Bottom's roles are too different from each other to be arranged into a harmonious "synthesis," Hegelian or otherwise, and yet Bottom assumes them all almost simultaneously and with such passion each time that he commits himself totally to each one simultaneously.

Inside Bottom, as in the uterus of their mother, there are always a Jacob and an Esau fighting for supremacy, and many other twins as well. Bottom cannot fail to be torn apart, literally shredded by all these totalitarian claims upon his undivided attention. His is the *diasparagmos* of the actor, his mimetic passion.

Beyond a certain threshold, the feverish impersonations of Bottom impinge upon one another as the multiple images in a cinematic film and breed a whole host of monsters. Then the swirl becomes so dizzying that another threshold is reached, and Bottom himself becomes the monster, first in the eyes of his fellows, then in his own eyes as well, mimetically.

As new impersonations keep crowding in, the whole system becomes destabilized, then explodes into fragments that tend to reorganize in weird bits and pieces like a mosaic of broken glass. Bottom is "translated" into a sparkling jumble of fragments from his various roles, with a unifying preponderance of the original ass.

* * *

What is the relationship between the two subplots? Can the craftsmen have anything in common with the four mixed-up lovers? The first have gathered to perform a play, the others to love and hate one another. Does their Eros have an affinity for the frantic theatrical impersonations of a half-crazed Bottom?

It certainly does. In order to justify this assertion, I must summarize the argument of an earlier essay about the four lovers.[3]

With the help of Theseus, Hermia's father seeks to prevent his daughter from marrying Lysander. The boy and girl flee to the woods. On their heels comes Demetrius in hot pursuit of Hermia, whom he still loves even though she no longer loves him. On his heels comes Helena in hot pursuit of Demetrius, whom she ardently loves even though he has never loved her.

It seems that the first two lovers have a sound enough reason to flee their Athenian homes. Fleeing one's parents and other oppressive political forces is a comic prop so traditional that it is taken at face value. It is never examined, and yet this time the theme is deceptive in the sense that there is a more convincing cause for the troubles of the lovers. The parental figures are no more responsible for getting the frenzy started than the fairies, a little later, for making it worse.

Even in the case of Lysander and Hermia, "true love" needs no parental or supernatural interference to run into trouble. Shakespeare slyly informs us that, until Lysander appeared upon the scene, Hermia was happy enough to marry Demetrius. Her father's choice was her own choice.

This information is unnecessary to the plot, but it is highly suggestive of an instability among the four lovers that cannot be blamed on the older generation or even on the disruptive influence of the midsummer spirit.

Lysander may well be the original troublemaker. It would be wrong, however, to attach too much importance to him personally, or to anyone else for that matter. In this play, individuals as such do not matter. The traditional critics correctly observed their lack of personality and their interchangeability, but they mistakenly regarded it as a weakness of the play, as something unintended that Shakespeare would have remedied if he had been able to.

In reality, Shakespeare is in complete control of his literary effects, but his goal is the opposite of the only one these traditional critics could conceive, which was the creation of stable character differentiations. Shakespeare wants to show the pressure of fads and fashions inside a group of idle young aristocrats. It can become so intense that it extends to matters of the heart.

Shakespeare portrays what happens to adolescents who read too many romances and choose to live in a world of literary imitation. Taking fictional heroes as models predisposes them to real-life experiments with erotic mimicry, and the results can be simultaneously disastrous and comical. They become a "living theater."

Everybody feels compelled to choose what everybody else has already chosen. The two boys are never in love with the same girl for long, but at any given time they are both in love with the same girl—Hermia first, Helena later. Neither one can desire anything that the other one will not immediately desire as well. Even the girls are carried away in the end by the dominant desire—the one fashionable desire—and compelled to yield to the mimetic pressure of uniformity. This is the reason Helena, at the beginning, seems to desire Hermia even more than Demetrius. The reason is that Hermia is already desired by the two boys; she is the star of the entire show, and Helena feels irresistibly attracted by her success.

All characters do their falling in love according to the falling in love in the vicinity. They remind us of these modern consumers who already have everything and never experience a real need, therefore, but who cannot hear that a product is "popular" or see people standing in line to buy something without rushing themselves to join that line. The longer the line, the more valuable the prize seems at the end of it. But the line can dissolve as quickly as it will re-form behind something else. The queue that forms behind Hermia at the beginning will shift to Helena in the middle of the night for no reason whatever.

Let us listen to the first encounter of Helena and Hermia in act 1, scene 1:

> *Hermia.* God speed fair Helena! whither away?
> *Helena.* Call you me fair? That fair again unsay.
> Demetrius loves your fair, O happy fair!
> Your eyes are lodestars, and your tongue's sweet air
> More tuneable than lark to shepherd's ear
> When wheat is green, when hawthorn buds appear.
> Sickness is catching; O, were favor so,

[Yours would] I catch, fair Hermia, ere I go;
My ear should catch your voice, my eye your eye,
My tongue should catch your tongue's sweet melody.
Were the world mine, Demetrius being bated,
The rest I'll give to be to you translated.

The homosexual flavor is undeniable. Shakespeare certainly wanted it there. For this, we cannot pin the blame or the merit—whichever term we choose—upon some authorial "unconscious." The only serious critical question is: why did the author do it? I doubt very much that he wanted to demonstrate the cleverness of Jacques Lacan, or even of Sigmund Freud. I also doubt that he wanted to promote an "alternative life-style." Shakespeare must have had a purpose of his own when he wrote these lines.

There is a passage in *Coriolanus* with an even more unmistakable homosexual flavor, but this time the two characters are male. *Vis-à-vis* Coriolanus, his sworn rival, Aufidius expresses sentiments similar to those of Helena for Hermia.

If you compare the two passages, you will see that the only common feature is the mimetic rivalry of two characters, male or female. The gender makes no difference at all. Quite as ardently as Helena, Aufidius desires something his rival possesses in great abundance, military glory. Aufidius wants the many victories of Coriolanus. Helena wants the many lovers of Hermia, her superior erotic glory. In front of Coriolanus, Aufidius feels like a failure. In front of Hermia, Helena feels like a failure.

A few lines after our passage, Helena is alone and, in a soliloquy, vents her bitterness against her rival. She claims that she is just as pretty as Hermia. Should we conclude that her mood has changed, or that she was a hypocrite in the previous scene? The answers are a little more complicated. Helena's worship of Hermia is more than a polite compliment. It is just as genuine as the hatred of a moment later. Aufidius also feels ambivalent towards Coriolanus.

The mimetic model is worshipped as a model and hated as a rival. The duality is inescapable; desire cannot mimic its friends without turning them into irritating obstacles, but the mimetic lover never seems to understand the self-generated process of his/her own frustration and keeps complaining that someone else is interfering with "true love."

To Helena, Hermia is perceived as a paragon of success, the true goddess of everything a normal girl may wish—elegance, wit, glamor, erotic triumphs . . . How can Hermia fail to be more interesting than either of the boys since she dominates both of them, at least for the time being . . .

The homosexual connotations must be acknowledged but must not blind our critical eyes to the context. Helena's fascination for Hermia is part of a larger story, the story of the mimetic rivalry. In an erotic triangle, the obsession can become so acute that the rival of the same sex tends to supersede the object of the other sex.

Demetrius, the object of Helena's desire, rates only half a line in this passage, which is not much compared to the eleven lines dedicated to Hermia. This type of inbalance gets worse and worse as the mimetic crisis intensifies and the obsession for the rival increases. Here again, the midsummer night is a description of a deepening crisis.

Beyond a certain threshold of intensity, the veritable object becomes the model. If we conclude that Helena has to *be* a homosexual in the same sense that she is a tall, blonde girl, or Hermia short and a brunette, we freeze solid a relationship that should be kept light and airy. We surrender our wits either to the current pedantry of sexuality or to the former puritanism. The two are equally disastrous for the understanding of what Shakespeare is talking about, which we would all understand intuitively if we were dealing with it in a real-life situation.

A Midsummer Night's Dream is much more like a real-life situation than people with their heads full of nihilistic critical theory will ever realize. The final predominance of the model means that the ultimate goal of mimetic desire is that model's "being." This ontological mirage is a must, of course, in a play that is a veritable encyclopedia on the subject, written by the greatest expert ever:

> Were the world mine, Demetrius being bated,
> The rest I'll give to be to you translated.

The last verse sums up and transcends the erotic poem that we quoted before, in the same sense that the metaphysical dimension sums up and transcends the more physical aspects of mimetic desire.

Those who desire mimetically are really trying to exchange their own despised being against the glorious being of their victorious model. Like Bottom, they seek a total metamorphosis, and ultimately their wish will be granted in the same paradoxical fashion.

How can Helena hope to reach her goal? How can she be *translated* to Hermia? Through imitation, of course: the exchange that follows makes it abundantly clear that the only technique of metaphysical desire is *mimesis*:

> O, teach me how you look, and with what art
> You sway the motion of Demetrius' heart.

We must take this language literally. "Teach me how to impersonate you" is what Helena is asking Hermia. We should not regard this effort at impersonation as a mere consequence of some preexisting desire. We should not regard it only as a cause, either. It is really a circular process in which Hermia's choice of Demetrius, before Lysander's arrival upon the scene, is both a cause and a consequence of Helena's own choice.

Helena would like to resemble her model in everything; she wants every feature of her body to be an exact replica of Hermia's. Her ultimate desire is to worship herself rather than Hermia, but the only conceivable method to achieve that goal seems to be to worship the more successful Hermia first and to become a perfect duplicate of the person she really wants to be.

This is what magazines and books about fashionable people are, in our world anyway. They are how-to books. This is a recurrent problem with self-worship. The would-be worshipper always ends up worshipping someone else.

When Helena's hour of success finally arrives, it is too late for her; she can no longer enjoy it. She has been buffeted too much during the midsummer night. She believes she is the victim of some kind of hoax. Her newly found lovers are as sincere as they always were, and yet she is right not to trust eight one. Each new combination proves more unstable and short-lived than the previous one.

Everybody ends up equally frustrated. The final outcome is conflict, failure and despair for everybody. No desire is ever fulfilled, and no desire is ever reciprocated, because all desires are one and the same. In order to respond to one another, desires must be differentiated; identical desires will all converge on the same object and can only *cross* one another.

Why is the system of mimetic desire so unstable? Why must the long-suffering Helena finally exchange places with Hermia and become everybody's idol while Hermia now is universally loathed? The reason lies with the universal dependence on *imitation*. The unanimous mimetic convergence seems enormously convincing because it does, indeed, convince everybody. It seems destined to last forever, and yet it is anchored in a pure mimetic effect rather than in anything concrete and objective. It floats half an inch above the ground, and in one instant, the same wind of fashion will topple the idol that it had erected a few instants before.

Ultimately this universal snobbery of imitation constitutes a surrender to pure randomness. The dabbing of the "wrong eyes" with the magical potion is unnecessary as a method of accounting for the fickleness of the lovers, but, like all mythical themes, it half reveals the disquieting truth that it dissimulates. We choose to desire mimetically, but then mimetic desire chooses for us; it deprives us of all power to choose and discriminate. This is what the operation of the love juice suggests quite explicitly. It makes Titania as well as the young people fall in love at *random*:

Oberon. Having once this juice,
I'll watch Titania when she is asleep,
And drop the liquor of it in her eyes;
The next thing then she waking looks upon
(Be it on lion, bear, or wolf, or bull,
On meddling monkey, or on busy ape),
She shall pursue it with the soul of love.

The name of the potion thus introduced in act 2, scene 1—*love-in-idleness*—is a satirical barb at the type of people portrayed in the play. Only youngsters with nothing to do, like the aristocrats of Shakespeare's time, or the entire well-to-do middle class in our day, can waste their time playing such self-destructive games as our four lovers.

The laws and patterns of mimetic desire govern the entire theater of Shakespeare, I believe, if only negatively, in such plays as *As You Like It* that do conform much more consistently than *A Midsummer Night's Dream* to the conventions of traditional romance. Much of the play runs completely counter to these laws, but in a spirit of caricaturally slavish obedience to the mystique of "true love" that really amounts to another form of satire, and therefore another assertion of mimetic desire.

Other plays of Shakespeare illustrate only certain aspects of mimetic desire, fragments of the entire crisis-and-resolution pattern. *A Midsummer Night's Dream* represents the whole dynamic cycle in a speeded-up version that can fit the time frame of a single night.

This is the same fundamental process as in the great tragedies. In their common desire to distinguish themselves from one another, the four lovers engage in a mutual imitation that brings about a warring confusion of everything and ultimately would result in violent murders, were it not for the "supernatural" intervention of Puck and Oberon.

The characters' interpretation of what happens is very much like that of the average spectator, totally blind to the logic of mimetic desire and open, therefore, to suggestions of scapegoating on the one hand and supernatural intervention on the other. The one and the other enable the victims of mimetic desire to not identify mimetic desire as the real culprit and to substitute someone or something else as an explanation.

Their view of the mimetic process is the very reverse of the truth. As all the characters become more and more alike in their undifferentiated frenzy, they perceive an immense difference between themselves and their models. As a result, they themselves feel more and more inferior, or beastly, and they perceive their models as more and more superior and divine. Between these two extremes, emptiness prevails and common humanity is on the way out.

Physical violence enters the picture, and the four wander at the edge of the inhuman. Their language reflects the shift. When they speak of themselves they use images of animality and confuse their models with various supernatural figures and even gods.

As the night advances, these images become more insistent. During this last evolution, the four seem to lose control entirely; they feel dizzier and dizzier; their perception becomes blurred. They are moving closer to the trance-like condition of the participants in orgiastic rituals. Shakespeare is obviously writing his own playful reconstitution not so much of the rituals themselves as the type of hysterical mimetic conflicts that must lie behind them.

This is what we already observed in the case of the craftsmen. As the cauldron boils over, the lovers lose their ability to distinguish their over-worked metaphors from real beasts and real divinities. Beyond a certain threshold, these metaphors assume a life of their own, but not an "independent" life in the sense of their being well separated from one another. The system is too unstable for that; the substitutions and recombinations are occurring too rapidly.

The youngsters start taking their beasts and their gods seriously at the point when they can no longer tell them apart. Gods and beasts are on the way to forming these weird assemblages that we call mythical monsters. As a result of the dismembering and disorderly *remembering* of normally differentiated creatures, with no regard for the original differentiation, all sorts of fantastic creatures appear.

We already know which ones actually appear. We are back with our old friends, the ass-headed Bottom, Puck, Oberon, Titania and all the fairies. The subplot of the four lovers constitutes a gradual genesis of the mythical metamorphoses that parallels the genesis in the subplot of the craftsmen.

This invasion of the four lovers' speech by animal images corresponds to the excessive preoccupation of Bottom and his companions with the lion and to the early metamorphoses of that terrible beast. In both subplots the images of infrahuman and superhuman creatures prepare the ground for a final metamorphosis that is the same in the two subplots.

After the four lovers wake up and leave the wood, they give Theseus and Hippolyta their own account of what happened during the night. This account is not given on the stage because it would be a repetition of everything that has occurred to both groups during the midsummer night. In other words, the four lovers end up "dreaming" more or less the same "dream" as Bottom and his friends. Even though the two groups are not aware of one another's presence in the woods, they both participate in the genesis of the same mythology, and that is why the fairies are supposed to interfere with both groups.

The craftsmen and the lovers take a not-so-different road to end up in exactly the same place. This comes as no surprise to us. We found, indeed, that the erotic desire of the lovers was no less mimetic than the impersonations of the actors. The tendency for the idolatrous *imitatio* to focus not on one adolescent permanently but on this one now, then on another, then on a third, constitutes the equivalent of Bottom's urge to play all the roles and turn *Pyramus and Thisby* into a one-man show.

In each case, it is the same *hybris*, the same desire to dominate everyone and everything, that ends up destroying the goal it tries to reach because it destroys the very order that makes domination significant. This is the demise of "degree" in Ulysses' speech in *Troilus and Cressida*. This is the essence of tragedy.

What Shakespeare sees better than the Greeks is the reason why *hybristic* pride is self-defeating at the individual level. Mimetic desire is a desire for self-centeredness that cannot be distinguished from mimetic "de-centering," from the desire to "be" the model. A more radical alienation cannot be conceived. It lies at the root of the subject and depends on no sexual, economic or other determinations—unlike all the partial alienations of Marxism, Freudism and other contemporary theories. The four lovers resemble Bottom in their desire for turning the group into a one-man show and their ultimate inability to do so.

We can understand why Shakespeare resorts to the same word to express what the lovers desire and what happens to Bottom in the middle of the rehearsal. The lovers desire to be *translated* to their models. When Bottom turns into the ass-headed monster, Quince says to him: "Bottom, thou art translated."

Translation expresses both the desire for the *being* of someone else, and the paradoxical "success" of that desire, the monstrous metamorphosis. In both subplots the metamorphosis is the reward or, rather, the punishment for this desire.

The two subplots are closely patterned on one another. In both instances, the first scene is a distribution of roles. In principle, each character is supposed to play a single role, but in each case, signs of instability and disintegration immediately appear.

In both instances, as the crisis worsens, we shift from the city of Athens to the wood nearby. This is what the young people in England were supposed to do on midsummer nights. The wilderness is the right place, ritually speaking, for the two escalations of mimetic frenzy and the commingling between human and supernatural beings, the temporary destruction of civilized differentiation.

In both instances we have the same two levels of interpretation that I distinguished *à propos* of the craftsmen: 1) the dramatic level takes the monsters and fairies at face value, regarding them either as a genuine apparition or as a gratuitous product of a purely *individual* imagination, which is what Theseus does in his great speech; 2) a "genetic" level sees these same monsters and fairies as the product of mimetic impersonation gone mad, mimetically affecting all the characters in the two subplots.

Everything is alike in both subplots. Shakespeare makes the whole scheme of mimetic desire obvious to the point of caricature, and then he channels it into a dramatic effect that disguises it, for the benefit of those—the immense majority—who would rather not acknowledge the existence of mimetic desire. As in the case of the actors, the mimetic behavior produces the very mythology that it needs to transfigure its own folly into the mischievousness of Puck.

The author must maintain the illusion that a "true" pairing of the quartet exists. There must be a "right" combination: the myth of "true love" demands it. If it does not have the permanence required, or if it cannot be found at all, we can always pin the blame on the "fairies," or, better still, on the Oedipal father represented by Egeus, or on the power of the state represented by Theseus. These are the only fairies in which a modern critic is allowed to believe, the Freudo-Marxist fairies.

The happy ending of a comedy is one of these conventions that must be respected. The author does not want to offend the possible censors in his audience, or the really pure at heart. Unlike our modern demystificators, even in his most daringly cynical plays, Shakespeare always allows for the possibility of innocence, as if there were no deep resentment in him, or as if it were somehow transcended.

* * *

The characters in the two subplots have no contact at all during the night. They come together only during the play within the play. The craftsmen are on stage and the lovers in the audience. It is traditional as a result to regard the two subplots as unrelated or loosely related. The comical antics of the craftsmen serve as an introduction to the play within the play, but their relevance to the work as a whole remains problematic.

The play is about monsters and has often been regarded as a trifle superficial, an elegant but somewhat empty fantasy, a mosaic of unrelated themes. The current fashion of incoherence and discontinuities has made this view more popular than ever, and yet it is completely false. But the formidable coherence of the play is of a sort that traditional criticism has never suspected.

With the blessing of its author, the play turns into a serious theory of its own mythological aspects, which most spectators and critics have always interpreted and will continue to interpret as a pure fantasy, arbitrarily super-imposed on the more realistic aspects of the work. The force of the mythical metamorphosis ultimately stems from the craftsmen's and lovers' excessive taste for "translation," or for a type of "identification" that must be identified with *mimesis*, imitation, both because it is Shakespeare's view, and because it accounts for everything in the play. Shakespeare's own theory is the best theory of the play and of the anthropology behind it.

The proof that I have Shakespeare's blessing when I speak as I do is to be found in the smart reply of Hippolyta to the rather stodgy positivism of Theseus in act 5, scene 1, when he tells her what she should believe regarding the cause of the midsummer night. Like Polonius, Theseus does not say anything that is not true, and yet he understands nothing. Hippolyta understands everything. In my earlier article, I have quoted her in connection with the lovers only; I will quote her here once again more appropriately, in connection with the craftsmen as well:

> But all the story of the night told over,
> And all their minds transfigur'd so together,
> More witnesseth than fancy's images,
> And grows to something of great constancy;
> But howsoever, strange and admirable.

Shakespeare reveals the patterns of mimetic desire and their relation-ship to mythic creation so powerfully in the subplot of the four lovers that the case for its presence can be made on internal evidence only. No help is needed from the other subplot, the theatrical *mimesis* of Bottom and his friends.

But this help is always available, and a comparison of the points the two subplots have in common is enormously enlightening. Mimetic desire remains controversial, no doubt, but since Plato and the *Poetics* of Aristotle, *mimesis* has been the major concept of dramatic criticism. In the Renaissance, the mimetic interpretation was not simply the preferred interpretation, it was just about the only one.

In *A Midsummer Night's Dream*, the presence of *mimesis* as a Shake-spearean theme is unquestionable. I assume, therefore, that my readers will have no difficulty agreeing with me on this point: the subplot of Bottom and his friends entails a perpetual and perfectly explicit reference to *mimesis*.

Mimesis is certainly part of the picture in the case of the craftsmen, but something else is needed to complete that picture. The aesthetic *mimesis* of the philosophers and the critics does not explain why the craftsmen decided to perform *Pyramus and Thisby*. They are not professional actors. They did not embark on their theatrical enterprise for aesthetic reasons primarily, or to make a living, or even out of a sense of obligation to the duke. To celebrate the wedding of Theseus, they might have come up with something better suited to their cultural shortcomings. Why did they choose to do a play?

The obvious answer is: personal ambition, narcissism, desire, mimetic desire. Since all the craftsmen show up every time they are summoned, since not one of them is ever missing, the same desire for impersonation must possess each and every one of them, including the most timid, the ones who stand at the other extreme of Bottom and act out the part of the reluctant actor. The reluctance of the reluctant actor means the same thing, ultimately, as the extreme eagerness of Bottom.

Bottom, we found, could never settle on any role, not even the leading one, the most flattering to his ego. His avidity was finally punished, or rewarded, by his metamorphosis into a monster.

Most people enjoy watching a play, but the more they enjoy it, the more they also enjoy being watched by others and therefore performing as actors. The craving for impersonation corresponds to a perfect fusion of *mimesis* and desire.

The desire for the theater consists not in imitating some specific model but in the undifferentiated avidity of Bottom that inevitably conflicts with the pretentions of Quince and the other actors, just as the desires of the four lovers must necessarily "cross" one another.

In the case of the lovers, the one component that is identified most easily is desire. The critic does not have to demonstrate that desire belongs in the picture. But here again, this is not the whole picture; something more is needed to account for the systematic and almost algebraic aspect of the lovers' antics.

If we have *mimesis* plus desire in the case of the craftsmen, we must have desire plus *mimesis* in the case of the lovers. The second component must be imitation or impersonation. The picture is reversed, but to Shakespeare, obviously, it is fundamentally the same picture.

If *mimesis* is really present in the case of the actors, the case for a *mimesis of desire* that would belong to Shakespeare's own conception of both subplots and of the entire play becomes inescapable. A mimesis of desire can always reverse itself into a desire for mimesis. The two subplots are *perfect* mirrors of one another, and together, they breed the fairies. This triunity is the unity of *A Midsummer Night's Dream*.

Unlike the ancient and modern students of imitation, unlike the Freudian students of desire, Shakespeare is not merely aware that imitation and desire cannot be divorced from each other; he realizes that, far from being the bland ingredient that the modern world sees in it, a source of sheepish gregariousness in society and of a platitudinous "realism" in the arts, *mimesis* (because of its admixture of desire) is an explosive combination. It constitutes the disruptive factor par excellence of human relations, the major reason for the fragility of even and especially the closest friendships and the most tender erotic relationships. The closer the friends, the more likely they are to imitate one another's desires and therefore to turn into enemies. This is Shakespeare's tragic as well as his comic insight par excellence, and it is undistinguishable from the fusion of mimesis and desire that he perpetually portrays.[4]

Notes

1. William Shakespeare, *A Midsummer Night's Dream*, in *The Riverside Shakespeare*, ed. G. Blakemore Evans (Boston: Houghton Mifflin Company, 1974). All subsequent quotations in the text are taken from this same source.

2. René Girard, *Violence and the Sacred* (Baltimore: Johns Hopkins University Press, 1978).

3. "Myth and Ritual in Shakespeare: *A Midsummer Night's Dream*," in *Textual Strategies*, ed. Josue Harari (Ithaca: Cornell University Press, 1979), 189–212.

4. This essay should lead to a consideration of the play within the play. The theme is too rich, however, and too long for the present essay; it will be instead the subject of a separate essay, the third in a three-part study of *A Midsummer Night's Dream*. The author apologizes for his long delay in treating the fascinating encounter between the two types of mimetic actors.

WILLIAM W. E. SLIGHTS

The Changeling in A Dream

Midway through the first scene of Act II in *A Midsummer Night's Dream*, Oberon, King of the Fairies, begs "a little changeling boy" of Titania. She responds, "The fairy land buys not the child of me" (II.i.120, 122), and from this exchange—or non-exchange—follows a highly determined though minimally textualized custody battle.[1] After a great deal has been done and said about the nature of love and marriage, and a quantity of flower juice has been squirted about, Oberon again "ask[s] of her her changeling child," and "straight" Titania gives it to him (IV.i.59–60), not because the snaky scales of feminine insubordination have fallen from her eyes, but because Oberon has caused her to become infatuated with a very funny-looking local weaver who is also not her husband. The quarrel over the changeling boy is powerful but also peripheral, erratically described, and never properly resolved. These and similar anomalies in Shakespeare's treatment of the changeling boy make it difficult to see how the other characters, followed by a group of usually reliable critics, can say with such fierce (over-)determination just what the boy and the fairy discords focused on him are all about. Although the text never calls for this "character" to appear on stage, theatrical directors, taking matters creatively into their own hands, tend to beg the question by assigning the changeling's "part" to some small member of the company. In the case of such a shadowy figure as the changeling in *A Dream*, however,

From *Studies in English Literature* 28, no. 2 (Spring 1988): 259–72. © 1988 by *Studies in English Literature*.

29

we need to proceed with some care in order to be sure that what we are interpreting is, in some sense, *there.*

There are just six direct references to the changeling boy in the text, three of which I have already quoted. In another, Puck, that perpetually amused vulgarizer of relationships, voices his view that the changeling is stolen goods that "jealous" Oberon wants to possess. He tells an unnamed fairy that Titania

> as her attendant hath
> A lovely boy stolen from an Indian king;
> She never had so sweet a changeling.
> And jealous Oberon would have the child
> Knight of his train, to trace the forest wild;
> But she, perforce, withholds the loved boy,
> Crowns him with flowers, and makes him all her joy.
>   (II.i.21–27)

From these lines we learn that the boy, who started life as an Indian prince, is "lovely," "sweet," and "loved" by Titania.[2] Oberon's competing and exclusive claim suggests that perhaps, as Puck implies, no one in fairyland has a rightful claim to him. Anyone who wants the changeling, for whatever purpose, may have to withhold him "perforce," that is, forcibly. On the other hand, the line, "she, perforce, withholds the loved boy," also opens the possibility that Titania herself is acting under some form of compulsion.

While Puck's account of the changeling boy raises the problems of compulsive behavior and custodial rights among thieves, Oberon's way of seeing the matter is that he has suffered an intolerable injury (II.i.147) at the hands of a "wanton" wife (II.i.63).[3] To punish this act of sexual and social insubordination he employs the aphrodisiac juice of the flower called love-in-idleness, thereby creating a "hateful imperfection [in Titania's] eyes" (IV.i.63) that makes her lust after Bottom the ass. Eventually he chastens her and, we are to suppose, drives her back to his own conjugal bed with a second flower drug, "Dian's bud o'er Cupid's flower / [Having] such force and blessed power" (IV.i.73–74).

Titania's view of the changeling boy is altogether different from Puck's and Oberon's. To her, caring for the boy is an act of loyalty to a woman with whom she had shared the most intimate and delightful female companionship, until the fatal moment of the child's birth:

> His mother was a vot'ress of my order,
> And in the spiced Indian air, by night,
> Full often hath she gossip'd by my side,

And sat with me on Neptune's yellow sands,
Marking th' embarked traders on the flood;
When we have laugh'd to see the sails conceive
And grow big-bellied with the wanton wind;
Which she, with pretty and with swimming gait,
Following (her womb then rich with my young squire)
Would imitate, and sail upon the land
To fetch me trifles, and return again,
As from a voyage, rich with merchandise.
But she, being mortal, of that boy did die,
And for her sake do I rear up her boy;
And for her sake I will not part with him.
    (II.i.123–37)

The passage captures the pleasure the two women take in gently mocking the world of marine commerce with the richer joys of sorority and pregnancy.[4] However perplexing we may find the phrase "a vot'ress of my order,"[5] the lines describe a relationship of deep understanding and trust based on their feelings as women. The experience of perfect empathy is expressed in the metaphoring, unmetaphoring, and remetaphoring of the big-bellied sails. What is conceived and imitated here is the very idea of conception. The sails, impregnated by the inspiring breath of the wind, transform the trading vessels into women great with child, one of whom (Titania's votaress and the mother of the changeling boy) in turn humorously imitates a merchandise-laden vessel by gliding gracefully across the land "with pretty and with swimming gait." One need only exchange the terms and, handy-dandy, which is the tenor, which the vehicle in this fully conceived metaphor? Ruth Nevo remarks wittily that "Oberon might mend his marriage more effectively by getting Titania with child than by trying to get Titania without child."[6] Though there is something vaguely absurd in the critic turning marriage counsellor to the Fairy King, Nevo has rightly seen that parenting emerges as central to Titania's consciousness. The Fairy Queen places herself in loco parentis when the Indian queen dies in childbirth. Now she must nurture and protect a child who, to her mind, is more adopted than kidnapped from the human realm. In Titania's eyes, the fact that he straddles the border between human and fairy in no way obviates his need for mothering.

Understanding what happens on the psychic boundary between human and fairy kind is a prime interpretive challenge in *A Dream*. The changeling boy, who in my view exists rather precariously in this bordering state, has seemed to some critics to provide a clear case of a lesson learned in fairyland and transferred back into the human realm. The lesson is largely concerned with the hypothesized superiority of reason (identified as a male strength) over will (identified as a female weakness) in Renaissance psychology, the dominant position of husbands over their wives in Renaissance society, and the advisability of graduating boy-children from women's care to men's hunting parties.[7] The difficulty with these claims is that they assume or assert a kind of particularity about the nature and function of the changeling boy that—as we have already seen from the conflicting views of Puck, Oberon, and Titania—Shakespeare's text does not provide. The changeling is an absent presence, existing only as a series of competing claims on his company. As such, he illustrates a principle of indeterminacy evident in many parts of the play.

The concept of indeterminacy has gained considerable currency over the past three decades, largely through the work of Ferdinand de Saussure, Jacques Derrida, and other semantic philosophers. One version of the concept grows out of Derrida's efforts to break down the simple model of one signifier and one thing signified by suggesting that signifiers may just go on indefinitely referring to other signifiers. Jonathan Culler is at pains to point out that this is not the same thing as arguing that any interpretation is as good as any other. He writes, "The combination of context-bound meaning and boundless context on the one hand makes possible proclamations of the indeterminacy of meaning—though the smug iconoclasm of such proclamations may be irritating—but on the other hand urges that we continue to interpret texts, classify speech acts, and attempt to elucidate the conditions of signification."[8] It is in this sense and spirit that I invoke the principle of indeterminacy. I do not propose to make common cause with those who, like Bottom, believe that "Man is but an ass, if he go about t'expound this dream" (IV.i.206–207). Expounding is a large part of the business of criticism as I practice it. What makes asses of us all, including the characters in *A Dream*, is announcing that we possess the sole, uncontestable truth, particularly about an area of experience as unstable as the one Shakespeare dramatizes in this play. As interpreters, we must always be prepared to deal with contending, contingent truths about matters as apparently simple as weather-reporting and as decidedly complex as love and marriage. While offering us a variety of insights into such topics as these, the play always slips free of formally restrictive readings. The changeling boy receives a wide range of responses from characters in the play and invites even more complex, unsettling responses from the audience.

Consider for a moment an apparently banal topic, the weather. Titania's account of the weather in a distinctly anglicized Athens and environs achieves mythic proportions but precious little fixity:

> never, since the middle summer's spring,
> Met we on hill, in dale, forest, or mead,

By paved fountain or by rushy brook,
Or in the beached margent of the sea,
To dance our ringlets to the whistling wind,
But with thy brawls thou hast disturb'd our sport.
Therefore the winds, piping to us in vain,
As in revenge, have suck'd up from the sea
Contagious fogs; which, falling in the land,
Hath every pelting river made so proud
That they have overborne their continents.
The ox hath therefore stretch'd his yoke in vain,
The ploughman lost his sweat, and the green corn
Hath rotted ere his youth attain'd a beard.
The fold stands empty in the drowned field,
And crows are fatted with the murrion flock;
The nine men's morris is fill'd up with mud,
And the quaint mazes in the wanton green,
For lack of tread, are undistinguishable.
The human mortals want their winter here;
No night is now with hymn or carol blest.
Therefore the moon (the governess of floods),
Pale in her anger, washes all the air,
That rheumatic diseases do abound.
And thorough this distemperature, we see
The seasons alter: hoary-headed frosts
Fall in the fresh lap of the crimson rose,
And on old Hiems' thin and icy crown
And odorous chaplet of sweet summer buds
Is, as in mockery, set; the spring, the summer,
The childing autumn, angry winter, change
Their wonted liveries; and the mazed world,
By their increase, now knows not which is which.
And this same progeny of evils comes
From our debate, from our dissension;
We are their parents and original.
        (II.i.82–117)

This perplexing set-piece of visionary verse moves from logic to chaos, from a precise time-frame to a seasonal jumble, from a complaint about infertility to a complaint about a "progeny of evils," from precise signs denoting natural objects, causes, and consequences to a "mazed world [that] knows not which is which." This sounds a good deal like a working definition of indeterminacy. Titania's catalogue of inclemency—fog, flooding, failed crops, decimated flocks, polluted air, and unseasonable temperatures—carries an implicit self-accusation of being either merciless (literally without clemency) or irresponsible towards the people whose weather she is making. But Titania is no bubble-headed woodland deity heedlessly upending the seasons. The thrice-repeated logical connective, "therefore," lends force to the carefully deployed argumentative structure aimed at forcing Oberon to accept joint responsibility for the weather, if not for the changeling child. For all that the fairies seem to be a source of disorder in the play, Titania here provides an orderly explanation of that very disorder. From the precisely defined "middle summer's spring" Titania plunges us into a *wintry* world incongruously crowned with "sweet summer buds," despite her assertion midway through the speech that "mortals want their winter here." Though phrases such as "wanton green" and "lap of the crimson rose" convey, as C. L. Barber points out, a strong "amorous suggestion" (p. 147), others such as "childing autumn," "progeny of evils," and "parents and original" create an equally strong maternal suggestion. As she arrives at her conclusion regarding the debate over the changeling child, she leaves us with an overwhelming sense that, for all her logical explanation, the progeny of evils remains a paradox, an indeterminate truth, and we a part of that "mazed world [that] knows not which is which."

Extending the indeterminacy of Titania's account of the grief caused by the struggle for custody of the changeling boy is the fact that no one else in the play seems to notice any bad weather. However much the Athenian lovers quarrel, not so much as a cloud emerges on their horizons. It is not an adequate response to this observation to say that Titania's lines apply only to the lofty idealities of fairyland and are not intended as a description of ordinary human reality when she has gone to such lengths to locate all that mud in the nine men's morris and to de-rhapsodize her speech with the sweat of redundantly "human mortals." René Girard amusingly demystifies the play's meteorology: "Scholars assume that the weather must have been particularly bad in the year Shakespeare wrote the play; this, in turn, gives some clues to the dating of the play. It must be true, indeed, that Shakespeare needed some really inclement weather to write what he did."[9] Girard goes on to argue that what lies behind all this literalized weather forecasting is the deeper problem of "conceptual undifferentiation" (p. 203), concluding with tongue in cheek that in the play's happy ending, "Good weather is back, everything is in order once more" (p. 208). The effect of omitting from the mimetic dimension of the play any corroborating text about the weather is to call into question the notion of a single, authorized version of reality, even though that version emanates from a royal source. Here is no privileging of the text but a willingness to launch the text on to the uncertain seas of human emotion.

If something as ordinary as the weather becomes a source of conflicting evidence in the play, we may expect a still higher degree of uncertainty to be generated around the presentation of love and marriage. It would be reasonable to conclude after reading the play or seeing it performed that love is the major source of indeterminacy, not quarreling, as Titania contends. It is hard to get a straight answer from a lover to even the simplest question: How do you like Athens, Hermia?

> Before the time I did Lysander see,
> Seem'd Athens as a paradise to me;
> O then, what graces in my love do dwell,
> That he hath turn'd a heaven unto a hell!
> (I.i.204–207)

Not only does the weather around Athens remain uncertain, the city itself evokes diametrically opposed responses in the same person, this time under the compulsion of love.

Some of this violent changeability can be credited to Shakespeare's Ovidian treatment of love. Love, especially youthful love, can never remain fixed for long in the *Metaphorphoses*. Similarly, Lysander's account of the course of true love broods with *Romeo and Juliet*–like awareness over the fate of a passion that is

>   momentary as a sound,
> Swift as a shadow, short as any dream,
> Brief as the lightning in the collied night,
> That, in a spleen, unfolds both heaven and earth;
> And ere a man hath power to say "Behold!"
> The jaws of darkness do devour it up:
> So quick bright things come to confusion.
> (I.i.143–49)

That four of Shakespeare's bright young things quickly come to confusion in the night wood may be attributed to their youthful inexperience. Indeed, the skittishness of lovers becomes synonymous with childishness in the play. The two Athenian youths and their girlfriends are initially thought to be as much in need of parenting as the changeling boy. They are not fully formed persons but rather exude the still undetermined potential of childhood.

In the non-human world of *A Midsummer Night's Dream*, love's fickleness has not one but three childish faces. "Love [is] said to be a child" (I.i.238) in the iconographic tradition that transmitted the Cupid myth from classical times to the Renaissance, a tradition summarized in some detail by Helena (I.i.232–45). With delicate literalness, Shakespeare translates the erratic power of Cupid's arrows into the magic juice of Oberon's narrative of the fiery shaft that missed Diana's "imperial vot'ress," who figures the chaste Eliza, striking instead the flower called love-in-idleness (II.i.148–74). Oberon places Cupid's powerful drug in the hands of another "waggish boy," Puck, who, though himself no lover of mankind, is vastly amused by the emotional instability generated by his newly acquired ability to make people tumble in and out of love. The third is our old friend the changeling boy, who likewise represents no uniform or fixed approach to the meaning of love.[10] In each case, these spirits pose a threat to established hierarchy and its protective institution of marriage.

A widely accepted interpretation of the play's comic resolution is that the young people's unrealized potential for love is eventually given adult definition by traditional marriage celebrations in Act V.[11] The fullest and most persuasive account of this approach to determining the meaning of the play is Paul Olson's essay, "*A Midsummer Night's Dream* and the Meaning of Court Marriage."[12] After tracing a social and iconological tradition of marriage from the garden of Eden to the court of Elizabeth, Olson concludes that "In the total conceptual scheme of the play, the king and queen of the woods dramatize the two poles of the scale of values which gave meaning to marriage. They are types of the forces of Reason and Passion which in a more complex and human manner move through Theseus and Hippolita respectively" (p. 111).

One problem with this kind of reading is that it is clear both from literary and non-literary sources of the late sixteenth and early seventeenth centuries that marriage performed a great many functions besides subjecting women's passions to the control of men's intellects.[13] Some marriages were for gain, some for companionship, some for love, some for convenience. Some were equally shared, some enforced, some secret, and some nasty, mean, brutish, and short. Furthermore, given the favored male pastimes referred to in *A Midsummer Night's Dream* (war and the hunt), it is difficult to believe that Shakespeare was trying to depict Reason as an exclusive male preserve. Although Olson explains with admirable fullness and subtlety the significance of various literary representations of marriage, he overreads the text of Shakespeare's play. He refers, for example, to Titania's "erotic games with . . . the changeling" (p. 111), assignations we neither see nor hear about.

Far more prominent in the play than "the celestial love which preserves chaste marriages and keeps the cosmos in order" (Olson, p. 109), are the uncontrollable, carnivalesque impulses operating despite the best efforts of several patriarchs to rearrange or suppress the natural impulses of youth. As one recent critic points out, "the play represents several stories of resistance and discord, counter-models of the reconciliation and accommodation Theseus proposes."[14] Not only does the play confront us with the willful rebellion of a quartet of teenagers, but it sets in motion the maddest of low-life subplots, including Bottom's anarchic synesthesia (IV.i.204–19) and even in the fifth-act resolution the topsy-turvy indeterminacy of "very tragical mirth" (V.i.57) in the mechanicals' performance at court. The challenge for all the audiences, on-stage and off, is to hold in mind at once pairs of terms and concepts that point in opposite directions. It has become customary to discuss the reconciliation of opposites or *concordia discors* in *A Midsummer Night's Dream* in terms of a patriarchal triumph over female waywardness in the most obvious of institutional joining of opposites, holy matrimony.[15] This is the great Elizabethan humanist settlement for the problem of conflicting stories and emotional states in the play: Titania is forced to see the folly of her infatuation with the changeling boy by being made to fall in love with a second and more monstrous changeling, one that even she can eventually perceive as inferior to her proper husband. Like Helena, Hermia, and Hippolyta, she is taught that the only true concord for the sexes requires her to acknowledge the central fact of benign (and, by analogy, divine) male superiority in a patrilineal-patrological culture. Titania, in fact, acknowledges nothing of the kind when she gives up the changeling boy. All she says is that she now loathes the sight of the transfigured Bottom (IV.i.79). It can be argued, then, that in its pursuit of comic conflicts Shakespeare's play does more to unsettle than to inscribe traditional assumptions of courtly culture concerning marriage.

Traditional readings of *A Midsummer Night's Dream* do, of course, allow that conflicts exist within the hierarchical social structure depicted in the play, but they maintain that discord exists only to be chastized, corrected, and subsumed by a higher order. For a number of reasons I believe, on the contrary, that the indeterminacy of Shakespeare's text permits the characters to perpetuate their amorous and festive madness with all the illogic of a dream through and even beyond its formal end. Though the young lovers awake in Act IV as if from a dream, their present waking reality is as unfixed as their labyrinthine sleepwalking:

> *Her.* Methinks I see these things with parted eye,
> When every thing seems double.
> *Hel.* So methinks;
> And I have found Demetrius like a jewel,
> Mine own, and not mine own.
> 　　(IV.i.189–92)

Shakespeare poses as a problem for his fictional persons as well as his would-be understanders outside the play, the proposition that any attempt to make something firmly one's own, whether it be a changeling boy, an eligible bachelor, or a unique interpretation of a text, is to expose the vaguely ridiculous limitations of the human condition. No tyrannical assertion of authority by a father, a duke, a lover, or a critic can manage to avoid the problem.

In writing a comedy that takes place almost wholly beyond the reach of ordinary domestic locales, exploring the haunts of Endymion rather than Gammer Gurton, Shakespeare ignores the centrality of traditional male power and respectability, instead mapping the terrain that Robert Frost in his poem "West-Running Brook" calls "lady-land." The male authority figures, Egeus and Theseus, cease to exert their powers of constraint after Act I. The genuine sources of human vitality and insight in Shakespeare are not to be found at the safe center of government or in the quiet domains of marriage but rather in the world of Falstaff and Hal at the Boars Head, Lear and his fool on the heath, Perdita in her garden, Prospero and Caliban on their uneasily shared island—places that harbor the mooncalves and changelings of the world. *A Midsummer Night's Dream* is not a celebration in the same genre as Jonson's court masques. It is not focused on the literal or even the symbolic seat of royal power but rather on the largely uncharted territory on the fringes or "margents" of society where the rules of power tend to break down, often with imaginatively liberating and extremely amusing results. Here, Hippolyta's view that "the story of the night ... grows to something of great constancy" (V.i.23–27) can brush aside Theseus's condescending and authoritarian pronouncements, leaving intact the claims of the imagination.

The point about discords in this marginal world is that they remain stimulatingly discordant. The changeling boy, so insubstantial in the text and so variously perceived as a source of conflict, is a prime example of the indeterminacy that the play postulates as the essential condition of people who love and people who dream. Try as they may to remain wrapped "In maiden meditation, fancy-free" (II.i.164), like the Imperial Virgin protected by chaste moonbeams from Cupid's fiery shaft, ordinary mortals are seldom free in their fancying. Even the perceptions of the Queen of Fairy can be constrained by the siren call of the strange mortal, Bottom:

> I pray thee, gentle mortal, sing again.
> Mine ear is much enamored of thy note;
> So is mine eye enthralled to thy shape;
> And thy fair virtue's force (perforce) doth move me
> On the first view to say, to swear, I love thee.
>   (III.i.137–41)

Here are a woman and a piece of text about as determined as they can be. Bottom's perceived good looks, his "virtue," are closely shadowed by the root sense of *virtú*, power or force. A force perforce forces Titania triply to swear to a love that will evaporate from her eye and her tongue in the space of a single act. The real forces celebrated in the play would seem to be not marital restraint, chastity, or even, perhaps, constancy, but natural sexual impulses and radically unstable sense-perceptions. As Michael Andrews argues, the dewy tears that materialize in the "pretty flouriets' eyes" (IV.i.55) when Oberon upbraids Titania for bedecking first the changeling boy and then Bottom with flowers, are as likely to be shed for love repressed than, as usually glossed, for chaste women ravished.[16] Enforced chastity is no wellspring of joy in *A Midsummer Night's Dream*. Instead, the play gives full scope to desires that struck Puritan preachers and authors of courtly entertainments alike as anathema to Christian marriage and good government.

Still, matrimony has its hour when the moon is full, the rustics are fooling at the height of their bent, and the fairies are in gentle attendance. The troublesome changeling child, violator of the shifting but ever-present boundary between human and other worlds, has apparently been forgotten in the wake of the new amity between Titania and Oberon. This is not to say that the differences of perception regarding the changeling have been resolved, any more than the conflicting infatuations of the Athenian lovers or Hermia's dispute with her father have been "resolved." They have merely been swept to one side like the dust that Puck is sent to sweep behind the door on the wedding night. There the unpleasantnesses and competing truths will coexist with the joys of marriage and those of the comic stage. No single or higher truth emerges from the play but rather a slightly bewildering and highly amusing collection of apparently willful reinterpretations of the experience of being in and out of love. Like the changeling boy, *A Midsummer Night's Dream* itself is a masterwork of what I have called indeterminacy and what Keats called "*Negative Capability*, that is when man is capable of being in uncertainties, Mysteries, doubts, without any irritable reaching after fact & reason."[17]

Notes

William W. E. Slights, Professor of English at the University of Saskatchewan, has recently completed a study of early printed marginalia in relation to contemporary socio-linguistic theories of *marginalité* (forthcoming in *Renaissance Quarterly*). He continues to work on Jonson and Shakespeare as reformers of literary genres.

1. Quotations from *A Midsummer Night's Dream* are from *The Riverside Shakespeare*, ed. G. Blakemore Evans, et al. (Boston: Houghton Mifflin, 1974).

2. "The changeling," according to Minor White Latham, "seems to have been peculiar to the 16th-century fairies of England" (*The Elizabethan Fairies: The Fairies of Folklore and the Fairies of Shakespeare* [New York: Columbia Univ. Press, 1930],

rpt. New York: Octagon Books, 1972, p. 150). The still more peculiar feature of this particular changeling is that he is not the usual deformed child left behind by the fairies to create consternation among distraught human parents, but instead the handsome young prince vied for on the far side, the fairy side.

3. In his article, "Titania and the Changeling," *ES* 22 (1940): 66–70, Donald C. Miller argues with single-minded determination that several epithets attached to Titania's name, including "proud," "rash," and "jealous," are synonymous with "wanton." Largely on this basis, he concludes that "Titania has made the boy her lover" (p. 66). As will become clear, I view the relationship very differently.

4. I cannot agree with David Marshall's assertion that in this speech Titania "is perpetuating rather than rejecting terms that inscribe people in a system of economic relations." The tenderness of her language has little in common with characters such as Shylock whose purpose actually is so to "inscribe" people. See David Marshall, "Exchanging Visions: Reading *A Midsummer Night's Dream*," *ELH* 49 (1982): 568. A more sensitive and persuasive reading of the lines is C. L. Barber's in *Shakespeare's Festive Comedy* (Princeton: Princeton Univ. Press, 1959), pp. 136–37. Louis Adrian Montrose reads the speech as an exclusively female version of carrying sons and argues that it "counterpoints" Theseus's account of how men, without the mediation of women, leave their imprint on their daughters (I.i.47–51). The upshot of this contest between male and female fantasies of parthenogenesis, according to Montrose, is repeated "male disruption of an intimate bond between women" (p. 71), a disruption that the play's comic form eventually sanctions and, in doing so, "neutralizes the forms of royal power [in particular, the potent myth of the Virgin Queen] to which it ostensibly pays homage" (p. 85). See "'Shaping Fantasies': Figurations of Gender and Power in Elizabethan Culture," *Representations* 1 (1983): 61–94.

5. Ernest Schanzer, with refreshing candor, admits his bafflement at the phrase: "The order of the fairy queen? With human votaresses? It does not make sense . . . the words 'vot'ress of my order' seem oddly chosen. Perhaps some topical allusion is the answer to the puzzle, with Titania at least in this episode standing for the Queen and the votaress perhaps for one of her ladies-in-waiting" ("The Moon and the Fairies in *A Midsummer Night's Dream*," *UTQ* 24 [1955]: 241–42). More relevant to today's readers than surmised topicality is the sense of stability, as opposed to wantonness, conveyed by the word "order."

6. Ruth Nevo, *Comic Transformations in Shakespeare* (London: Methuen, 1980), p. 104.

7. In addition to Ruth Nevo's book, which I have already cited, and Paul Olson's essay, which I will discuss later, the following works read the play as endorsing certain sexist assumptions of Shakespeare's society: Paul N. Siegel, "*A Midsummer Night's Dream* and the Wedding Guests," *SQ* 4 (1953): 139–44; James L. Calderwood, "*A Midsummer Night's Dream*: The Illusion of Drama," *MLQ* 26 (1965): 506–22; David P. Young, *Something of Great Constancy: The Art of "A Midsummer Night's Dream"* (New Haven: Yale Univ. Press, 1966); Anca Vlasopolos, "The Ritual of Midsummer: A Pattern for *A Midsummer Night's Dream*," *RenQ* 31 (1978): 21–29; and Alan W. Bellringer, "The Act of Change in *A Midsummer Night's Dream*," *ES* 64 (1983): 201–17.

8. Jonathan Culler, *On Deconstruction: Theory and Criticism after Structuralism* (Ithaca: Cornell Univ. Press, 1982), p. 133.

9. René Girard, "Myth and Ritual in Shakespeare: *A Midsummer Night's Dream*," in *Textual Strategies: Perspectives in Post-Structuralist Criticism*, ed. Josué V. Harari (Ithaca: Cornell Univ. Press, 1979), p. 199.

10. For an interpretation that finds a fixed, indeed a theoretically predetermined, pattern of behavior in the way adults and children relate to one another, see Vicky Shahly Hartman, "*A Midsummer Night's Dream*: A Gentle Concord to the Oedipal Problem," *AI* 40 (1983): 356–69. Norman Holland's application of Freudian theory to the play ("Hermia's Dream," in *Representing Shakespeare: New Psychoanalytic Essays*, ed. Murry M. Schwartz and Coppelia Kahn [Baltimore: Johns Hopkins Univ. Press, 1980], pp. 1–20) avoids some of the problems of overdetermining the text that Hartman's essay exhibits. Paul Stevens argues from a rich matrix of allusion that the psychological origin of childishness in the play is the fancy uninformed by reason. See his *Imagination and the Presence of Shakespeare in "Paradise Lost"* (Madison: Univ. of Wisconsin Press, 1985), pp. 15, 85–87, et passim.

11. The connection between this play about marriage and an actual aristocratic marriage of the mid-1590s has often been postulated, but the evidence for linking *A Midsummer Night's Dream* to one or another specific marriage is so far inconclusive.

12. Paul A. Olson, "*A Midsummer Night's Dream* and the Meaning of Court Marriage," *ELH* 24 (1957): 95–119.

13. The fourth chapter of Keith Wrightson's *English Society, 1580–1680* (London: Hutchinson, 1982) presents evidence of some highly companionable marriages drawn from a variety of shires and social classes.

14. Michael D. Bristol, *Carnival and Theater: Plebeian Culture and the Structure of Authority in Renaissance England* (New York: Methuen, 1985), p. 172. On the basis of Harold Brooks's source work with Plutarch and Seneca in the Arden edition, Louis Montrose argues that "sedimented within the verbal texture of *A Midsummer Night's Dream* are traces of those forms of familial violence which the play would suppress" ("Shaping Fantasies," p. 75).

15. Hippolyta's lines concerning the hounds of Sparta suggest a possible analogue to this process:

> Never did I hear
> Such gallant chiding; for besides the groves,
> The skies, the fountains, every region near
> Seem all one mutual cry. I never heard
> So musical a discord, such sweet thunder.
> (IV.i.114–18)

16. See Michael Cameron Andrews, "Titania on 'Enforced Chastity,'" *N&Q* 31 (1984): 188.

17. *John Keats: Selected Poems and Letters*, ed. Douglas Bush (Boston: Houghton Mifflin, 1959), p. 261.

JAY L. HALIO

Nightingales That Roar:
The Language of A Midsummer Night's Dream

In an essay called "On the Value of *Hamlet*," Stephen Booth has shown
how that play simultaneously frustrates and fulfills audience expectations
and otherwise presents contradictions that belie or bedevil the attempts of
many a reductionist critic to demonstrate a coherent thematic pattern in
Shakespeare's masterpiece. Booth's commentary is particularly directed to
the language and action of act 1 which, from the very outset, arouse in the
audience a "sensation of being unexpectedly and very slightly out of step"
with the drama that the players unfold. "In *Hamlet*," Booth says, "the audience does not so much shift its focus as come to find its focus shifted."[1] The
end result, though initially disturbing, is not finally so: "People see *Hamlet*
and tolerate inconsistencies that it does not seem they could bear. . . . Truth
is bigger than any one system for knowing it, and *Hamlet* is bigger than any
of the frames of reference it inhabits. *Hamlet* allows us to comprehend—to
hold on to—all of the contradictions it contains."[2]

The kind of linguistic and dramatic complexity that Booth describes,
while preeminently demonstrable in *Hamlet*, is by no means limited to that
play. It is far more prevalent than perhaps has been recognized, although several critics before and since Booth's essay have tried to show similar situations
in other plays. David Bevington, for example, has shown how in *A Midsummer
Night's Dream* the debate between Oberon and Puck in act 3, scene 2 "reflects a

From *Traditions and Innovations: Essays on British Literature of the Middle Ages and the
Renaissance*, edited by David G. Allen and Robert A. White, pp. 137–49. © 1990 by
Associated University Presses.

fundamental tension in the play between comic reassurance and the suggestion of something dark and threatening."[3] In "Titania and the Ass's Head" Jan Kott argued that *A Midsummer Night's Dream* is "the most erotic of Shakespeare's plays" and nowhere else is the eroticism "expressed so brutally."[4] Kott's focus is largely upon the animal imagery and erotic symbolism. The metaphors in Helena's speech to Demetrius in which she proclaims herself his "spaniel," his "dog" (2.1.203–10), Kott regards as "almost masochistic." Contrary to the romantic tradition, reinforced by Mendelssohn's music, the forest in *Dream* represents anything but a version of Arcadia, inhabited as it is by "devils and lamias, in which witches and sorceresses can easily find everything required for their practices."[5] Titania caressing the monster with the head of an ass is closer to the fearful visions of Hieronymous Bosch, in Kott's view, than to the gentler depictions of Chagall and countless other illustrators of Shakespeare's dream play.

Like Bevington, we need not go as far as Kott does. We need not imagine Titania's court consisting of toothless old men and shaking hags, "their mouths wet with saliva" as they, sniggering, "procure a monster for their mistress."[6] But there is a good deal more going on beneath the play's surface than many have been willing to notice, or have deliberately been persuaded (or lulled) into not noticing. This surely was the point, in part, of Peter Brook's 1970 production: to shake us out of complacency. In much of the poetry, indeed in some of the most celebrated passages, there is a repeated undercutting of the tenor by the vehicle Shakespeare chooses, or a subverting of the overall tone by the actual sense of the language employed. Although this point is related to Kott's, it is, I think, a more general one and characterizes similar phenomena in other plays.

As so often in Shakespearean drama, the first clues come early, in the very opening speeches. Theseus tells Hippolyta that their nuptial hour approaches and he is, like any bridegroom, impatient for the event. But the specific language suggests a crass motive and includes images that are otherwise scarcely flattering to his bride, who is, like Theseus, somewhat advanced in years:

> Four happy days bring in
> Another moon—but O, methinks how slow
> This old moon wanes! She lingers my desires,
> Like to a stepdame or a dowager
> Long withering out a young man's revenue.
>   (1.1.2–6)[7]

Hippolyta's response, meant to be reassuring, yet includes the simile of a "silver bow / New-bent in heaven" that reminds Theseus in his turn how he wooed her with his sword and won her love by doing her injuries. He promises to wed her in "another key," but suggestions of discord have already been sounded, and many more will follow before Oberon's final benediction and Puck's epilogue—and their interesting peculiarities.

One such discord occurs immediately with the entrance of Egeus, Hermia, and her two suitors. It is a situation not unlike the opening scenes of *Othello*, and Egeus's complaints against Lysander are similar to Brabantio's accusations of the Moor: the young man has "bewitched" the old man's daughter with rhymes and presents, "messengers / Of strong prevailment in unhardened youth" (34–35). As the dialogue develops, however, it is clear that if any bewitching has so far occurred—some will certainly occur later—it has been Hermia who has enchanted the affections of both young men. Nevertheless, Egeus's determination to have his way, or his daughter's death, is more than a little disconcerting. It is Theseus—not Egeus—who recalls a third alternative that he makes sound, in this dramatic context, less attractive than a more orthodox view requires. Hermia, after all, can become a nun:

> Therefore, fair Hermia, question your desires,
> Know of your youth, examine well your blood,
> Whether, if you yield not to your father's choice,
> You can endure the livery of a nun,
> For aye to be in shady cloister mewed,
> To live a barren sister all your life,
> Chanting faint hymns to the cold fruitless moon.
> Thrice-blessèd they that master so their blood
> To undergo such maiden pilgrimage;
> But earthlier happy is the rose distilled
> Than that which, withering on the virgin thorn,
> Grows, lives, and dies in single blessedness.
>   (67–78)

Anachronisms apart, Theseus's description of a "thrice-blessèd" life is shall we admit, rather forbidding. The whole conception of devotion—filial, religious, amorous—is further subverted a few lines later when Lysander mentions Helena's love for Demetrius, who has jilted her:

> she, sweet lady, dotes
> Devoutly dotes, dotes in idolatry
> Upon this spotted and inconstant man.
>   (108–10)

And, strangely enough, Theseus sets his own wedding day as the date on which Hermia must make her fateful decision:

Take time to pause, and by the next new moon—
The sealing day between my love and me
For everlasting bond of fellowship—
Upon *that* day either prepare to die
For disobedience to your father's will,
Or else to wed Demetrius, as he would,
Or on Diana's altar to protest
For aye austerity and single life.
    (83–90; my italics)

Left with the three alternatives that Theseus enumerates, the lovers look for consolation from each other. Lysander tries to comfort Hermia with a disquisition upon the theme, "The course of true love never did run smooth." The stichomythia in which they then engage reveals only the most obvious way Lysander's words of "comfort" are undercut: "O cross! . . . O spite! . . . O hell!" begins each of Hermia's comments. She eventually allows herself to be persuaded by the lesson Lysander seems to be emphasizing—"Then let us teach our trial patience"—only to discover, contrary to his explicit assent, that this is not what he really has in mind at all. His "therefore" (156) leads in quite a different direction, wherever his earlier logic might have been pointing, as he presents to Hermia his plan to elope.

Hermia's ready agreement to the plan concludes with what is, again given the dramatic context, a most curious set of oaths. It begins conventionally enough, but then something happens to the conventions, or rather some oddly inappropriate ones intrude:

I swear to thee by Cupid's strongest bow,
By his best arrow with the golden head,
By the simplicity of Venus' doves,
By that which knitteth souls and prospers loves,
And by that fire which burned the Carthage queen
When the false Trojan under sail was seen,
By all the vows that ever men have broke—
In number more than ever women spoke,—
In that same place thou hast appointed me
Tomorrow truly will I meet with thee.
    (169–78)

Hermia may be merely teasing her lover, so sure she is of him, as Alexander Leggatt says, and the joking does no harm.[8] But teasing always contains a barb, and (not only in light of what comes later) the allusions to male infidelity are ominous, to say the least. In any event, the rhetoric of the first eight lines is neatly undercut by the final couplet, whose jingling and prosaic simplicity collapses the soaring quality of what precedes it. This may all be part of the comic effect intended, and Lysander's flat "Keep promise, love," while confirming the anticlimactic effect, at the same time suggests by its peremptoriness that he may be caught a little off balance by Hermia. But before we can ponder this exchange further, Helena enters with paradoxes of her own.

Consider her lines on love and the imagination. Although earlier she laments how Demetrius is misled in large part by Hermia's external beauty, here Helena complains of the transforming power of the imagination under the influence of love:

> Things base and vile, holding no quantity,
> Love can transpose to form and dignity.
> Love looks not with the eyes, but with the mind,
> And therefore is winged Cupid painted blind.
> Nor hath love's mind of any judgement taste;
> Wings and no eyes figure unheedy haste.
> And therefore is love said to be a child
> Because in choice he is so oft beguiled.
>   (232–39)

Throughout her speech Helena shows remarkable maturity of insight, except of course that all of her insight helps not a jot to correct her own love's folly. She errs as badly as Demetrius, by her own admission. Nor is she correct about visual susceptibility. As much of the central action of the play demonstrates, the eyes decidedly lead—or mislead—lovers. The capacity for transposing "things base and vile" to "form and dignity" is not in the imagination, or "mind," but in the fancy, which as she indicates is devoid of judgment. Shakespeare shows the relation between eyesight and fancy (or love) in a song from *The Merchant of Venice*:

> Tell me where is fancy bred,
> Or in the heart or in the head?
> How begot, how nourished? Reply, reply.
> It is engendered in the eyes,
> With gazing fed; and fancy dies
> In the cradle where it lies.
>   (3.2.63–69)

Later, in a speech notable for its dramatic irony, Lysander justifies his sudden passion for Helena by an appeal to his reason, which he claims has led his will, or desire (2.2.121–23). But like others in the Athenian forest, he is led by his eyes, influenced by Puck's misapplied herb juice, which has engendered his fancy. And it will be through his eyes also that his fancy, his infatuation for Helena, will die. Although the terms were often used interchangeably by Shakespeare and his contemporaries, the power of the imagination *could* be distinguished from the fancy, as some Elizabethans knew two centuries before Coleridge's *Biographia Literaria*. It is, moreover, this power, fancy (or phantasy), that Theseus unfortunately calls "imagination" in his famous fifth act speech, which connects the lunatic, the lover, and the poet.[9]

The frequent malapropisms of the rude mechanicals' dialogue also add to our growing sense of linguistic (and other) disorder. Here Bottom is the most notorious, because the most pretentious; but he is not the only one. Wanting the role of Lion, as well as the roles of Pyramus *and* Thisbe—and Ercles, too, if that "part to tear a cat in" could somehow be worked into the play—he pleads that he will use moderation in his roaring so as not to frighten the ladies in the audience:

> But I will aggravate my voice so that I will roar you as gently as any sucking dove. I will roar you an 'twere any nightingale.
>
> (1.2.76–78)

Peter Quince, the stalwart impresario, also gets tangled up in his language, not only in failing to stand upon his points in the Prologue, but earlier, speaking more accurately than he realizes, when he explains how moonlight can be provided for their play. As an alternative to leaving the casement window open, he suggests "one must come in with a bush of thorns and a lantern and say he comes to *disfigure* or to present the person of Moonshine" (3.1.53–55; my italics). When it is finally staged before the court, the "*most lamentable comedy . . . Pyramus and Thisbe*" will function on various levels of significance well prepared for by the kinds of linguistic subversion that appear elsewhere in the play.

The sense of disorder that characterizes much of *A Midsummer Night's Dream* is, in one way, explained by the conflict between Oberon and Titania. These adept lovers, when they meet in act 2, upbraid one another with accusations of jealousy, philandering, insubordination, and downright meanness. As a result of their quarrel, Titania complains that everything in nature has turned topsy-turvy (2.1.81–117). The vagaries of love have power, apparently, in these supernatural beings to make the seasons alter:

> ... hoary-headed frosts
> Fall in the fresh lap of the crimson rose,
> And on old Hiems' thin and icy crown
> An odorous chaplet of sweet summer buds
> Is as in mockery set.
>   (107–11)

But the disorder is conveyed in other, more subtle ways than in this image of old Hiems and his fragrant chaplet. Immediately after Oberon vows to "torment" his queen for her injurious behavior, he calls upon his "gentle" Puck. Again, as he describes hearing a mermaid on a dolphin's back "uttering such dulcet and harmonious breath / That the rude sea grew civil at her song," he notes that at the same time "certain stars shot madly from their spheres / To hear the sea-maid's music" (2.1.150–54). How can it happen both ways: the rude sea grows civil, but certain stars go mad in the firmament? The subsequent magnificent passage describing the "fair vestal throned by the west" concludes with the sad plight of the once milk-white flower, love-in-idleness, stained purple, which will provide Oberon with the magic he needs for his plot against Titania. The epitome of this kind of double-speak occurs in the famous passage where Oberon describes his plan in detail:

> I know a bank where the wild thyme blows,
> Where oxlips and the nodding violet grows,
> Quite overcanopied with luscious woodbine,
> With sweet muskroses and with eglantine.
> There sleeps Titania some time of the night,
> Lulled in these flowers with dances and delight.
> And there the snake throws her enamelled skin,
> Weed wide enough to wrap a fairy in.
> And with the juice of this I'll streak her eyes,
> And make her full of hateful fantasies.
>   (2.1.249–58)

As Harold Brooks remarks, the lines are "famous for their melody, as well as for their imagery, which is no less lyrical."[10] The mellifluousness of the verse, the lulling rhythms of the end-stopped lines, but especially the beauty of the images combine to hide for the reader or spectator almost entirely the edge of Oberon's real malice. If the image of the snake is hardly an image here that repels, its appearance is at least problematical—whatever generic relation it may have to Hermia's dream of the crawling serpent on her breast after Lysander deserts her in the next scene. Jan Kott has noted a parallel in the fairies' lullaby in act 2 where the linguistic effect is reversed:

> You spotted snakes with double tongue
> Thorny hedgehogs, be not seen.
> Newts and blindworms, do no wrong
> Come not near our Fairy Queen.
> Philomel with melody
> Sing in our sweet lullaby,
> Lulla, lulla, lullaby; lulla, lulla, lullaby.
> Never harm
> Nor spell nor charm
> Come our lovely lady nigh.
> So good night, with lullaby.
> Weaving spiders, come not here;
> Hence, you longlegged spinners, hence!
> Beetles black, approach not near
> Worm nor snail, do no offence.
> Philomel with melody. . . .
> (2.2.9–24)

Despite its invocation to Philomel in the refrain, this is not the sort of lullaby to forecast or inspire pleasant dreams. But the harmonies of sound, especially enhanced by music (as in many lullabies), do everything—or almost everything—to hide from us the actual horrors. The same point can be illustrated where Titania explains her opposition to Oberon's demand for the changeling Indian boy:

> His mother was a votress of my order,
> And in the spicèd Indian air by night
> Full often hath she gossiped by my side,
> And sat with me on Neptune's yellow sands,
> Marking th'embarked traders on the flood,
> When we have laughed to see the sails conceive
> And grow big-bellied with the wanton wind;
> Which she with pretty and with swimming gait
> Following—her womb then rich with my young squire—
> Would imitate, and sail upon the land
> To fetch me trifles, and return again
> As from a voyage, rich with merchandise.
> And she, being mortal, of that boy did die,

And for her sake do I rear up her boy;
And for her sake I will not part with him.
  (2.1.123–37)

The beauty of the passage—"spiced Indian air," the imagery of conception, and the mocking gait of the pregnant young woman—bears the full
emphasis, and the serious point of the speech—the mother's childbirth
death, leaving her son an orphan—becomes almost anticlimactic, certainly
less emphatic, though to Shakespeare's audience the dangers of childbirth
were quite real.

Bottom's meeting with Titania also offers some surprising paradoxes.
Can Oberon really mean to have himself cuckolded by an asinine country
bumpkin? We may laugh, and are surely meant to do so, when Titania greets
Bottom's rustic song: "What angel wakes me from my flowery bed?" (3.1.122).
But Bottom goes on, providing some interesting clues to what actually is
about to happen:

The finch, the sparrow, and the lark
  The plainsong cuckoo grey,
Whose note full many a man doth mark
  And dares not answer "Nay"—
for, indeed, who would set his wit to so foolish a bird? Who
would give a bird the lie, though he cry "cuckoo" never so?
  (123–129)

Cuckoos and cuckolds—need one remark?—traditionally have a strong
association, which modern audiences may miss, but Shakespeare's would
not. Oberon plans to punish Titania and succeeds—not without some cost
to himself, however, which he may ignore or perhaps relish ("This falls out
better than I could devise!" he says to Puck at 3.2.35). But Bottom's song
and comment point to what the cost actually is.[11]

These linguistic and dramatic complexities and contradictions serve, as
Stephen Booth has said about *Hamlet*, to keep us from simplistic reductions
of experienced situations, specifically the play's mirrored experiences of reality, to say nothing of its own reality. As such, they force us out of, rather
than into, an artificial prison that R. P. Blackmur has (in another connection)
described as a tendency to set artistic unity as a chief criterion of excellence.[12]
Coherence, existentially considered, is more, much more, than rhetorical
cohesiveness, though to some extent that kind of coherence is also necessary.
But however necessary, it is not a sufficient condition of great art, such as
Shakespeare's. The point can be illustrated as well by examples from the great

literature of music, such as the late Beethoven quartets. But (to remain with Shakespeare) let me expand the reference to other plays of the same period as *A Midsummer Night's Dream*.

In an essay on "Shakespeare and the Limits of Language," Anne Barton some years ago contrasted Richard II's verbal adeptness with Bolingbroke's political skill to show how, despite his manifold successes, Shakespeare did not allow language, the efficacy of the word, an "unexamined triumph."[13] In the deposition scene, for example, Barton shows how it is the weak king who insists upon inventing a rite, creating a litany that will, through words, invest the transference of power with meaning. The speech she specifically cites uses the well metaphor as its controlling device:

> Here, cousin, seize the crown.
> On this side my hand, and on that side thine.
> Now is this golden crown like a deep well
> That owes two buckets, filling one another:
> The emptier ever dancing in the air,
> The other down, unseen, and full of water.
> That bucket down and full of tears am I,
> Drinking my griefs, whilst you mount up on high.
>   (4.1.181–88)

As Barton says, Bolingbroke's submission is "oddly qualified"; he reaches out his hand, but verbally he will not cooperate; his blunt inquiry—"I thought you had been willing to resign"—tears through and destroys the validity of the metaphor.[14] Or does it? We can see Bolingbroke containing himself in patience while Richard goes through his ceremonies of self-debasement, for Bolingbroke fully understands the political might he now controls. Richard's wit is keener than Bolingbroke suspects, or lets on. The well metaphor, like much else in this scene, carries more than an acknowledgment of Richard's defeat and Bolingbroke's success. Richard, the heavier bucket, down and unseen, is also fuller, weightier; Bolingbroke, the high bucket, is also lighter, emptier, frolicking in the air as in a dance. The word, as Richard delivers it then, in this speech as in others, is hardly impotent. Its triumph is not an unqualified one, but neither is Bolingbroke's. Many of Shakespeare's plays make the same point.

In the last act of *The Merchant of Venice* the equations appear reversed. Some of the same verbal inconsistencies that analysis of *A Midsummer Night's Dream* revealed occur in the opening speeches between Lorenzo and Jessica, creating the initial tension that leads indirectly to the tensions created by the ring trick that Portia and Nerissa have played upon their husbands. Or are all of these tensions, as Jonathan Miller's production (with Laurence Olivier as Shylock) seemed to argue, actually the result, or aftermath, of those generated in the previous act, where Shylock learns the meaning of justice as taught him by Portia and Antonio and the rest?

Lorenzo and Jessica are sitting outside Portia's house in Belmont. Lorenzo speaks:

> The moon shines bright. In such a night as this,
> When the sweet wind did gently kiss the trees
> And they did make no noise, in such a night
> Troilus methinks mounted the Troyan walls
> And sighed his soul toward the Grecian tents,
> Where Cressid lay that night.
>   (5.1.1–6)

The first three lines set both the scene and time and prepare for the lovely passage fifty lines later that begins, "How sweet the moonlight sleeps upon this bank!" But here as later a discordant note slips in, even as the mellifluousness of the lines, the soft alliterations and rhythm beguile the listener—the less attentive audience, at any rate—but not Jessica. She follows Lorenzo's allusion to the tragedy of Troilus and Cressida with:

>   In such a night
> Did Thisbe fearfully o'ertrip the dew,
> And saw the lion's shadow ere himself
> And ran dismayed away.
>   (6–9)

And so on, back and forth, through Dido and Medea until Lorenzo openly teases Jessica about stealing away with him to Belmont, and she retorts in kind. Only the entrance of a messenger apparently halts the contest; but later, as they await Portia's return and Lorenzo describes the music of the spheres, Jessica feels compelled to say: "I am never merry when I hear sweet music" (69). And so on, again, throughout the scene concords find discords, discords concord, in a seemingly unending series. Although the overall tone is joyful and the teasing playful, Shakespeare does not let us forget the more somber aspects of human relationships, which can and do intrude.

The same kind of linguistic and dramatic strategy is at work in the final act of *A Midsummer Night's Dream*. Philostrate's list of possible wedding entertainments is an odd one, beginning as it does with "The battle with the

Centaurs, to be sung / By an Athenian eunuch to the harp" (5.1.44–45). His fourth possibility brings us to

"A tedious brief scene of young Pyramus
And his love Thisbe; very tragical mirth."
    (56–57)

Theseus's reaction summarizes ours:

Merry and tragical? Tedious and brief?
That is, hot ice and wondrous strange snow.
How shall we find the concord of this discord?
    (58–60)

Philostrate's condescending reply to the question does not probe deeply enough, of course: How indeed shall we find the "concord of this discord"? Not, I submit, by simply acquiescing in the general merriment of the stage spectators while the playlet is in progress, beginning with the "tangled chain" of Quince's Prologue. Even if we grant that the play was first performed at an actual wedding celebration, with fun and laughter very much in the spirit of the occasion, we cannot stop there. However well things may turn out for Theseus and Hippolyta, Lysander and Hermia, Demetrius and Helena, Oberon and Titania, there is still one couple whose fortunes do not end happily. Within the happy framework of this celebration, the solemn notes of tragedy still intrude, all but obliterated by peals of mirth that the simple rustics inspire, but nonetheless there.

Critics have been at some pains to show how Shakespeare "brilliantly reconciles opposites"[15] in his dream-play. The usual reference is to the passages on Theseus's hounds in act 4, scene 1, lines 109–26, specifically to "So musical a discord, such sweet thunder" that their baying offers. Not remarked often enough, perhaps, is the providential role that characters like Oberon and Theseus enact in bringing about the concord between the jarring couples in the play. (Shakespeare as playwright is of course the relevant analogy here.) But my purpose has been to show that the concords exist at only one level, and that one not the most profound. The thunder may be "sweet," but it is still thunder. Oberon overmasters Titania, reduces her to tears, and has his way finally. Theseus suavely ignores the law Egeus and he himself have invoked in act 1 to enable the young couples to be married, and Egeus (with whatever silent, grudging acceptance) goes along: Theseus quite frankly tells him "I will overbear your will" (4.1.178). Shakespeare is hardly as direct, but in effect he overbears ours as well, lulling or beguiling us into an acceptance of concord and amity, however achieved, through the artistry of his verse and the adeptness of his comic genius. But he has left sufficient pointers (for those willing to recognize them) that this is artifice, after all; that a benevolent providence does not always or inevitably enter into human affairs to make things right. His most significant indication of that fact is in the play-within-the-play, where no providential solution to Pyramus and Thisbe's plight appears. The "thunder" there may be nearly drowned out by laughter and jollity, but it still rumbles. And what the thunder says is *not* a message of concord or reconciliation of opposing wills.

Of this situation Marjorie Garber has commented that the play-within-the-play is "ultimately nothing less than a countermyth for the whole of *A Midsummer Night's Dream*, setting out the larger play's terms in a new and revealing light."[16] If the playlet "absorbs and disarms" the tragic alternative to the happy outcome that the other couples have experienced, it is nevertheless present to remind us of what we all know but usually prefer to ignore or forget, especially on such occasions as this. By framing the images of nightmare terrors in "an illusion within an illusion," as James Calderwood has said, Shakespeare here dissolves their threat in laughter. But the laughter is generated, Calderwood continues, at least in part by the act of self-recognition that follows from the transformation of "subjective vagueness" into the "objective clarity" of dramatic form.[17]

As "the iron tongue of midnight" summons the couples to bed, with Theseus's anticipation of yet a fortnight of "nightly revels and new jollity," Puck steals in and reminds us that

> Now the hungry lion roars
> And the wolf behowls the moon,
> Whilst the heavy plowman snores
> All with weary task foredone.
> (5.1.361–64)

Not that the fairies' work is done, and Puck is "sent with broom before / To sweep the dust behind the door" (379–80). Perhaps that is the best image for Shakespeare's strategy in this play. As every housewife knows, sweeping the dust behind the door, or under the rug, may hide it for awhile, but does not get rid of it. In *A Midsummer Night's Dream* Shakespeare, like Puck, is busy with his broom, but we do not altogether lose sight of his, or the world's, dust.

Notes

1. In *Reinterpretations of Elizabethan Drama*, ed. Norman Rabkin (New York: Columbia University Press, 1969), 143.

2. Booth, "Value of *Hamlet*," 175.

3. "But We Are Spirits of Another Sort: The Dark Side of Love and Magic in *A Midsummer Night's Dream*," *Medieval and Renaissance Studies* 7 (1975): 81.

4. *Shakespeare Our Contemporary*, trans. Boleslaw Taborski (Garden City, N.Y.: Doubleday, 1964), 212.

5. Ibid. 218.

6. Ibid. 219.

7. Quotations are from the New Penguin Shakespeare, ed. Stanley Wells (Harmondsworth, England: Penguin, 1967).

8. *Shakespeare's Comedy of Love* (London: Methuen 1974), 95. The New Arden editor, Harold Brooks, also refers to Hermia's "tender teasing."

9. See David P. Young, *Something of Great Constancy* (New Haven: Yale University Press, 1964), 126–41. For an acute analysis of Helena's speech, cf. Ruth Nevo, *Comic Transformations in Shakespeare* (London: Methuen, 1980), 98–99.

10. Introduction to *A Midsummer Night's Dream*, New Arden ed. (London: Methuen, 1979), cxxx. Cf. Leggatt, *Comedy of Love*, 96, on the experiences of the Athenian lovers in the forest: "Over and over, the violence of the ideas is lightened by jingling rhythm and rhyme."

11. On the other hand, as Bevington notes, these gods "make a sport of inconstancy." Out of her love for Theseus, Titania has helped him to ravish Perigouna, break faith with Aegles and with others; while Oberon has made love with Aurora as well as, apparently, with Hippolyta. "This is the sort of mysterious affection," Bevington says, "that only a god could practice or understand." See "Spirits of Another Sort," 90.

12. *Form and Value in Modern Poetry* (New York: Doubleday, 1957), 83. Cf. Stanley Wells's comments on the theme of concord in his introduction to *A Midsummer Night's Dream*, 31. He says that the baying of Theseus's hounds is "a symbol of the possibility of a unity that is not sameness, an agreement that can include disagreement." Cf. Young, *Great Constancy*, 86.

13. In *Shakespeare Survey* 24 (Cambridge: Cambridge University Press, 1971), 20.

14. Barton, "Limits of Language," 22.

15. Wells, introd. to *A Midsummer Night's Dream*, 28. Cf. Leggatt, *Comedy of Love*, 114: "But the artistic vision itself, which draws these disparate experiences together, is also limited."

16. *Dream in Shakespeare* (New Haven: Yale University Press, 1974), 81.

17. "*A Midsummer Night's Dream*: The Illusion of Drama," *Modern Language Quarterly* 26 (1965): 522. Cf. Madeleine Doran, *Shakespeare's Dramatic Language* (Madison: University of Wisconsin Press, 1976), 16, on *Pyramus and Thisbe* as a suitable antimasque for the wedding ceremony.

JAMES L. CALDERWOOD

A Midsummer Night's Dream:
Anamorphism and Theseus' Dream

1. Anamorphic Doubling

Anamorphism, a visual device well known and much used by Renaissance painters, is a perspectival technique designed to present one image if viewed from directly in front of the painting and another if viewed from an angle. The most famous instance is Holbein's *The Ambassadors*. Looked at straight-on, the painting displays the familiar figures of the two Frenchmen and, in the foreground between them, an indistinguishable image, a kind of elongated pale blur that might be a flying saucer with holes in it but that, if the puzzled viewer moves to the right and glances back and down, turns out to be a skull lying at the ambassadors' feet.[1] The eye sockets of the skull are large and distended, and their vacant gaze seems to focus nowhere and everywhere, taking in the ambassadors but also the side-angled viewer of the painting and, beyond, all who think they see without being seen. The uncanniness of the painting comes not just from the unexpected appearance of death in it—*Et in Arcadia ego*—but from the association of death with being-seen-seeing. In the very moment of power, while taking possession of the painting visually, the viewer is, as it were, seen and nullified. The effect is like that sought by the director Carl Dreyer for his film *Vampyr*: "Imagine that we are sitting in an ordinary room. Suddenly we are told that there is a corpse behind the door. In an instant the room we are sitting in is completely altered: everything in it has taken on another look; the light, the atmosphere

From *Shakespeare Quarterly* 42, no. 4 (Winter 1991): 409–30. © 1991 by Folger Shakespeare Library.

have changed, though they are physically the same. . . ."[2] As with the painting, the room takes on "another *look*," acquiring a gaze as well as a different appearance, both of which are in excess of the sheer physical facts, which remain precisely as they were. Nothing changes, and everything changes.

In *A Midsummer Night's Dream* Shakespeare does something similar to what Holbein does by creating a linear version of anamorphosis, converting the painting into a play that the audience sees from three different perspectives.[3] We don't have to change seats during a performance to find the proper anamorphic angle; Shakespeare does our moving for us by making the "seen"—that is, the scene—change, in effect presenting us with a painting in three panels. First he gives us a straight-on look at Athens, then shifts our perspective by obliging us to consider the forest, then brings Athens back in the third panel and says, "Look again." The anamorphic effect arises from the fact that the forest world, though not exactly a grinning skull lying at the base of Theseus' palace, is a kind of crazed mirror of the Athenian world.

Because Shakespeare is adapting a graphic technique to a linear form, the anamorphic acquires a parenthetical quality. Since the affairs in Athens can't be entirely resolved until the day of the wedding, what happens in the forest is a kind of embedding or, more precisely, a recursive function. The play puts Athens on "hold" while a more urgent "call" is taken concerning marital insurrections in fairyland and dislocations in nature. The two calls are more than merely modally related. If the Athenian problem can't be addressed until the fairyland problem is solved, it's not just because the latter is more urgent but because the two are causally connected; fairyland is a phase in the Athenian plot.

What, then, does fairyland cause in Athens? Most obviously, it brings about the corrective realignments among the lovers that prepare for the multiple-marriage finale. However, Puck's and Oberon's machinations only make the lovers at the end of Act 4 *willing* to marry. That they *can* marry is a result of Theseus' surprising dismissal of the law. "Surprising" because in Act 1 the law was said, by Theseus himself, to be irrevocable. "Fit your fancies to your father's will," he told Hermia, "Or else the law of Athens yields you up—/ Which by no means we may extenuate" (1.1.118–20).[4] But at the end of Act 4, when Egeus invokes that same law, Theseus doffs it aside with a cryptic "Egeus, I will overbear your will" (4.1.178). Why so great a change? Who knows—we've neither seen nor heard of Theseus since his exit in the opening scene.

Or have we?

Perhaps we have—but from an anamorphic angle.

That is, one way to explain Theseus' cavalier dismissal of the law is by registering the full effect of Shakespeare's device of doubling the roles of Theseus and Hippolyta with those of Oberon and Titania. I say "Shakespeare's" because this practice, which has become almost automatic in the late twentieth century, issues from the playwright as much as it does from inventive directors like Peter Brook or Robin Phillips.[5] The effect of this doubling is that the actors who play the paired parts become visual puns. Listen to Oberon and Titania upbraiding one another about their love for Hippolyta and Theseus in 2.1, then cock your head to one side and, despite differences in costume, you see the bodily presence of Theseus and Hippolyta themselves. Or, rather, of the actors who play them. But since we have already assigned the names *Theseus* and *Hippolyta* to these actorly bodies, when they appear as Oberon and Titania they can't help evoking ghostly images of their Athenian counterparts. All the more so because just when we are asking ourselves "Isn't that Theseus, and isn't that Hippolyta?" we are also asking ourselves "Isn't this the same subversion of hierarchical and patriarchal order that we just saw so ruthlessly dealt with in Athens?" For in Athens we heard that Theseus has won Hippolyta's love "doing [her] injuries," and we saw Egeus, Demetrius, and the law combine in an effort to win Hermia's love doing *her* injuries, and now we see Oberon trying to win Titania's love doing *her* injuries. It's all Athens in another key or mode.

To make the parallel with anamorphism more exact, let me take another angled glance at the opening scene and observe that Oberon and Titania are invisibly present there in the persons of Theseus and Hippolyta. Not that Theseus and Hippolyta are blurred the way Holbein's skull is in *The Ambassadors*; we see the duke and his betrothed as clearly as we do the French ambassadors. Yet something is there that we can't see or fully make sense of—Oberon and Titania.

Naturally, this seems a perverse claim: how can we expect to see Oberon and Titania when they have yet to make an entrance as characters? Ah, but the anamorphic is perverse by nature—that is to say, by artifice: how can we expect to see Holbein's skull when we have yet to move to a position from which it's visible? Nevertheless, when we first encounter *The Ambassadors* straight-on, the skull is there, in the white paint that came from Holbein's brush; and while we watch the opening scene of *A Midsummer Night's Dream*, the fairy king and queen are there too, in the stuff Shakespeare painted his plays with, the bodies of actors.

2. Dream Visions in Fairyland

Let me trace out the anamorphic effect of this curious doubling, with the aim of seeing how it affects Theseus' dismissal of the law in Act 4. Most immediately, if Oberon and Titania are present in the opening scene in shadowy shape, that is, in actorly shape—"The best in this kind are but shadows" (5.1.210)—then we get a glimpse of a different, more troubled other-side to the seemingly cheerful obverse shown us by Theseus and Hippolyta in this scene. But nothing can be discerned until we have a change of scenes and costumes, and a quarreling exchange in which Oberon is accused of loving Hippolyta and Titania of loving Theseus (2.1.63–80). Elliot Krieger supplies a perceptive gloss on this:

> The suggestion of an erotic connection between the rulers of the fairy world and the rulers of Athens transforms the fairies into spiritual manifestations of the sexual drives of Theseus and Hippolyta: Titania represents in the realm of spirit Theseus's physical desire, held in abeyance during the four-day interval before the wedding, for Hippolyta; Oberon represents Hippolyta's desire for Theseus. The destructive jealousy with which Oberon and Titania confront each other replaces, then, the injury, the actual martial opposition between their two races, with which Theseus "woo'd" Hippolyta.[6]

If we factor in the implications of theatrical doubling, these erotic connections between fairyland and Athens suggest a rather sharp discord within the pre-marital harmonies of Theseus and Hippolyta in Act 1. If Oberon's difficulties reflect Theseus' state of mind, then the somewhat Chaucerian Theseus of the opening scene, duke of bright corners and exemplar of order and government, he whose rough courtship has brought the Amazonian queen so properly to heel that he can refer to it with urbane self-assurance[7]—

> Hippolyta, I woo'd thee with my sword,
> And won thy love doing thee injuries;
> But I will wed thee in another key,
> With pomp, with triumph, and with reveling
>   (1.1.16–19)

—this same duke may nevertheless be hearing in some corner of his mind unnerving fore-hints of Horace Walpole's remark about comedies ending in marriage because after that the tragedy begins. After all, winning love by doing injuries is not the most auspicious form of courtship in the best of cases, and it would seem particularly questionable when one's beloved is an Amazon. Consider, for example, some Amazonian precedents.

In his account of the life of Theseus, Plutarch says that at one point in the continuing conflict between the Greeks and the Amazons, the latter invaded Athens and very nearly conquered it.[8] Had this invasion succeeded, dreadful consequences would surely have ensued. If not killed outright, the Athenian stalwarts might well have suffered the fate of the men captured by Spenser's Radigund, the evil Amazon who obliged her male captives to wear feminine attire and spend their days at women's work.[9] Perhaps Theseus would have been reduced to spinning flax and tow like the wretched Artegall, until some sojourning female warrior like Britomart freed him and set the earth back on its axis again.

Fortunately, Theseus was spared such humiliations. Still, he may have other anxieties about his duchess-to-be. After all, the Elizabethan view of Amazons was somewhat anamorphic. From one perspective they appeared as noble, valiant, beautiful, and chaste as their goddess, Diana.[10] From another they were cunning, cruel, tyrannous-possessed, Spenser wrote, of a "wandring fancie [that] after lust did raunge" (5.5.26). Thus Artegall says he fights Radigund because of "the faith that I / To Maydenhead and noble knighthood owe" (5.4.34); and when Britomart kills Radigund, chastity and marriage triumph over lust and "licentious libertie" (5.5.25). Given the unnatural disobedience and sensuality to which some of these Amazons were prone, Theseus can hardly rest easy despite having conquered Hippolyta and persuaded her to marriage. Who knows whether she will replace his crown with a set of horns, or his throne and scepter with a joint stool and distaff?

Not that Hippolyta says anything to suggest as much. Her first speech seems perfectly accepting of the coming "solemnities." But it's hard to know how she responds to the unpleasantness with Hermia. As a woman, especially an Amazonian woman, she can hardly regard with indifference this show of masculine force. As a bride-to-be for whom marriage is the gate to Athenian citizenship, can she simply hold Theseus' arm and smile as he decrees death or virginity for women who reserve some right of choice in marital matters? Does she see in Hermia's resistance a rebuke to her own submissiveness? Or is she submissive? Is Theseus' "Come, my Hippolyta. What cheer, my love?" (1.1.122) merely routine solicitude, or has he sensed something amiss with Hippolyta, and if so, what—outrage, dismay, fear, shame? But Hippolyta keeps her counsel, and so remains an enigma to us as well as to Theseus.[11]

What cheer, then, for the anxious duke? What cheer especially four nights later when he is scheduled for another engagement with this man-woman whose sexual desire is a mystery? Who knows the extent of her requirements? Perhaps she will demand more than he has to give—or, worse, as a devotee of Diana disdain all he has to offer—or, worse yet, insist on assuming an "Amazon-on-top" position! What does a warrior-monarch do in such a case besides casting uneasy glances at his betrothed and murmuring "What cheer, my love?"

Well, as W. Thomas MacCary suggests, perhaps he dreams about his plight, or rather has a nightmare about it.[12] In his nightmare he finds himself transformed into a fairy king married to a fairy queen even more uncontrollable than he fears his Amazonian queen may turn out to be. This stubborn imperi-ous creature, refusing to honor either his masculinity or his royalty by yielding a changeling boy, instead makes "[the child] all her joy," forswears his own bed and company, and spends her time dancing in the wood with her elves. Not much cheer here for Oberon. Nor for Theseus, whose ducal body fits within the fairy king's robes far too snugly for comfort—especially when Hippolyta's body is so visible in Titania's.[13]

In fact, since Hippolyta's body is every bit as visible in Titania's as The-seus' is in Oberon's, is she not dreaming too? After all, it's she of whom The-seus asks "What cheer, my love?" And certainly she has as much reason as he to be troubled about their forthcoming marriage, especially after observing how things are done in Athens. Hence what happens to Titania is as much Hippolyta's nightmare-dream as it is Theseus'; and as a result affairs in fairy-land must be interpreted from two perspectives. Let me try to simplify this by dividing the experience of Hippolyta-Titania into two phases, before and after she is charmed by Oberon. The first phase focuses on the dispute over the changeling child.

3. "I do but beg a little changeling boy"

Why does Oberon beg a little changeling boy? To serve, he says, as his squire. But Oberon needs a squire the way Portia needs a ring when she demands hers back from Bassanio at the end of *The Merchant of Venice*. That is, Ober-on's desire for the boy is an example of what Lacan calls *demand*: "Demand in itself bears on something other than the satisfactions it calls for. . . . [It] annuls (*aufhebt*) the particularity of everything that can be granted by trans-muting it into a proof of love. . . ."[14] Oberon's demand "annuls . . . the partic-ularity" of the boy by transforming him into a symbol of what Oberon really desires, the gift of Titania's love and obedience. From an Hegelian-Sartrian point of view, it appears that the boy is a subject reduced to an object (a slave) in a contest for marital dominance—even, some have argued, a sexual object, not for Titania but for Oberon.[15] However, if Shakespeare intended the boy as a Ganymede figure for a pederastic Oberon or meant him to have any importance in his own person, surely he would have put him onstage. By not doing so, he does to him theatrically what Oberon and Titania do to him rhetorically—transform him into a signifier in a system of communication.[16] For Titania also wants him less for himself than as a token of love. She tells Oberon exactly why she will not surrender the boy:

> Set your heart at rest.
> The fairy land buys not the child of me.
> His mother was a vot'ress of my order,

And, in the spiced Indian air, by night,
Full often hath she gossip'd by my side,
And sat with me on Neptune's yellow sands,
Marking th' embarked traders on the flood,
When we have laugh'd to see the sails conceive
And grow big-bellied with the wanton wind;
Which she, with pretty and with swimming gait,
Following—her womb then rich with my young squire—
Would imitate, and sail upon the land
To fetch me trifles, and return again,
As from a voyage, rich with merchandise.
But she, being mortal, of that boy did die;
And for her sake do I rear up her boy,
And for her sake I will not part with him.
      (2.1.125–37)

Titania describes a fellowship with her votaress Indian queen as idyllic as that enjoyed by Hermia and Helena or, more to the Theseus-as-Oberon point, by Hippolyta in her Amazonian past—a feminine world rich with all the mysteries of fertility, conception, pregnancy, and birth that women can treat with easy familiarity but that can be conveyed to Oberon only through imperfect analogies to masculine trade and moneymaking. The analogies work both ways: the sails of the merchantmen imitate pregnancy by conceiving and growing big-bellied with the wanton wind, and the pregnant votaress, seeing this, imitates the ships by sailing upon the land "as from a voyage, rich with merchandise." But although a profitable rhetorical trade is conducted here between women's and men's "business," there is no question which has priority in terms of nature and grace. Pregnancy is primary and ideal; it can only be imitated by merchantmen, who are then imitated in turn, with light mockery, by the Indian queen.

This is a picture that Oberon, who sees no sign of himself or even of the Indian king in it, can hardly be expected to admire.[17] His response is curt: "How long within this wood intend you stay?" For her part, Titania takes obvious but melancholy pleasure in the recollection. For the skull in the corner is the child in the womb. Male of course, it kills the mother and brings an end to Titania's idyll, just as the arrival of men has curtailed the idylls of the other women in the play.[18] And now, for Titania, here is another man, a fairy-man, demanding of her as stepmother another kind of birth and death, that she yield up the boy and let the past die.

Thus the fairyland dispute, like that in Athens in the opening scene, is a displaced version of the oedipal crisis. The Athenian version of the crisis took a Father-Lover-Daughter configuration, with Egeus' paternal "No" delivered to Hermia with respect to marriage. In fairyland we have the classic Father-Mother-Child triangle, except that the child is a changeling and the parents are step-parents. Because the child is absent from the scene here, the theatrical focus falls on the "mother's" reaction to the paternal "No" that would separate the child from her. Titania, not the child, suffers symbolic castration; she has to surrender not only a desire for the phallus of masculine privilege but also her symbolic association with her beloved votaress. Like Hermia and Helena, she longs for a paradisal feminine past prior to or outside of marriage; and so her desire, like theirs, is founded on loss, made even more irremediable in her case by death. To part with the changeling is to acknowledge this loss and the futility of trying to perpetuate an imagined completeness associated with pregnancy by playing step-mother to the boy. Life with Oberon will not compensate Titania for the loss of these illusions; but on the assumption that fairyland has turned Protestant during the Reformation, she will find her likeliest compromise in companionate marital love.[19]

From Oberon's standpoint, acquiring the changeling child erases the point of contentious difference between him and Titania by dissolving her ties to an idealized female past. Similarly, Hippolyta's marriage to Theseus will represent a castration of her Amazonian attempt to possess the phallus. Ceasing to live a life of masculine privilege, she will submit to her role as Athenian wife (though just how submissive she will be is the point at issue). Thus Titania's giving up a male child seems the dream equivalent to Hippolyta's giving up a masculine life.

But this is to stress merely one aspect of Theseus' anxieties about his Amazonian bride. Such sacrifices guarantee the duke an obedient wife, under which heading chastity presumably falls too. But if we key on Titania's speech about the pregnant votaress, the stress falls not just on obedience but also on motherhood. Amazons, after all, were hardly model mothers. According to Elizabethan authorities, "Not only did the Amazons refuse to suckle their sons but—according to their enemies—they often slew them at birth. At best they banished them to the fathers for rearing. Or—a third account, preferred by violent antifeminists—these outrageous mothers dislocated the boys' joints and then enslaved the cripples at spinning."[20]

This is a far cry from the attitude expressed by Titania in recounting the scene on the beach. Immortal herself (accented by her line "But she, being mortal, of that boy did die"), she does what immortals inexplicably do from time to time, envy humans. It comes as something of a surprise that Titania, the beautiful queen of fairyland, can want for anything; but of course immortals have always found themselves wanting—why else would Apollo chase Daphne so, or Aphrodite dote on Endymion, or Zeus descend swan-like upon

Leda? What Titania lacks and yearns for here is not sex but pregnancy. She gazes on the Indian queen as Helena gazes on Hermia in the opening scene, desiring "to be to [her] translated" (1.1.191). Indeed she depicts her votaress in full sail with such imaginative sympathy that she seems to make the experience her own—and surely she (and by means of her, Hippolyta) must imitate this voyaging onstage as she tells of it, herself the votaress and Oberon perforce the fairy queen to whom the trifles are given—but not the boy.

Thus Hippolyta-as-Titania experiences a moment when the phallus is not male but female.[21] Her story about her votaress proceeds as if she had been present during the opening scene and heard Theseus' patriarchal account of conception (1.1.47–51)—as of course in the form of Hippolyta she had. As though in retaliation, her story is as devoid of husbands as his was of wives, though hers gives at least a rhetorical nod in the direction of men. Delightful as all this is, it has a certain pathos too, inasmuch as Titania's desire focuses on that specific feature of humans that marks their greatest lack. Creatures that give birth must die, as the fate of the Indian queen makes clear. With her death, the phallus of femininity is lost to Titania, replaced by the boy whom she can only "step-mother." Real motherhood is barred to her by death—the death of the Indian queen but also, more fundamentally, the death an immortal would have to become subject to, and by definition cannot, to enter a world in which children are created, not stolen.

Thus in her role as Titania, Hippolyta experiences a past quite different from her own, one in which she longs for and imitates not male behavior but femininity and motherhood. For Titania, motherhood was never possible, and even her imaginative association with it through the Indian queen is lost; how irretrievably is evidenced by her inability to express it except in the rhetoric of masculine trade. When she begins her speech by saying "The fairy land buys not the child of me," she has already conceded the game by thinking of the boy not as a heartfelt be-all and end-all but as a commodity to be bartered for.[22] After all, as Puck said, "She never had so sweet a changeling" (2.1.23), which implies that the Indian boy is merely another item in a series and risks raising questions like "How many changelings had Queen Titania?" Whatever the answer, stepmotherhood is apparently as close as fairy queens can get to biological motherhood.

Not so, however, for Amazonian queens like Hippolyta, once the moon has beheld the night of her and Theseus' solemnities. But will an Amazonian queen even want to be a mother? Presumably she will, once she has passed through the dream of fairyland in the shape of Titania. For on this view Titania's loss and the desire it occasions represent the unconscious loss and desire of the Amazonian queen as well. They represent, that is, precisely what Hippolyta has had to repress in order to *be* an Amazon and what must be readmitted to consciousness, therefore, if she is to become, as she is soon to become, not merely the wife of Theseus but also the mother of Hippolytus.

4. "My mistress with a monster is in love"

The second phase of Hippolyta's nightlife role as Titania is stage-managed by Theseus-Oberon, who gets his will by magical means. If his own imperial gaze has proved ineffectual, he will capture Titania's gaze and refocus it with an aimlessness that would have gratified Cupid:

> The next thing then she waking looks upon,
> Be it on lion, bear, or wolf, or bull,
> On meddling monkey, or on busy ape,
> She shall pursue it with the soul of love.
>   (2.1.179–82)

According to Jan Kott, this prepares the way not merely for an arousal of "animal love" in Titania but for its consummation in her bower.[23] In this vein David Ormerod reminds us that Pasiphaë was just such a lascivious matron and suggests that the encounter of Titania and the onocentaurian Bottom in a labyrinthine wood carries overtones of monstrous doings beneath the palace at Knossos;[24] and Homer Swander attributes to Titania a "savage, knowingly destructive lust" that is consummated with Bottom in an offstage fairyland bower beyond the woods.[25]

Swander's argument situates the supposed ravishment of Bottom decorously offstage, primarily because that is the only place it could occur. His argument makes much of the fact that Titania's bower is not the same as the flower-canopied bank "where the wild thyme blows" and where, according to Oberon, "sleeps Titania sometime of the night" (2.1.249, 253). If it *were* the same, Swander says, then "it is especially easy and attractive to believe that no sexual act occurs between the Queen and the Ass." Since he believes such an act should occur, he argues that her bower is really in fairyland, which is distant from the wood, and that it's there where Bottom is taken and there where he is ravished.[26]

Peter Brook was not so delicate in his famous production of 1970. Roger Warren describes his staging of the pre-ravishment phase:

> As [Titania] fell in love with Bottom, she lay on her back and curled her legs around his, clawing at his thighs, gasping and gabbling in sexual frenzy as she said:
>   And I do love thee. Therefore go with me.
>   I'll give thee fairies to attend on thee,

> And they shall fetch thee jewels from the deep,
> And sing while thou on pressed flowers dost sleep . . .
—whereupon Bottom jumped on top of her.[27]

Whereupon many critics jumped on top of Peter Brook, crying that what is really being raped here are Shakespeare's text and theater. As for the theater, a Titania jumping Bottom, or a Bottom jumping Titania, is hardly what Shakespeare could have had in mind for his manor-house production, certainly not what the Office of the Revels would countenance for court performances, and not even what the Shoreditch Theatre in the licentious liberty of Holywell could display. All of Shakespeare's (and any other Elizabethan playwright's) bed-tricks occurred invisibly, offstage.

As for the text, any bedding of Bottom would have to be hidden not only from Elizabethan audiences but from Oberon as well. That the fairy king, twice said to be "jealous" of Titania (2.1.24, 81), should be willing to gain a squire at the expense of acquiring horns, especially when his rival is an ass, strains credulity. Of course the conjuring Oberon could not have known Titania would dote on an ass; what he had in mind was "ounce, or cat, or bear, / Pard, or boar with bristled hair" (2.2.30–31). The creatures he cites are all noted for their ferocity and hence would be the most likely to repel, not invite, sexual overtures. Hence his charm calls for Titania not to enjoy her new-found love, whatever he or it may be, but to "love and *languish* for his sake" (l. 29) or, as he said earlier, to "*pursue* it with the soul of love" (2.1.182). On learning that Titania "wak'd and straightway lov'd an ass," Oberon says, "This falls out better than I could devise" (3.2.34–35), thereby revealing, Brook says, the "hidden play": "It's the idea, which has been so easily passed over for centuries, of a man taking the wife whom he loves totally and having her fucked by the crudest sex machine he can find."[28] That such an idea was passed over for centuries comes as no great surprise, since Oberon, not a man but a fairy king, does not choose a "sex machine" or anything else, as John Russell Brown points out.[29] What is surprising is that Oberon would opt to be present at the time—as the stage direction at the opening of 4.1 implies: "Enter Queen of Fairies, and Clown, and Fairies; and the King, behind them"[30]—and that afterwards, looking upon the now-sleeping couple, he could merely observe wryly to Puck, "See'st thou this sweet sight?" (l. 45). Either we critics and directors mistaketh quite, or fairy kings regard such matters very differently from other Shakespearean husbands, most of whom express some anxiety about their wives' fidelity and none of whom assumes that the best way to teach a wife obedience is to encourage her to make a cuckold of him.

A third deterrent to this ravishing interpretation is Bottom himself, to whom I'll return momentarily. Let me note first that part of the difficulty lies in Shakespeare's having composed something of an anamorphic picture of Titania's bower. Take, for instance, Titania's words as she gathers Bottom and herself for . . . for whatever she is gathering them for:

> Come wait upon him; lead him to my bower.
> The moon methinks looks with a wat'ry eye;
> And when she weeps, weeps every little flower,
> Lamenting some enforced chastity.
> Tie up my lover's tongue, bring him silently.
>   (3.1.192–96)

A straight-on look at the phrase "enforced chastity" yields an image of chastity forced or violated, in which case the watery-eyed moon must be Diana, goddess of virginity, who quite properly weeps on such unhappy occasions. Indeed her watery eye, reflected in the eyes of every little flower, disperses a panoptic sex-censuring gaze throughout nature—hardly the kind of gaze or the kind of goddess Titania would want to invoke if she had carnal designs on Bottom. Nor can one imagine a lunar Diana and myriad flowerets dripping with grief at the thought of Bottom yielding up whatever chastity he has to yield up; the speech would make better sense if a salacious Bottom were hauling Titania off to his hay-stall, not she leading him dumbly to her bower. Still, if we opt for a Titania so bent on ravishing Bottom that she can dismiss the moon's weepy protests, then her "Tie up my lover's tongue, bring him silently" would apparently be equivalent to "Enough said, let's get down to business."

So the straight-on meaning of "enforced chastity" is *chastity forced*. Looked at askance, however, it means just the opposite, *chastity compelled*, the kind Hermia would exemplify if she were to get herself to a nunnery, perhaps the kind she does briefly exemplify when out of deference to "human modesty" she obliges Lysander to sleep apart from her. This reading would invoke a different kind of moon altogether, one who grows teary-eyed when chastity is preserved: certainly not the prudish Diana but rather the more amorous Luna or Selene, who fell in love with Endymion long ago and who still inspires the lunacy of country lads and lasses in woodland bowers on the eve of May and at Midsummer Night. By this token the weepy flowerets are not "Dian's buds" but "Cupid's flowers" (4.1.72), who should have little cause to weep if a deflowering is forthcoming. Later on, when Oberon exhibits the sleeping Titania and Bottom to Puck, these flowers, now "flouriets," are weeping anew. For as Oberon reports,

> . . . that same dew, which sometime on the buds
> Was wont to swell like round and orient pearls,

Stood now within the pretty flouriets' eyes
Like tears that did their own disgrace bewail.
   (ll. 52–55)

What flouriets are these, and what is their disgrace? Surely they must be
Dian's buds bewailing the disgrace of having been transformed into Cupid's
flowers during the bower episode—bewailing, that is, the humiliation of
Titania, brought about not necessarily by the loss of her married chastity but
simply by her degrading but unconsummated desire for Bottom.

   Most arguments for a sexual consummation rely less on the text than on
mythic or fictional parallels (Pasiphaë and the bull, the sexual escapades of Apu-
leius) or simply on the director's capacity to divine a subtext. Yet there are a couple
of instances in which Titania appears to speak of country matters. The first is in
3.1 when she tells her fairies to light tapers for Bottom "To have my love to bed
and to arise" (l. 166). Anamorphically hidden within a simple statement about his
getting up after sleeping is a phallic arousal on Bottom's part, indeed *of* Bottom's
part. In the Brook production the line was chanted by the fairies as they led Bottom offstage, one of them thrusting an ithyphallic arm up between his legs.

   The next instance occurs after their reappearance in 4.1, when Titania
enfolds the drowsy Bottom in her arms and murmurs

So cloth the woodbine the sweet honeysuckle
Gently entwist; the female ivy so
Enrings the barky fingers of the elm.
Oh, how I love thee! How I dote on thee!
   (ll. 41–44)

Woodbine and honeysuckle are innocent enough, but the enringed finger
is a familiar Shakespearean metaphor for coition,[31] most explicitly in *All's
Well* when Bertram sets the conditions for Helena's becoming truly his wife
(3.2.57–60). And the ivy enringing the elm is a variation on a vine-and-elm
topos that Peter Demetz has charted from the first century B.C. to modern
times (though, surprisingly, without mentioning *A Midsummer Night's Dream*).
Beginning with Catullus, the marriage of feminine grapevine and masculine
elm signifies the fruitful union of husband and wife.[32] By the Renaissance
the topos had become widespread, only now it was "combined and contrasted
with the motif of the ivy, clinging to its tree in an amorous embrace of intense
sexual connotations."[33] Shakespeare employs both topos and countertopos in
A Comedy of Errors when the faithful Adriana encounters a man who looks
exactly like her husband and, embracing him, says, "Thou art an elm, my
husband, I a vine," adding that "If aught possess thee from me, it is dross, /

Usurping ivy, brier, or idle moss" (2.2.173, 176–77). Adriana is unaware that in fastening on a man who is not her husband she is herself the "usurping ivy." Similarly, as Titania clings to Bottom, her lines identify her as the invasive ivy enringing an elm that is not her husband. Of course if Adriana can play the usurping ivy role in broad daylight on the streets of Ephesus without betraying her married chastity, so can Titania in her bower.

This is not to deny that Titania is sensually taken with Bottom; she is. But the question is how far her sensuality goes, and indeed how far it can go. Surely a good part of Oberon's punishment of Titania centers in the physical and metaphysical impossibility of a fairy queen to couple with an ass. Add to this the impossibility of exhibiting such a coupling in Shakespeare's theater and, if we still opt for a sexual act, then it must be accomplished verbally, not actionally, in which case Titania's onstage metaphors here serve as verbal substitutes for the unstageable. It seems to me that Titania's sexually ambitious metaphors are evidence not of what she and Bottom did or are doing but of what at worst she thinks she would like them to be doing. Such metaphors, like those of treasure-laden merchant ships earlier, are the only way to express the mystery of desire as it goes about its strange business in the psyche of a fairy queen.

To expand on this a bit: insofar as desire presupposes lack, we must imagine that Bottom has something that Titania lacks. One glance at Bottom makes this seem absurd; and yet, as we saw earlier, Titania's admiring portrayal of the Indian queen implies a desire on her part to be an Indian queen, big with an Indian prince. But what has Bottom got that Titania could possibly desire? Perhaps the most obvious thing a fairy queen lacks and Bottom abundantly possesses—"mortal grossness." That is how she phrases it when she tells Bottom that she will "purge [his] mortal grossness so / That [he] shalt like an airy spirit go" (3.1.154–55). Unfortunately for her, the last way in the world Bottom could "go" is like an airy spirit; not even Titania has such transformative powers. And yet she cherishes him most passionately, not in any airy form but in his utmost physicality. This follows logically enough from her speech to Oberon expressing her admiration for "lower" things—a woman, a human, pregnancy, mortality—even as she neglected her allegiance to "higher" things—a "man," a royal husband, wifely obedience, immortality. It follows also from Oberon's accusing her of loving the mortal Theseus. Thus Oberon engineers a punishment that caricatures her desire: she is obliged to descend to the level of brute matter, to the very Bottom itself, and be enthralled by it. When she dotes on Bottom's "shape" (3.1.134), his "amiable cheeks" and "fair large ears" (4.1.2, 4), when she obliges her elves to cater to each of his corporeal needs, and finally when she winds his drowsy bestial body in her arms, what else is she doing but desiring his mortal grossness?

And not simply his "grossness" but his "mortal grossness," a significant addition. In a play in which death is often invoked but always shied away from or apparently transcended, except in *Pyramus and Thisbe*, Titania comes at it from the other side. Her "tragedy" is not like that of mortal lovers, whose grand but fatal passion is "short as any dream" because the jaws of devouring time do their business quickly (1.1.144). Unlike humans, Titania is not in flight from time and its henchman mortality; she flutters at their window like a moth at a lantern, trying to find her way into a world of sexuality, pregnancy, birth, and (the price of all the others) death, and being frustrated by her immortal ungrossness. Her love for Theseus, her wish to be the pregnant Indian queen, her stepmothering of the queen's child, and now her passion for Bottom: all reflect a desire for mortality. In this light her surrender of the changeling child marks her reconciliation not merely to Oberon and patriarchy but also to her immutable destiny as an immortal. Titania's "tragedy" is that she is ineligible for the role of tragic heroine; fairy queens can't fall—not at least into time and death.

Yet in a sense she does fall, not into time or death and not even into bed with Bottom, whose more-than-mortal grossness is its own impediment to any sexual derring-do in Titania's bower. As Edward Berry observes, "Of all the many incongruities in this episode, the subtlest, least expected, and most characteristically Shakespearean, is the bestial lover's lack of interest in sex."[34] Even Kott says, "Bottom appreciates being treated as a very important person, but is more interested in the frugal pleasure of eating than in the bodily charms of Titania."[35] Thus despite a major campaign in which she sends armies of elves to hop in his walks, gambol in his eyes, and fetch and feed and scratch as well, she can no more capture his loving glance than Oberon can hers. From the standpoint of Theseus' therapeutic "dream," this suggests that it's not Hippolyta-Titania's sexual desire alone that is being purged but the unseemly aggressiveness and desire to dominate men that, in his anxious imagination, might well attend it. Thus the presumptuously masculine Amazon becomes the presumptuous Queen Titania, who then becomes the aggressive lover of Bottom, so domineering as to disabuse us of the notion that tyranny is an exclusively masculine pursuit.[36] If Oberon has imposed his will on her with flowers and charms, she imposes hers on Bottom no less irresistibly, first tethering his body—"Out of this wood do not desire to go. / Thou shalt remain here, whether thou wilt or no" (3.1.146–47)—and later his unmelodious braying—"Tie up my lover's tongue, bring him silently" (l. 196). In between, the love she displays is imbued with regal narcissism:

> I am a spirit of no common rate.
> The summer still cloth tend upon my state;
> And I do love thee. Therefore, go with me.
>   (ll. 148–50)

This "I-therefore-you" style of love seems almost as self-centered and inconsiderate in its imperiousness as Bottom is in his bestial oblivion. But Bottom's oblivion outfaces Titania's; when her loving "therefore" takes aim at him, it turns into a non sequitur of heroic proportions. Thus in the bluntest way Titania is lessoned about the limits of queenly command, and Amazonian queens are asked to take note.

In fairyland, kings demand, command, punish, and finally forgive. When Oberon displays for Puck the sleeping queen and her entwined beloved, Oberon says, "See'st thou this sweet sight?" and goes on to tell how, "meeting her of late behind the wood," he upbraided Titania until she begged his patience and bestowed the changeling child upon him. "And, now I have the boy," he says, "I will undo / This hateful imperfection of her eyes" (4.1.45–62). The quality of mercy is not entirely constrained in Oberon, but it's by no means free and generous either, coming as it does only after he's gotten his humiliating way. Still, Titania's disgrace, reflected in the flouriets' weeping eyes, moves him to pity; and if pity depends on taking the perspective of others, of feeling what wretches feel, then Oberon's own vision has been modified for the better. His sarcastic "See'st thou this sweet sight?" summarizes his entire project to restore marital order by doctoring Titania's eyes and standing coldly by to observe her humiliation. This is his version of the smiling sadism Hermia's dream attributes to Lysander; and insofar as this is also Hippolyta's "dream," it represents *her* anxieties about a Theseus who won her love doing her injuries. But then, in a forecast of Prospero's "The rarer action is / In virtue than in vengeance," Oberon not merely sees Titania's disgrace but feels it, and so breaks his charm.

Unpleasant as Oberon's methods are, we can only judge them by Titania's response; and from the moment of her awakening she is not only unembittered but quick both to love—"My Oberon!" (4.1.75)—and also to obey: when he asks for music, she immediately cries, "Music, ho! Music, such as charmeth sleep!" (l. 82). Moreover, when the fairies reappear at the end of the play to bless the marriages, the king and queen are in such perfect accord that her troupe of elves merges with his train as harmoniously as the song she instructs them to sing:

> First, rehearse your song by rote,
> To each word a warbling note.

Hand in hand, with fairy grace,
Will we sing, and bless this place.
　　　[*Song and dance*]
　　(5.1.392–96)

Surely songs and dances of this sort will not only ward off moles, harelips, scars, and other "blots of Nature's hand," as Oberon assures us, but also persuade the angry moon to dry up contagious fogs, quiet the rambunctious winds, set the seasons in order, and restore fertility to beast and human. However, before such glorious restorations can be made, Theseus must dismiss the law—and to see clearly and obliquely why he does this, we have to return to the opening scene and another instance of anamorphism.

5. Anamorphism, Realism, and the Law

One thing the blatant trickery of the anamorphic teaches us is the more subtle trickery of the "natural." For the realism produced by linear perspective in our first straight-on view of Holbein's *The Ambassadors* is just as much the product of craft and art and the geometry of pictorial representation, including the precise placement of the viewer, as is the anamorphic unrealism of the skull. What is palpably apparent in, say, surrealism or cubism is kept hidden in realism: the skull of artifice, whose hollow-eyed glance says to the viewer what the skull says in Holbein's painting—"Caught you!" What has been caught and exposed is not our blithe sense of immortality but rather our blithe acceptance of the reality of what we thought we saw to begin with: all of the clearly recognizable objects in *The Ambassadors* apart from the anamorphic skull.

Because the skull is invisible in dedicated realistic works, we think we are not being watched. But there's the cunning of it. Knowing we'll come this way, realism sets a trap for our gaze as craftily as anamorphism does. Seeing us before we ever arrive on the scene, it takes our measure, cataloguing the regularity of our habits, what we want and expect to see—our tiresome predilection for recognizable hands and faces and bowls of fruit and French ambassadors—and, noting all of this, it lines us up just so, as if we were sitting for the painting instead of viewing it. There we stand, wide-eyed as a spotlighted deer. We never know what hits us—until anamorphism or some other perversely artificial device gives away the game.[37]

In the opening scene of *A Midsummer Night's Dream*, something is hidden also, and hidden in full view, just as the artifice of perspectival realism is. I don't mean the shadows of Oberon and Titania cast by the bodies of Theseus and Hippolyta, but rather the invisibly visible artifice of patriarchy embodied in the Law, in the Name of the Father. For the one thing everyone in this scene accepts, even Hermia and Lysander, is the authority of the law, which no one except Egeus seems to like but which everyone acknowledges as given and unalterable. This is what Pascal calls the "mystic basis of authority," the fact that authority is often honored simply because it exists, and continues to exist simply because it's honored. "Laws," he observes, "are obeyed not because they are just but because they are thought just: it's necessary that [justice] be regarded as authentic, eternal, and its beginnings hidden, unless we desire its imminent collapse."[38] Yet although it's wise to keep "beginnings hidden," it's also tempting to seek legitimacy in origins, especially natural ones, as Theseus does when he chides Hermia for not honoring her quasi-divine genetic source:

> To you your father should be as a god—
> One that composed your beauties, yea, and one
> To whom you are but as a form in wax
> By him imprinted and within his power
> To leave the figure or disfigure it.
>   (1. 1.47–51)

But this appeal only confirms Pascal's wisdom about keeping beginnings hidden; for it doesn't take much of a sidelong glance to see who is missing from this act of genetic composition. If patriarchal authority rests on the act of conception, then mothers have as natural a right to be considered "gods" as fathers.[39] What is glaringly absent from Theseus' justification of patriarchy calls our attention to what is glaringly absent from the scene itself—mothers. Glaringly absent, that is, now that we notice. Before Theseus' speech we might have vaguely sensed that something was missing from this scene, but the theatrically given—simply who is present onstage—is a kind of law in itself, so naturally persuasive that it takes an anamorphic glance, prompted unwittingly by Theseus, to reveal what ought to be there but isn't.

As this speech indicates, Shakespeare supplies us with plenty of patriarchal fathers in *A Midsummer Night's Dream*, and a decided absence of mothers, especially in the opening scene. That being the case, we ought to be taken aback somewhat to encounter also, or not to encounter, a missing father. Not, of course, that every father or mother or great-uncle who fails to appear in a play should be reported as missing. Nothing is missing unless its absence is somehow announced, the way the nonmaterializing battle of Gaultree Forest in *2 Henry IV* is, or as Hamlet's long-delayed revenge is. Here, the absence of Theseus' father becomes apparent to us in the opening scene, announced by the fact that his name is possessed by that acme of fatherhood, the man whose identity is totally absorbed by paternity, Egeus.

That is, any Elizabethan familiar with the Theseus of mythology would know that his father's name was Aegeus and could hardly help being momentarily puzzled when an older man appears onstage, cries "Happy be Theseus, our renowned Duke!" (1.1.20) and is called homophonically "Aegeus/Egeus" by the duke. For a moment or two the very notion of paternity and patriarchy is as blurred as the skull in Holbein's painting. Has the royal father come before his son the duke to lodge a complaint? If so, then surely the specialty of rule hath been neglected, and degree, both familial and political, is given a fearful shake. An even fearfuller shake is given to our sense of time if we recall that Aegeus ought by all rights to be underground, or rather underwater, instead of in court. For the scholars in the audience would know that Theseus' marriage to Hippolyta took place well after he killed the Cretan minotaur and, returning with Ariadne, forgetfully flew the black sail that caused his despairing father to fling himself into what became the Aegean Sea.

Gradually, however, this blur takes recognizable shape. "King Aegeus" evaporates, leaving the despotic father of Hermia. Nevertheless, the association between the two has been made and is reinforced by the fact that in upholding the law Theseus bows to the will of a man who represents, quite literally, *le nom du père*. Perhaps there is a skull in this scene after all, casting a ghostly authoritarian gaze on Theseus. For the law Theseus cannot abrogate is "the ancient privilege of Athens" (l. 41), a law he inherits from his father's reign, as he inherited it from his, and so on. The monarch Theseus is as ruled by patriarchy as his subjects.

Up to a point, anyhow. At the end of Act 4, when Egeus invokes the law again, with even better justification than before, Theseus cavalierly dismisses both father figure and patriarchal law without a hint of explanation. If the play is a kind of *fort/da* game writ large, the *da* that would normally represent a recovery of the lost mother becomes here a *fort* that does away with the commanding father. I mean "does away with" not entirely metaphorically. For Egeus' death is implicit in Theseus' overruling his demand for Lysander's death. The situation is very like that in *Othello* when Brabantio hales his would-be son-in-law before the Senate, demands his death, and is himself officially overruled (1.3). The consequences of this are not mentioned until late in the play when Gratiano addresses Desdemona's dead body: "Poor Desdemon! I am glad thy father's dead. / Thy match was mortal to him" (5.2.211–12). In *A Midsummer Night's Dream* Hermia's match is not mortal to Egeus but something evidently akin to it. When Theseus issues his judgment, Egeus turns abruptly silent, exits shortly thereafter, and disappears from the play. At the performance of *Pyramus and Thisbe* he is, or should be, as conspicuously absent as Hermia's mother was from the opening scene of the play.[40]

In freeing Hermia and Lysander from *le nom du père*, Theseus also frees himself, especially if we hear an echo of *Aegeus* in *Egeus*. The name of the father resides in the law itself, and to repudiate the law, if only in a particular instance, is to deny its total dominion and hence to expose the ghostly skull of its "natural" authority for what it is, a self-serving construction of patriarchal culture. To see this, however, Theseus must position himself differently, taking a sidelong Socratic glance at the law. That is just what the play has done for him by casting him in the role of Oberon during the middle of the play and obliging him, in his private version of a midsummer night's dream, to come to terms with his marital anxieties. Not only his marital anxieties, it would seem, but also his tendencies toward phallocratic tyranny—the Theseus who won Hippolyta's love doing her injuries. For one solution to his anxieties about Hippolyta is precisely the solution Egeus resorts to when his authority is called in question: sheer force, death, sequestration. As Egeus, with the uneasy acquiescence of Theseus, seeks to humiliate Hermia by force of law, so Oberon humiliates Titania by force of love-in-idleness. When Titania capitulates, Oberon recants. If the parallels hold, perhaps we can assume that authoritarian excess has been purged not only from fairyland but also from Theseus and Athens.[41] At any rate Theseus releases the awakened lovers from the power of the law in an act analogous to and, I suppose, consequent upon Oberon's release of them from the power of his spells.

Both acts of liberation depend on the earlier freeing of Titania from her entrancement with Bottom, which, along with the transfer of the change-ling child, marks a restoration of hierarchy in royal marriages. Titania can now pass almost seamlessly into Theseus' world, translated into Hippolyta by means of her doubled role. Having resumed her proper status as obedient and loving wife, she is twice addressed by Oberon as "my queen" (4.1.84, 94) just before, after a quick change of costume, she reappears onstage as Hippolyta and is addressed by Theseus as "fair queen" (l. 108)—which, given the duke's skepticism in such matters, is as close as his tongue can get to "fairy queen."

This confirmation of the presence of Titania in the body of Hippolyta affirms the rightness of Theseus' marriage. For if we go back to Oberon's jealous accusations about Titania's love for Theseus—

> Didst not thou lead him through the glimmering night
> From Perigenia, whom he ravished?
> And make him with fair Aegles break his faith,
> With Ariadne and Antiopa?
> (2.1.77–80)

—we can now see that Titania is cast in the role of desire itself, figured as a kind of sensual glimmering in the night that promises Theseus the ultimate in fulfillment just beyond Perigenia with Aegles, just beyond Aegles with Ariadne, just beyond. . . . Always just beyond; so it goes with desire. And there, just beyond all of these transient desires, flits Titania herself, beckoning. Why? If my argument about Titania's desire for mortality is plausible, then surely it's because Oberon's jealousy is justified. Titania does—or, by now, did—love Theseus, yearning across the gap separating immortal from mortal. As she wanted and imagined herself to be the pregnant Indian queen, so in furthering Theseus' love affairs, she wanted and imagined herself to be Perigenia and Aegles and Ariadne. But fairies being fairies, she could come no closer than imagining, following darkness like a dream. Nor, it seems, could Theseus himself. For this line of interpretation implies that the amorous hero was not really pursuing the mortal women he briefly loved and left but rather the enduring image of Titania that took up residence in each of them before drifting out of reach like desire itself.

This would bespeak a tragic love if it weren't for the fact that Titania now stands beside Theseus in the shape of Hippolyta. Through the magic of an actor's body, Titania finally achieves the corporeality she sought, and with it Theseus. And Theseus achieves the elusive Titania he sought, in the body of his queen to be. Thus Theseus' marriage to Hippolyta receives a kind of teleological certification; it was she all the time he longed for. And, thanks to the tyrannies of Oberon, his anxieties about her Amazonian desires in bed, in council chamber, and in the royal nursery have been put to rest. With Oberon assuming the role of stepfather to the changeling child, patriarchal authority is restored in fairyland, and hence can be relaxed in Athens.

But of course Theseus knows nothing about all this. When he dismisses the Athenian law, he exhibits much the same kind of irrationality as the male lovers in the wood. As a result, his famous speech extolling the virtues of reason takes on the character of Lysander's flowery-eyed explanation of why he suddenly loves Helena: because "The will of man is by his reason sway'd" (2.2.115). Theseus will have nothing to do with "antic fables" or "fairy toys" (5.1.3), although as a mythic character he is an antique fable himself and as a player he is an antic onstage,[42] indeed an antic twice over, having played a fairy king as well as an Athenian monarch. In this light, Hippolyta's musing comment—

> But all the story of the night told over,
> And all their minds transfigur'd so together
> More witnesseth than fancy's images
> And grows to something of great constancy;
> But, howsoever, strange and admirable . . .
>   (ll. 23–27)

—grows more meaningful if she, like the awakened Hermia, is seeing things "with parted eye, / When every thing seems double" (4.1.188–89) and is perhaps hearing echoes of her own double, the awakened Titania, murmuring "My Oberon! What visions have I seen! / Methought I was enamor'd of . . ." (ll. 75–76). Ah, but neither fairy queen nor Amazonian bride can tell what she thought she was enamored of. What she is enamored of is Duke Theseus, and all the rest is a dream. Perhaps they can get Peter Quince to write a ballad of this dream. It could be called "Theseus' Dream."

Notes

1. In his *Anamorphic Art* (trans. W. J. Strachan [New York: Harry N. Abrams, 1977]; originally *Anamorphoses ou magic artificielle des effets merveilleux* [Paris: Olivier Perrin Editeur, 1969]), Jurgis Baltrusaitis says that one must stand "very close, looking down on it from the right" to see the skull properly (p. 91). Having seen the painting only in relatively small reproductions, I'm obliged to take his word for it. Everyone I know has gotten cross-eyed trying to see the skull, and one suffered paper cuts on the nose for the sake of perspectival science. For the less daring, Baltrusaitis has a photograph showing how the skull appears in proper focus (p. 103): it lies on its right cheekbone, eye sockets to the left, jaw to the right, looking in fact very much like the viewer.

2. Quoted in Rudolf Arnheim, *Visual Thinking* (Berkeley: Univ. of California Press, 1969), p. 89.

3. Shakespeare may or may not have seen Holbein's painting, but as Ned Lukacher points out ("Anamorphic Stuff: Shakespeare, Catharsis, Lacan," *South Atlantic Quarterly*, 88 [1989], 863–98), it is very likely that he saw the anamorphic painting of Edward VI by a Holbein follower, one William Scrots, whose very name invites anamorphic glances. Citing Baltrusaitis, Lukacher writes, "Scrots's portrait hung in Whitehall Palace during the 1590s when Shakespeare's company, the Lord Chamberlain's Men, played there; this portrait was to be viewed through a viewing hole drilled through a screen off to the side of the painting" (p. 873).

That Shakespeare is playing with perspective in *A Midsummer Night's Dream* would be in keeping with his interest in anamorphism in *Richard II*, which was written around the same time (Lukacher, pp. 863–78; Christopher Pye, "The Betrayal of the Gaze: Theatricality and Power in Shakespeare's *Richard II*," *English Literary History*, 55 [1988], 575–98, esp. pp. 581–88).

4. The text I'm using is that of David Bevington in *The Complete Works of Shakespeare*, 3rd ed. (Glenview, Ill.: Scott, Foresman, 1980).

5. The four parts are so amenable to doubling that they seem designed for that purpose. The only difficulty is the need for a couple of quick costume changes when one pair exits just before the other enters—at 4.1.101 and at 5.1.365. But changing time for the latter occasion is supplied by Puck's speech about dread spirits and frolicsome ones (ll. 366–86), and for the former occasion it can be managed if the stage direction "Wind horn" were taken as authorizing several windings and perhaps a few musical discords and sweet thunderings from Theseus' hounds before the duke and his train put in an appearance. If the parts were doubled in Shakespeare's time, the practice was subsequently abandoned (at least there is no mention of it for two centuries), only to be recovered in recent years.

As Graham Bradshaw observes, "doubling [the roles of Theseus and Oberon] makes excellent dramatic, psychological and symbolic sense, because they are the respective representatives of reason and of those life mysteries which reason cannot encompass or control." Doubling "underlines the irony that these seemingly opposed realms are properly interdependent and need to be integrated, brought into harmony with each other" (*Shakespeare's Scepticism* [London: Harvester Press, 1987], p. 69). However, see Roger Warren's *A Midsummer Night's Dream: Text and Performance* (London: The Macmillan Press, 1983) for objections (pp. 60, 64), as well as for excellent analyses of the productions not only by Brook and Phillips but by Peter Hall and Elijah Moshinsky as well.

6. *A Marxist Study of Shakespeare's Comedies* (London: The Macmillan Press, 1979), p. 56. Krieger also believes that the discord between Oberon and Titania, which reflects the conflict between Theseus and Hippolyta, implies that the wars between the Athenians and the Amazonians have disrupted all nature. But this is to translate the Athens-fairyland metaphor into literal identity, leading Krieger to add that it "indicates Shakespeare's understanding of the strategies used by the ruling class to justify its power and its retention of centralized authority through hypothetical analogy with the forces of nature" (p. 56). Grounding one's authority on "nature" is a strategy no doubt employed by all ruling classes (not to mention parents, labor-union leaders, and English professors), and certainly Shakespeare understood as much. However, Theseus' anxieties seem less those of a ruler desperate to legitimate his political authority, which no one has challenged, than those of an about-to-be husband concerned about his sexual dominance. Of course sexual dominance can be an important element in domestic politics, and the politician who cannot rule in his own bedroom may not be able to rule elsewhere, as Antony discovered during the sea battle near Actium (*Antony and Cleopatra*, 3.10).

7. Among the benighted critics who have been taken in by this surface view of Theseus, I'm afraid I must number myself: "As most critics have emphasized, Theseus has a normative role in the play, at least as far as love is concerned; and his marriage to Hippolyta, the preparations for which structurally enclose the trials of the young lovers, operates as the social ideal against which other relationships are measured" ("*A Midsummer Night's Dream*: The Illusion of Drama," *Modern Language Quarterly*, 26 [1965], 506–22, esp. p. 510).

8. Geoffrey Bullough, ed., *Narrative and Dramatic Sources of Shakespeare*, 8 vols. (London: Routledge and Kegan Paul, 1957–75), Vol. 1, pp. 386–87. The Amazonian invasion is reported in Plutarch's "The Life of Theseus," available to Shakespeare in Sir Thomas North's 1579 translation of Amyot's 1559 version.

9. *The Faerie Queene*, ed. Thomas P. Roche, Jr. (Harmondsworth: Penguin, 1978), 5.4.21ff.

10. See Simon Shepherd, *Amazons and Warrior Women: Varieties of Feminism in Seventeenth-Century Drama* (Brighton: Harvester Press, 1981), pp. 13–14.

11. That is, Hippolyta remains an enigma to the interpreter of the script. But of course directors and actors must decide how she is to be played—somewhere along the spectrum from loving and obedient (the traditional presentation) to fiercely resistant (as in a 1967 Greenwich Village production by John Hancock in which she was "brought back in captivity, robed in leopard skins, was caged and guarded" [Allan Lewis, "*A Midsummer Night's Dream*—Fairy Fantasy or Erotic Nightmare?" *Educational Theatre Journal*, 21 (1969), 251–58, esp. p. 251]).

12. *Friends and Lovers: The Phenomenology of Desire in Shakespearean Comedy* (New York: Columbia Univ. Press, 1985), pp. 146–49.

13. An identification of Theseus and Hippolyta with Oberon and Titania is of course not dependent on doubling the parts, though much is lost, I think, if that is not done. But the identification is made when Titania reproves Oberon about "the bouncing Amazon, / Your buskin'd mistress and your warrior love," and he accuses her of loving Theseus and leading him from woman to woman (2.1.70–80). For Theseus to marry Oberon's beloved, with Oberon's approval, is tantamount to his being Oberon. And if Theseus is Oberon, then he is Titania's husband, and she a fairy version of Hippolyta.

14. *Écrits: A Selection*, trans. Alan Sheridan (New York and London: W. W. Norton, 1977), p. 286.

15. "That the Indian boy is an Eros figure," MacCary argues, "cannot be doubted, and by my definition that means he represents an archaic self-image. Thus the male facing marriage nostalgically returns to an earlier, easier pattern of desire" (p. 147). On this view, that is, the Indian boy represents the classical *eromenos*, or boy-beloved, of the older male *eraster*, and Oberon-Theseus is regressing to a more narcissistic and manageable kind of desire, easier than negotiating with a fairy queen. It's not clear whether MacCary means what he seems to say—what Jan Kott said in *Shakespeare Our Contemporary* (trans. Boleslaw Taborski [Garden City, N.Y.: Doubleday, 1964], p. 214) and what John P. Cutts implies in *The Shattered Glass: A Dramatic Pattern in Shakespeare's Early Plays* ([Detroit: Wayne State Univ. Press, 1968], pp. 49–55)—that Oberon reverts to pederasty. However, it's hard to see how this, or any solution involving a love for the boy, helps the Theseus who, in MacCary's otherwise persuasive argument, is experiencing this therapeutic dream. There is no Ganymede in Theseus' palace; and if the duke must resort to a simpler mode of love, it would more likely be to the series of nomadic heterosexual encounters cited by Oberon than to something homoerotic. It seems to me that the boy merely plays a symbolic role in the contest for power. See also Shirley Nelson Garner, who argues for an Indian boy in whom both Titania and Oberon are erotically interested ("*A Midsummer Night's Dream*: 'Jack shall have Jill; / Nought shall go ill,'" *Women's Studies*, 9 [1981], 47–63, esp. pp. 49–50).

16. If Oberon and Titania treat the changeling child as a signifier, they do no more than other parents do with their children, converting them into objects of symbolic exchange even before they are born. In "The Indian Boy's Dream Wherein Every Mother's Son Rehearses His Part: Shakespeare's *A Midsummer Night's Dream*," *Shakespeare Studies*, 20 (1988), 15–32, Allen Dunn regards the Bottom-Titania episode as the Indian boy's dream, a dream designed to defend himself against an oedipal expulsion from Titania's maternal bower by having Bottom expelled instead, while his "ultimate defense is his [own] absence" (p. 22). Eliciting a dream from a character who never appears onstage is no mean feat and may risk being called "The Critic's Dream," as may my own argument for regarding regal quarrels in fairyland as "Theseus' (and Hippolyta's) Nightmare." Nevertheless, Dunn's essay is an insightful exploration of oedipal crises in the play.

17. In a deservedly well-known article on the play—"'Shaping Fantasies': Figurations of Gender and Power in Elizabethan Culture" in *Representing the English Renaissance*, Stephen Greenblatt, ed. (Berkeley: Univ. of California Press, 1988), pp. 31–64—Louis Adrian Montrose shrewdly regards Titania's speech about motherhood as a counterpoint to Theseus' earlier speech about fatherhood (1.1.46–52), in

which Theseus overcompensates for the "*natural* fact that men do indeed come from women . . . [and] for the *cultural* facts that consanguineal and affinal ties *between* men are established through mothers, wives, and daughters" (p. 42).

18. The delightful scene described by Titania reveals what Helena's account of her and Hermia's childhood also reveals, the presence of difference within an idealized recollection of oneness. In Titania's case feminine friendship does not paper over hierarchic distinctions. What she chooses to remember is an occasion when the Indian mother playfully went about the beach "to fetch me trifles." No question who is fairy queen and who is votaress here.

19. Actually some Protestants, especially Puritans, regarded fairies as an invention of the Catholic Middle Ages, "devised by Popish priests to cover up their knaveries" (Keith Thomas, *Religion and the Decline of Magic: Studies in popular beliefs in sixteenth- and seventeenth-century England* [New York: Charles Scribner's Sons, 1971], p. 610). But this was unfair, as Thomas points out, because fairies antedated the Church and because the medieval Church had been hostile to such beliefs, not anxious to have competing deities and spirits. The existence of fairies was much debated, and among believers an effort was sometimes made to distinguish good fairies from bad ones; but most theologians, Protestant and Catholic, thought them all devilish. For a survey of the various opinions, see K. M. Briggs, *The Anatomy of Puck: An Examination of Fairy Beliefs among Shakespeare's Contemporaries and Successors* (London: Routledge and Kegan Paul, 1959), pp. 163–83.

20. Celeste Turner Wright, "The Amazons in Elizabethan Literature," *Studies in Philology*, 37 (1940), 433–56, esp. p. 453. For these claims, Wright cites Thevet's *New Founde World* (translated into English in 1568), Butler's *Feminine Monarchie* (1609), Gainsford's *Glory of England* (1618), Heywood's *2 Iron Age* (1632), Purchas's *Pilgrimes* (1613), Raleigh's *Discovery of Guiana* (1596), and Barckley's *Felicitie of Man* (1598), among others.

21. Lacan's notion of the phallus (*Écrits*, pp. 281–91) is difficult to set forth clearly. First, it is "neither a fantasy, nor an object, nor an organ (whether penis or clitoris), but a signifier—indeed the signifier of all signifiers" (John P. Muller and William J. Richardson, *Lacan and Language* [New York: International Univ. Press, 1982], p. 335). What this master signifier signifies is something like "being the object of desire," possessing the power to compel recognition, desire, love, respect. For the child, male or female, the original phallus is the mother, whom the child both wants and wants to be wanted by. At the oedipal crisis the child must repress the desire for the mother and for the mother's desire by transferring the phallus to the Name-of-the-Father, thus enabling his or her admission to the symbolic. From this time on the phallus is associated with the power and privilege of patriarchy, not because it should be but simply because in patriarchal cultures it is.

Lacan's apparent transcendence of biology in making the phallus a signifier rather than the penis is compromised by his very choice of the phallus to serve as this signifier and by his associating the "rise" (*Aufhebung*) and "fall" (repression) of symbolized desire with tumescence and detumescence (*Écrits*, p. 288). At one point he says the question is whether one physically "has" the phallus (men) or symbolically "is" the phallus, with or without having it (women or men).

22. "The changeling," as David Marshall notes in an unusually perceptive essay, "comes to represent all of the characters in the play who are traded or fought over as property. It also shows us that the other characters are changelings in the sense that the play's plot revolves around their exchanges: their substitutions and

their interchangeability" ("Exchanging Visions: Reading *A Midsummer Night's Dream*," *ELH*, 49 [1982], 543–75, esp. p. 568).

23. pp. 220–21 (cited in n. 15, above).

24. "*A Midsummer Night's Dream*: The Monster in the Labyrinth," *ShStud*, 11 (1978), 39–52. On the other hand, M. E. Lamb, in "*A Midsummer Night's Dream*: The Myth of Theseus and the Minotaur," *Texas Studies in Literature and Language*, 21 (1979), 478–91, also sees allusions to Pasiphaë and the bull without feeling that Titania's passion is consummated. See also Deborah Baker Wyrick, "The Ass Motif in *The Comedy of Errors* and *A Midsummer Night's Dream*," *Shakespeare Quarterly*, 33 (1982), 431–48, for a learned response to Kott's stress on the priapic connotations of the ass. As Wyrick says, "Thus, even as a sexual cipher the ass is unstable; under his shaggy skin lurks a remarkable ability to shift symbolic significance. The 'licentious ass,' the 'foolish ass,' and the 'admirable ass' inhabit one hide" (p. 438). I should add that Theseus shapes his dream in accord with the principle of Artemidoros Daldianus (second century A.D.), who in his *Oneirokritika* revealed the significance of dreaming of an ass: "Asses, if they carry a burden, obey their driver, are strong and walk quietly, bode good for marriage and partnership, for they indicate that the wife or partner will not be wasteful but obedient and compatible" (Naphtali Lewis, *The Interpretation of Dreams and Portents* [Toronto and Sarasota: Samuel Stevens, Hakkert and Company, 1976], p. 70). Thus a great virtue of watching *A Midsummer Night's Dream*, our theatrical dream about an ass in fairyland, is that we can return home to a "wife or partner [who] will not be wasteful but obedient and compatible."

25. "Editors vs. A Text: The Scripted Geography of *A Midsummer Night's Dream*," *SP*, 87 (1990), 83–108, esp. p. 102.

26. p. 92 ff. This all depends, however, on a Titania whom Swander regards as full of "wildly lust-driven desires" (p. 96)—desires made evident through stylistic devices so subtly meaningful as to boggle the imagination. For instance, of her lines "Out of this wood do not desire to go. / Thou shalt remain here, whether thou wilt or no" (3.1.146–47), he says, "Her sudden violent lust is all available in the arrangement of the 't-d-g' consonants, the basically monosyllabic diction, the opening trochee, the firm metrical regularity thereafter, and the caesura defined by the identical hard consonant ('d') on both sides" (p. 97). Even so, Swander's otherwise careful and interesting argument makes the best case yet for a ravishment of Bottom that does not require a wild disregard of the text.

27. pp. 57–58 (cited in n. 5, above).

28. Quoted in Peter Ansorge, "Director in Interview: Peter Brook," *Plays and Players*, 18 (1970), 18–19, esp. p. 18.

29. "Free Shakespeare," *Shakespeare Survey*, 24 (1971), 127–35, esp. p. 133.

30. In keeping with his argument that Titania's bower is in an offstage fairyland, Homer Swander takes this stage direction, with its "and the King behind them," to imply that Oberon may have followed the errant couple to the bower, spied upon them *in flagrante delicto*, and now, as they return for a few post-coital pleasantries, trails behind in dejected jealousy (p. 105). If, on the other hand, Titania's bower is the onstage "bank where the wild thyme blows," then the mismatched pair is entering her bower in this scene (4.1), and the ravishment, if there is to be one, must deal with the awkward presence of both Oberon and the audience.

31. See William C. Carroll's persuasively bawdy discussion of this issue in his *The Metamorphoses of Shakespearean Comedy* (Princeton, NJ.: Princeton Univ. Press, 1985), pp. 152–55.

32. "The Elm and the Vine: Notes Toward the History of a Marriage Topos," *PMLA*, 73 (1958), 521–32.

33. p. 526.

34. *Shakespeare's Comic Rites* (Cambridge: Cambridge Univ. Press, 1984), p. 122.

35. *The Bottom Translation*, trans. Daniela Miedzyrzecka and Lillian Vallee (Evanston, Ill.: Northwestern Univ. Press, 1987), p. 52.

36. J. Dennis Huston shrewdly observes that Titania's tyrannic bent is part of a more pervasive pattern of tyranny in the play, beginning with Egeus and the law but also including the despotism of love itself (*Shakespeare's Comedies of Play* [New York: Columbia Univ. Press, 1981], pp. 105–7).

37. In *Towards Deep Subjectivity* (New York: Harper and Row, 1972), Roger Poole cites an interesting example of sculptural anamorphism:

> Naum Gabo's "Spherical Theme" (1964) appears from directly in front of it to be a construction in one circular piece of metal. Only when one moves round it does it appear that there are two curved circles of metal bent and placed back to back. From a position at a ninety degree angle to one's first position, one can in fact look right through the two halves of what appeared at first to be a solid object. At forty-five degrees to one's original position, the ambiguity is perfectly established, as the rhythmic quality of the whole forbids a final decision as to whether or not the construction is in one piece.
> (p. 113)

Within the realistic sphere the most obvious example is pornography, which places the viewer in the position of a voyeur, seeing without being seen. But insofar as the picture has been staged to catch the gaze of the viewer, it has "seen" him before he sees it.

38. *Pascal's Pensées*, trans. Martin Turnell (New York: Harper and Brothers, 1962), p. 134.

39. Theseus would have been better off simply to assert the authorizing agencies of nature and God, like the well-known preacher William Whately, author of *A Bride-Bush; or, a direction for married persons* (1619), who admonishes women: "If ever thou purpose to be a good wife, and to live comfortably, set down this with thyself: mine husband is my superior, my better; he hath authority and rule over me; nature hath given it to him . . . God hath given it to him" (quoted by Lawrence Stone in *The Family, Sex and Marriage in England 1500–1800* [New York: Harper and Row, 1977], pp. 55–56). For a good analysis of Theseus' speech, see David Marshall (pp. 551–52 [cited in n. 22, above]).

40. Egeus is absent from the last act in Quarto 1. In the Folio, however, he appears and is given the lines assigned in Q1 to Philostrate. As critics have recently noted, whether Egeus is present or absent here can have a crucial effect. See Barbara Hodgdon, "Gaining a Father: the Role of Egeus in the Quarto and the Folio," *Review of English Studies*, 37 (1986), 534–42; Philip C. McGuire, "Egeus and the Implications of Silence" in *Shakespeare and the Sense of Performance: Essays in the Tradition of Performance Criticism in Honor of Bernard Beckerman*, ed. Marvin and Ruth Thompson (Newark: Univ. of Delaware Press, 1989), pp. 103–15. His absence implies his refusal to acknowledge Hermia's wedding and his alienation from

Athenian society, whereas his presence speaking Philostrate's lines implies his full acceptance of the marriage. His absence makes far better sense: in part because the radical reversal of attitude required by the Folio seems so implausible—for instance, an Egeus shedding "merry tears" (5.1.69) while watching a rehearsal of *Pyramus and Thisbe* taxes credulity—and in part because it parallels the earlier absence of the mother and, following logically upon the dismissal of the law, sweeps the stage clear of the harsher aspects of patriarchy.

41. Not, of course, that Theseus is wiping patriarchy off the cultural slate, only its most repressive features as represented by the tyranny of the law. After all, Athens and Elizabethan England *were* patriarchal, and although Shakespeare could movingly represent injustices brought about by and within the system, it is questionable whether he could entertain the idea of the kind of just social order that has only become politically imaginable in the late twentieth century.

42. See Philip Edwards, *Shakespeare and the Confines of Art* (London: Methuen, 1968), pp. 51–56; also Leonard Barkan, *The Gods Made Flesh: Metamorphosis and the Pursuit of Paganism* (New Haven: Yale Univ. Press, 1986), p. 252.

DAVID WILES

A Midsummer Night's Dream *as Epithalamium*

The closing speeches of *A Midsummer Night's Dream* constitute the kind of finale that we would expect to find at the end of a wedding masque. No other play by Shakespeare ends quite like it. *Love's Labour's Lost* and *The Tempest* celebrate a betrothal, not a wedding. In *As You Like It*, the appearance of Hymen in a kind of masque suggests that the couples should be understood as married rather than betrothed at the end of the play, but the moment of marriage is left vague. Orthodox ceremonial does not seem to belong in the Forest of Arden. The formality of the ending is the formality of a conventional theatrical finale, with four couples gathered on stage for a celebratory dance. Unlike these three plays, *A Midsummer Night's Dream* displays a complete lack of concern with the process of courtship. The rites of courtship—a first encounter in a romantic environment, the interchanging of love-tokens, the composing of love-verses—are all completed before the action of the play begins. The play is concerned with the actual physical union of male and female.

For comparison, let us return to Munday's *John-a-Kent and John-a-Cumber*. Almost certainly, the play was a major source for Shakespeare's plot structure. There seems no reason why we should not follow Greg and identify the play with *The Wise Man of Chester* (or *West Chester*), first produced by the Admiral's company in December 1594 and a big popular

From *Shakespeare's Almanac:* A Midsummer Night's Dream, *Marriage and the Elizabethan Calendar*, pp. 114–25. © 1993 by David Wiles.

success. The central figure in Munday's play is a 'wise' magician struggling to prove his supremacy over a rival, and the Chester setting receives much prominence.[1] It is easy to see how Munday could have inspired Shakespeare through the way he juggles levels of reality. In Munday's play we find a nocturnal elopement and a double wedding. A Puck-like figure serving a magician leads lovers astray by night, and makes them fall asleep. A group of clowns prepare a dramatic entertainment to mark the wedding. The Puck-figure intercalates himself in a performance. I suggested in the last chapter that the transformation of Bottom must be indebted to the scene in Munday where the magician is turned into a fool. For all the similarities, Munday's play is no epithalamium. It concludes not at the bedding but at the church door. The plot represents a power struggle for possession, and it is the tying of the legal knot that is at issue. While the humble players in *A Midsummer Night's Dream* intrude upon wedding night revels, where one would normally expect courtly masquers to be performing, the players in *John-a-Kent* perform where tenants should, in the open air. They welcome the bridegrooms on the evening before the wedding, and they provide a musical reveille the following morning to mark the brides' awakening. Further satirical entertainments, aristocratic and popular, take place on the castle green, when the brides have departed on their procession to the church and the men have yet to follow. The whole play is concerned with the public side of marriage rituals, and no heed is given to the private, carnal dimension. The use of an upper level lends support to the conclusion that Munday's play was written for the Rose playhouse, and not for a private gathering.

The finale of Shakespeare's play has all the attributes of an epithalamium. In Act IV we see a reveille, followed by a procession to the church. Unlike Spenser and Donne, Shakespeare omits the actual ceremony in the 'temple'. He does stage the wedding masque (in a grotesque inverted form), and he represents the departure of the bridal couples to bed. The events within the bedchamber, transposed and burlesqued, are represented through the encounter of Bottom and Titania. At the end of Shakespeare's play it is after midnight, the new day is waxing, and it is time for the consummation. Theseus and Hippolyta, Hermia and Lysander, Helena and Demetrius have all left and are supposed in bed. Puck evokes the noises and spirits of the night that Spenser warned of in his *Epithalamion*:

> Ne let the Pouke, nor other evil sprites,
> Ne let mischievous witches with their charms,
> Ne let Hobgoblins, names whose sense we see not,
> Fray us with things that be not.

Let not the screech-owl, nor the stork be heard:
Nor the night raven that still deadly yells
Nor damnèd ghosts called up with mighty spells.

When Shakespeare's Puck appears with his cleansing broom, he evokes the same 'screech-owl', the same 'sprites' arisen like ghosts from gaping graves. Unlike Spenser's Puck, Shakespeare's Puck alias 'Hobgoblin' (II.i.40) and his demonic companions cease to threaten and become instead protectors of the marriage bed.

Oberon and Titania arrive with a train of fairies who produce a 'glimmering light'. This implies that they arrive with torches, like the pages who always served as torchbearers in a masque. The Unton memorial portrait illustrates such child torchbearers, attending upon masked adult dancers, and bearing tapered poles with a small flame at the tip. (The semantic distinction between taper and torch is not altogether clear.) In 'The Haddington Masque', the torchbearers are twelve Cupids, each bearing two torches. At the wedding night of James' daughter, the torchbearers were sixteen winged spirits bearing torches of virgin wax in either hand. These last were described by Peacham as they waited to escort the bride from the hall:

With torches' light the children stay,
Whose sparks (see how) ascend on high
As if there wanted stars in sky.

These winged spirits encouraged Donne to interpret all the dancers as fairies:

The masquers come too late, and, I think, will stay
Like fairies, till the cock crow them away.[2]

Titania in the course of Shakespeare's play (III.i.162) instructs her fairies to make night-tapers out of beeswax (i.e. virgin wax as distinct from recycled wax or tallow) in order to escort Bottom to bed. There is no sign that the fairies produce such tapers to honour Bottom, but they do take on the role of torch-bearers at the finale. These tapers or torches perhaps continued to serve a ceremonial purpose once the play was over.

There is an obvious parallel, as we have seen, between the fairies who appear at the end of *A Midsummer Night's Dream* and those who appeared in the midnight masque at the end of *Merry Wives of Windsor* in April 1597, dancing the shape of Carey's Garter ribbon, and departing to bless St George's Chapel. In *Merry Wives* the fairies wear 'rounds of waxen tapers on their heads' (IV.

iv.50), leaving them free to lock hands in the dance. Tapers in *A Midsummer Night's Dream* have a different symbolism and are clearly hand held. In *Merry Wives* the tapers are used for a trial by ordeal, but in *A Midsummer Night's Dream* they are the torches of the masque and procession to the bed-chamber.

The question arises as to who performed the parts of these fairies. An analysis of the casting suggests that *A Midsummer Night's Dream* is written for a standard complement of sixteen actors: four boys to play Hermia, Helena, Titania and Hippolyta, and twelve adults to play Bottom and the five mechanicals, Lysander and Demetrius, Oberon and Theseus, Egeus and Puck. Philostrate would double with Puck, and the other five speaking fairies would double with the five mechanicals. Supernumeraries would seem to be required to play the trains of Oberon and Titania.[3] The role of these supernumeraries is not to act, but to sing and dance, and it is a role that would suit a group of choristers from an aristocratic household. These circumstances would help to explain why two dances seem to be omitted from our text of *A Midsummer Night's Dream*, along with an exit for Oberon's train in Act II.[4] The state of the surviving text is consistent with the hypothesis that the original dances and songs were attenuated when *A Midsummer Night's Dream* was performed in the public theatre, without an available group of boys and without a wedding night context.

The two 'trains' of dancers, choristers or torchbearers are kept apart in Act II, when Oberon refuses to keep company with Titania and dance in her 'round'; in Act II scene ii, Titania's fairies sing a lullaby around their somnolent mistress; and the two trains return only at the finale. It seems reasonable to infer that Oberon's train must comprise male fairies and Titania's train female fairies. Peaseblossom, Cobweb, Moth and Mustardseed are male, of course, but the logic of the doubling required that these speaking roles should be written for adult actors, not for boy actors.

Oberon cues a lively dance when he instructs both groups ('every elf and fairy sprite') to perform a dance that might be a galliard or corranto ('hop as light as bird from briar … and dance it trippingly'). Titania then seems to introduce not the same but a different dance with the speech which follows:

> First rehearse your song by rote,
> To each word a warbling note,
> Hand in hand, with fairy grace,
> Will we sing and bless this place.

This song is slower ('warbling') and formal ('by rote'), and fulfils Oberon's earlier promise that the fairies would at midnight 'solemnly' dance in Theseus' house (IV.i.87). A circular dance would have particular significance because of the link between fairies and fairy rings. Titania's fairy has been delegated to 'dew her orbs upon the green', and a circular dance at the finale would lead naturally into Oberon's distribution of dew. The dialogue therefore suggests two unscripted dances, followed by Oberon's speech

> Now until the break of day
> Through the house each fairy stray . . .

which appears to introduce and explain the next action in the play. The problem is that no stage directions in the Quarto at any point offer guidance as to the nature and timing of the dances. In the Folio, Oberon's speech 'Now until the break of day . . . ' is headed 'The Song' and italicized, suggesting that this is indeed the 'ditty' which Oberon requires the fairies to sing 'after me' as they dance trippingly. Yet the speech starts and ends with instructions, and scarcely seems to fit the term 'ditty'. The Folio heading may have been introduced in the printing house (along with the italics, which are unlikely to be a feature of the manuscript). Alternatively, the Folio text may reflect the way the actors solved the problem of performing the play without an adequate number of child supernumeraries.

The latent choreographic structure that we glimpse in the Quarto text is consistent with the conventions of the wedding masque. In *Hymenaei* a group of female masquers balances the male group. When the two opposed forces which the dancers represent are reconciled, the males pair off with females. The dancing rises to an energetic climax with galliards and corrantoes, which is then followed by a solemn circular dance as two concentric circles are formed around Reason. 'Lord Hay's Masque' represents the norm in having a single group of male dancers, but the piece finishes likewise with galliards and corrantoes, followed by a symbolic round.[5] In *A Midsummer Night's Dream*, the formal reconciliation of male and female fairies within the dance would have brought the theme of elemental conflict to a visually appropriate conclusion. The use of two choruses strengthens the idea that the play is concerned not with psychologically distinct individuals but with types of male and female.

The purpose of the final dance is to 'bless this place', and the 'place' in question seems to have a double identity:

> Now, until the break of day,
> Through this house, each fairy stray.
> To the best bride bed will we:
> Which by us shall blessed be:
> And the issue, there create,
> Ever shall be fortunate:

This 'best bride bed' which Oberon and Titania intend to bless appears to be that of a real bridal pair. If Shakespeare did not have a real wedding in mind, it is odd that he should have referred to a single 'best' bed rather than to three beds. The famous issue of Theseus and Hippolyta was of course the tragic Hippolytus, as Shakespeare knew from Seneca, but the drift of the text does not seem to be towards this mythic outcome. Shakespeare continues:

> So shall all the couples three
> Ever true in loving be

indicating quite explicitly that the three couples of the play are differentiated from the occupants of the best bride-bed.

The fairies now begin to resemble the amoretti whom Spenser visualized as a beneficent presence around his bride-bed:

> an hundred little wingèd loves,
> Like divers feathered doves,
> Shall fly and flutter round about your bed.

Oberon sends the fairies off with 'field dew consecrate'. This dew, as we have seen, acquires its symbolic potency through association both with the moon and with May Day. It comes now to symbolize the holy water used in the old Catholic ritual of blessing the marriage bed. Using rather similar language, Shakespeare's Catherine of Aragon, as a good Catholic, wishes that the 'dews of Heaven fall thick in blessings' on her daughter Mary.[6] We may turn for analogies to Herrick. In Herrick's epithalamium to Sir Robert Southwell and his lady, a poem that is classical rather than Christian in its references, it is not the bed which has to be anointed but the door-frame of the bed-chamber through which the reluctant bride has to be forced. When the couple are safely installed in bed, Herrick wishes that the blessing of the spheres may 'fall like a spangling dew'. The dew acquires distinctly seminal associations.[7]

There is a certain irony in the fact that fairies bestow the blessing in Shakespeare's play, since one would normally expect a blessing to ward off the influence of fairies. Chaucer's Wife of Bath, for instance, complains that, because of the popularity of blessings, the Elf Queen and her fairies have vanished from the land.[8] Oberon promises that

> the blots of Nature's hand
> Shall not in their issue stand:
> Never mole, hare-lip, nor scar,
> Nor mark prodigious, such as are

Despised in nativity,
Shall upon their children be.

His blessing gains force from the fact that fairies were held responsible for handicapped children. Gill in the *Wakefield Second Shepherds' Pageant*, to quote a well-known example, explains the sheep found in her cradle as a changeling:

He was taken with an elf
I saw it myself
When the clock struck twelve
Was he forshapen.

Shakespeare's King Henry IV had a theory that Hal was a substitute for Hotspur, and had been placed in the royal cradle by 'some night-tripping fairy'. Jonson describes Queen Mab, the Fairy Queen, as one who deceives midwives and 'empties cradles, / Takes out children, puts in ladles'.[9] The particular role of fairies in substituting deformed changelings for healthy babies must have meant that, in the context of a wedding night, the evocation of fairies touched an emotional chord.

Oberon ends with a compliment to the host of the wedding:

And each several chamber bless
Through this palace with sweet peace;
And the owner of it blest,
Ever shall in safety rest.

It seems odd that Theseus should be blessed at this point, separating him as the Duke of Athens from his propertyless bride. There is no reason why his 'safety' should be more important than that of his wife. The real host of a real wedding is a more plausible addressee. In masques, a closing reference to the real host is entirely conventional. Jonson in *Hymenaei* bids the masquers salute James, who has hosted the wedding at court:

As you, in pairs, do front the state,
With grateful honours, thank His Grace,
That hath so glorified the place.[10]

Likewise in 'Lord Hay's Masque' the chorus concludes:

Yet, ere we vanish from this princely sight,
Let us bid Phoebus and his states good-night . . .

The masquers removed their masks as they approached the state. The same protocol is described in the two masques performed at the Somerset wedding in 1613.[11]

Puck's epilogue would appear to have been written for performance in the public theatre, where the blessing of the 'owner' would have had little force as an ending. Harold Brooks argues in the New Arden edition that the actors' promise to 'mend' in future if they are pardoned now makes sense in the context of performance before a regular clientèle.[12] It is hard to conceive that a wedding audience might insult their host by hissing the actors ('the serpent's tongue'). Puck's promise to 'make amends ere long' seems to look forward to the jig which followed the play in the public playhouse. Whatever the status of the epilogue, we should note that neither with nor without it does the finale make any reference to the presence of the Queen, unless the Queen be the 'owner' of the place where the play is performed. If the Queen were present, the actors could scarcely bless the host at the end of the play and ignore her. The idea that *A Midsummer Night's Dream* could have been written for a performance at which the Queen was principle guest is not compatible with the protocol that we find in the extant text.

Within the body of Shakespeare's play, Titania's bower is an obvious symbol of the marriage bed. We have seen how Spenser merges the concepts of the 'bridal bower and genial bed' by virtue of the herbs and flowers placed inside the bed-chamber. Wither in his 'Epithalamion' of 1613 rouses the bride in the morning because the 'Bride-Chamber lies to dressing'.[13] Jonson in *Hymenaei* speaks of 'the nuptial-room' as 'the chaste bower, which Cypria strows / With many a lilly, many a rose'. In 'Lord Hay's Masque', roses are plucked from Flora's bower and strewn about the stage, and the masquers all pass into the bower after they have removed their green garments of chastity. It is easy to see the link between bed and bower when we recall that Elizabethan beds were surrounded by curtains. In performance, whether in the public playhouse or in a private dining hall, Titania would most likely have led Bottom behind a curtain. By extension, a 'bower' commonly becomes a metaphor for the enclosing body of the woman, and we have seen how this idea is exploited in 'Lord Hay's Masque'.

The encounter between Bottom and Titania can be seen as an inversion or burlesque of the real consummation that will occur after the play is over. Like the secluded marriage bed blessed by holy water, Titania's bower is described as 'consecrated' (III.ii.7). Bottom like Spenser will sleep on pressed flowers. Titania confidently promises Bottom sexual satisfaction in her bower when she promises to purge his mortal grossness, and to have pearls fetched from the deep. In a double entendre, she tells her fairies to escort Bottom 'to bed, and to arise'. Bottom's escort of male fairies can be equated with the bridegroom-men whose role would be to lead the groom to the bedchamber. The four fairies are instructed to dance and to feast Bottom before lighting him to bed. Their duty is to ensure that he does not have 'sleeping eyes' (III.i.166), but is sexually aroused. The names of the fairies suggest sexual attributes. Bottom's attention passes from Cobweb—used to staunch bleeding—to Peaseblossom—a flower which will grow into a phallic peascod—and finally to Mustardseed—the tiny potent seed which grows into a huge tree. When Jan Kott interprets peaseblossom, mustardseed, cobweb and moth as ingredients for an aphrodisiac, he misses only the element of parody, for these are folk remedies for common complaints.[14] We might recall the electuaries which Chaucer's January took in a vain attempt to make himself capable of a bridegroom's duties. Bottom, like January, is the antithesis of the model bridegroom.

When the pair finally re-emerge from the bower, consummation must be deemed to have taken place. Many productions have succeeded in eliminating this possibility by conflating the off-stage bower with the on-stage flowery bank, and so keeping the couple safely in view.[15] The text lends no support to this chaste interpretation. Bottom's garland of roses plucked from the bower symbolizes his sexual conquest. Titania still has appetite for more, but Bottom only wants to sleep. Sexually exhausted, he seeks a filled honeybag. Titania offers him 'new nuts'.[16] Sensing that it is morning, and time to shave ('I am marvellous hairy about the face'), he accepts the offer of breakfast, with rough music to accompany the reveille. The details owe not a little to *The Merchant's Tale*, where Chaucer refers to the bristly chin of January in the wedding bed, to his breakfasting and singing in the morning before he falls asleep, to his 'coltish' behaviour, and grotesque appearance with nightcap and lean, sagging neck.

The encounter between Bottom and Titania is a parodic inversion. A real bride should be modest, not sexually voracious, a virgin and not sexually experienced. The real groom should display more sexual enthusiasm, yet not surrender to animal instinct. Jonson is clear about the man's duty:

> Tonight is Venus' vigil kept.
> This night no bridegroom ever slept;
> And if the fair bride do,
> The married say 'tis his fault too.[17]

Bottom's failure to stay awake is conceived as the ultimate form of inappropriate behaviour in a nuptial context. In the context of a real wedding, we can see how the parody would have a social function of some importance. The night is to be an initiation for both parties, and is a rite of passage that has no modern equivalent. A couple who have only met each other a few times in relatively formal circumstances are suddenly going to meet naked under the sheets, with an obligation to give a good account of themselves the next morning.

The shyness and distress of the bride is a stock motif in epithalamia. Spenser urges:

> Let no lamenting cries, nor doleful tears,
> Be heard all night within nor yet without.

Jonson in *Hymenaei* pictures a 'faint and trembling bride' on her sacrificial altar, and he urges the thirteen year old girl:

> Shrink not, soft virgin, you will love
> Anon what you so fear to prove.[18]

For Herrick the bride is afraid of the physical experience which lies ahead, and the groom must be persistent:

> O Venus! thou, to whom is known
> The best way how to loose the zone
> Of virgins! Tell the maid,
> She need not be afraid:
> And bid the youth apply
> Close kisses, if she cry:
> And charge, he not forebears
> Her, though she woo with tears.

Herrick suggests that the bridesmaids are also likely to be weeping, faced with the loss of youth and companionship. He associates the grief of the bridesmaids with a festive cycle which, as we saw in the last chapter, is linked to rites of passage. A girl goes out with a partner in May, but if she has not secured a husband by Midsummer Eve, she tries at that point to foretell who she will be paired with in the coming spring.

> Virgins, weep not; 'twill come, when,
> As she, so you'll be ripe for men.
> Then grieve her not, with saying
> She must no more a-Maying:
> Or by Rose-buds divine
> Who'll be her Valentine.[19]

While Titania is the antithesis of the shrinking bride in *A Midsummer Night's Dream*, Hermia is the embodiment. She denies Lysander 'bed-room' and insists that they behave as 'Becomes a virtuous bachelor and a maid' (II. ii.58). Her subsequent Freudian dream of a snake demonstrates her fear of sexuality. Her maidenly modesty, combined with a desire to sleep, results in her losing the love of Lysander. In the peculiar context of a wedding night, Hermia's behaviour becomes no more acceptable than that of Titania. A real bride is required to perform a dialectical miracle, and find an intermediate mode of behaviour that avoids both evils: modesty and lust.

Once the sexual act has taken place in Titania's bower, Oberon is able to obtain from Titania that which he most wants, the boy. Titania's withholding of the boy is the source of all the dissent in Fairyland, and the chaotic inversion of the seasons. Pregnancy is vividly and rapturously evoked, likened to the way a sail grows 'big-bellied with the wanton wind' (II.i.129). Titania is custodian of the boy, but after her consummation with Bottom, she transfers the boy to Oberon's bower. The symbolism is clear in an epithalamic context. The boy sought by Oberon parallels the male heir which all bridegrooms seek from their brides. The poets are explicit on this subject. Spenser hopes that Cynthia, who has charge of 'women's labours' may 'the chaste womb inform with timely seed'. Genius is asked to ensure that the 'timely fruit of this same night' arrives safely. Jonson calls for 'the birth, by Cynthia hasted' in the epithalamium to *Hymenaei*, and in the epithalamium after the 'Haddington Masque' he calls for a babe who will 'Wear the long honours of his father's deed'. The masculine pronoun seemed self-evident. Herrick echoes the theme, and we notice how dew is again associated with procreation:

> May the bed, and this short night,
> Know the fullness of delight!
> Pleasures, many here attend ye,
> And ere long, a boy, Love send ye,
> Curled and comely, and so trim,
> Maids (in time) may ravish him.
> Thus a dew of graces fall
> On ye both; goodnight to all.[20]

Aristocratic marriages were undertaken in order that a family line could be continued. Brides were under enormous psychological pressure to yield up a male child. The pressure which Oberon places upon a reluctant Titania echoes that urgent social demand. The entire central action of the play is a dreamlike (or nightmare) evocation of a wedding night. The Athenian scenes are associated with the public, patriarchal aspect of marriage. The young lovers have to obtain parental consent at the start of the play, and in the last act they conform to the social expectation that males will be capable of witty banter, females will be modestly silent. The woodland scenes are associated with the private, nocturnal, female-dominated aspect of marriage. The wood, closely associated with the maying ceremony, functions as an extended May/nuptial bower. As in a nuptial, it is 'deep midnight' when the lovers escape to the secrecy of the 'bower'. Here they fall prey to Puck and other malicious spirits. The long-delayed sexual act is suggested mimetically by the dance when Oberon and Titania hold hands and 'rock the ground whereon these sleepers be' (IV.i.85). In the morning when the lovers are woken to the rough music of the hounds, they receive a humiliating reveille. The reveille, as we have seen, was a time when the newly-married couple had to give an account of themselves, and satisfy interrogators that intercourse had taken place. As in the dream, so in reality a hunting song was often used to awaken the newly-weds.[21] What the lovers in the play have learned from their experience is not clear, but in the extra-theatrical world of the audience, an actual bridal couple may well have done their share of learning and adjusting. It was not only the Queen who found the conflict between Venus and Diana very hard to reconcile. Every young bride was expected on her wedding night to put aside the cult of chastity and in an instant become a votary of Venus.

NOTES

1. See pp. lxiv–lxvi of the New Arden edition, which gives a summary of Coghill's fundamental study.

2. Campion 'Lords' Masque': *Works*, ed. W.R. Davis (New York, 1967) 255; Peacham *The Period of Mourning . . . together with Nuptial Hymns* (London, 1789) 35; Donne 'Epithalamion on the Lady Elizabeth and Count Palatine', *Complete Poetry and Selected Prose*, ed. J. Hayward (New York, 1946) 105.

3. The fundamental study of doubling is William A. Ringler 'The number of actors in Shakespeare's early plays' in G. E. Bentley (ed.) *The Seventeenth-Century Stage* (Chicago, 1968). For the suggestion that choir boys were used, see E.K. Chambers *William Shakespeare* (Oxford, 1930) ii.86. T.J. King in *Casting Shakespeare's Plays* (Cambridge, 1992) does not accept the doubling of fairies and mechanicals. His method of setting up a distinction between major and minor roles seems arbitrary in relation to *A Midsummer Night's Dream*. Snug has few lines but a demanding role.

4. The view outlined here follows that of Dr Johnson, accepted in outline by the New Arden editor. See Brooks' long note 3 to p. cxxiii of the New Arden edition.

5. *Works*, 226, 230. The final song refers to a 'round', and to a 'centre'.

6. *Henry VIII*, IV.ii.133. For the dew as holy water, see C.L. Barber *Shakespeare's Festive Comedy* (Princeton, 1959) p. 139, and the fuller discussion in F. Douce *Illustrations of Shakespeare* (London, 1807) i.180.

7. *Poetical Works*, 56.

8. *The Wife of Bath's Tale*, 857–881. David Young notes Shakespeare's 'reversal' in *Something of Great Constancy* (New Haven, 1966) 22.

9. *The Second Shepherds' Pageant*, 616–19; *Henry the Fourth Part One*, I.i.87; Jonson *Entertainment at Althorpe*, 65–70; cf. Keith Thomas *Religion and the Decline of Magic* (London, 1971) 612–13. For survivals of this belief, see K.M. Briggs *The Vanishing People: A Study of Traditional Fairy Beliefs* (London, 1978) 93–103.

10. *Hymenaei*, 420–2.

11. John Nichols *Progresses of King James I* (1828) ii. 713–714, 723–724.

12. Note to V.i.416. Brooks does not consider the possibility that the actors may be addressing a regular spectator in the form of their patron.

13. George Wither *Juvenilia* (Spenser Society, London, 1871) 469.

14. Jan Kott *Shakespeare Our Contemporary* (London, 1965) 182; L.A. Reynolds & P. Sawyer 'Folk Medicine and the Four Fairies of *A Midsummer Night's Dream*', *Shakespeare Quarterly*, 10 (1959) 518–21.

15. See Homer Swander 'Editors vs. text: the scripted geography of *A Midsummer Night's Dream*', *Studies in Philology* 87 (1990) 83–108. Robert Lepage in his 1992 production at the National Theatre went to the opposite extreme, allowing Titania and Bottom to copulate on a bed.

16. Although 'nuts' was not a regular slang term for testicles in the Elizabethan period, the metaphorical implications are clear, and were well brought out in Brook's production. See David Selbourne *The Making of A Midsummer Night's Dream* (London, 1982) 305.

17. 'Haddington Masque' 367–70.

18. *Hymenaei*, 369, 408–9.

19. *Poetical Works*, 56.

20. 'The Good-night or Blessing' in *Poetical Works*, 124–5.

21. L.E. Pearson *Elizabethans at Home* (Stanford, 1957) 359.

Works Cited

Barber, C.L., *Shakespeare's Festive Comedy* (Princeton, 1959)

Briggs, K.M., *The Vanishing People: A Study of Traditional Fairy Beliefs* (London, 1978)

Campion, Thomas, *Works*, ed. W.R. Davis (London, 1969)

Chambers, E.K., *William Shakespeare* (Oxford, 1930)

Chaucer, Geoffrey, *The Riverside Chaucer*, ed. L.D. Benson and F.N. Robinson (3rd edition, Boston, 1987)

Coghill, N., *Shakespeare's Professional Skills* (Cambridge, 1964)

Donne, John, *Complete Poetry and Selected Prose*, ed. J. Hayward (London and New York, 1946)

Donne, John, *The Epithalamions, Anniversaries and Epicedes*, ed. W. Milgate (Oxford, 1978)

Douce, William, *Illustrations of Shakespeare* (London, 1807)

Herrick, Robert, *Poetical Works*, ed. L.C. Martin (Oxford, 1956)

Jonson, Ben, *Ben Jonson*, ed. C.H. Herford, P. and E. Simpson (Oxford, 1925–52)

King, T.J., *Casting Shakespeare's Plays* (Cambridge, 1992)

Kott, Jan, *Shakespeare Our Contemporary*, tr. B. Taborski (London, 1965)

Munday, A., *John a Kent and John a Cumber*, ed. M. St Clare Byrne (Malone Society, Oxford, 1923)

Nichols, John, *The Progresses, Processions and Magnificent Festivities of King James the First* (London, 1828)

Peacham, Henry, *The Period of Mourning . . . together with Nuptial Hymns* (London, 1789)

Pearson, L.E., *Elizabethans at Home* (Sanford, 1957)

Reynolds, L.A. and P. Sawyer, 'Folk Medicine and the Four Fairies of *A Midsummer Night's Dream*', *Shakespeare Quarterly*, 10 (1959), 518–21

Ringler, William, 'The Number of Actors in Shakespeare's Early Plays' in *The Seventeenth-Century Stage*, ed. G.E. Bentley (Chicago, 1968), 110–34

Selbourne, David. *The Making of a Midsummer Night's Dream* (London, 1982)

Shakespeare, William, *A Midsummer Night's Dream*, New Arden edition, ed. Harold F. Brooks (London, 1979)

Spenser, Edmund, *Works*, Variorum edition, ed. E. Greenlaw, C.G. Osgood, F.M. Padelford and R. Heffner (Baltimore, 1932–49)

Spenser, Edmund, *Fowre Hymns and Epithalamion*, ed. E. Welsford (London, 1967)

Swander, H., 'Editors vs. Text: The Scripted Geography of *A Midsummer Night's Dream*', *Studies in Philology*, 87 (1990), 83–108

Thomas, Keith, *Religion and the Decline of Magic* (London, 1971)

Wither, George, *Juvenilia* (Spenser Society, London, 1871)

Young, David P., *Something of Great Constancy* (New Haven, 1966)

STANLEY WELLS

Translations in A Midsummer Night's Dream

A Midsummer Night's Dream is profoundly and constantly—though also
delicately and humorously—concerned with processes of change, of translation from one state to another, and its audience is frequently made aware
that for human beings translation—any kind of translation—is likely to
be a difficult process requiring that obstacles be overcome, and that it may
involve loss as well as gain. The most prominent, and most frequently discussed, aspect of translation in the play is from the unmarried to the married
state. In no other play by Shakespeare is the process of courtship leading to
marriage so central a concern. Almost all his comedies portray attempts to
overcome obstacles to marriage, but at the end of most of them marriage
is deferred, not accomplished. This play, however, opens with preparations
for marriage, continues with the story of wooings at first thwarted but then
successfully concluded, and ends with the celebration of not one but three
marriages. But the transition from the unmarried to the married state is
not the only form of translation with which the play is concerned, and I
shall consider the idea less in relation to the lovers than to the labourers, or
mechanicals, and especially Bottom. 'Bless thee, Bottom, bless thee', says
Peter Quince at a climactic moment, 'Thou art translated' (III.i.113). But
Bottom is a translator as well. I shall look at both roles, and I start with the
passive rather than the active.

From *Translating Life: Studies in Transpositional Aesthetics*, edited by Shirley Chew and Alistair
Stead, pp. 15–32. © 1999 by Liverpool University Press.

At the moment of his translation, Bottom's appearance wearing an ass's head comes to Quince and his fellows as a total, and unwelcome, surprise. It is a surprise for the audience, too, though one for which there has been, in Shakespeare's usual manner, a good deal of subtextual preparation. We know of Oberon's plot to drop the liquor of love-in-idleness on Titania's eyes so that

> The next thing then she waking looks upon—
> Be it on lion, bear, or wolf, or bull,
> On meddling monkey, or on busy ape—
> She shall pursue it with the soul of love. (II.ii.179–82)[1]

We have seen him squeeze the juice on her eyes with the invocation,

> What thou seest when thou dost wake,
> Do it for thy true love take;
> Love and languish for his sake.
> Be it ounce, or cat, or bear,
> Pard, or boar with bristled hair,
> In thy eye that shall appear,
> When thou wak'st, it is thy dear.
> Wake when some vile thing is near. (II.ii.33–40)

More recently, we have seen Robin Goodfellow moving invisibly among the mechanicals at their rehearsal, looking for mischief—'I'll be an auditor—/ An actor too, perhaps, if I see cause'—and then following Bottom off stage with the threat that at his reentry he will appear 'A stranger Pyramus than e'er played here'. Bottom, in training to translate himself into Pyramus, has gone supposedly into the hawthorn-brake that serves him and his fellows as a tiring-house, but presumably, in Shakespeare's theatre, into the actual tiring-house. He re-enters a few moments later '*with the Asse head*', as the Folio direction has it, and speaking the ironically appropriate words, 'If I were fair, fair Thisbe, I were only thine' (II.ii.98).

Around thirty different animals have so far been named in the play, but Shakespeare has cunningly refrained from having anyone speak of an ass until the moment of Bottom's translation. For the audience, this is a moment that permits a reaction at least partly comic: we see now where Oberon's plot is leading, it seems appropriate enough that Bottom, like his close relative Dogberry, should be writ down an ass,[2] and we have the pleasure of observing the theatrical mechanics of the transformation. A history of asses' heads in *A Midsummer Night's Dream* would form an entertaining chapter of theatre history in itself. Trevor R. Griffiths provides a concise survey in his 'Shakespeare in Production' edition,[3] and the variety of expedients that have been adopted, ranging from realistic full heads with working ears and mouths to mere skull caps with ears attached, bears witness to the fact that this is not an easy moment to bring off effectively. Partly this is because Shakespeare, as often in his early plays, does little to integrate action into dialogue. The translation of Bottom into an ass is abrupt; nor is it total. Bottom needs to look enough like an ass for us to sympathize with those who believe him to have been transformed, but at the same time the actor has to be perceptible enough for us to register facial expression.

William C. Carroll, in his excellent study *The Metamorphoses of Shakespearean Comedy*, describes Bottom's translation as 'the only onstage physical man-to-beast transformation in all of Shakespeare's plays',[4] but of course it is not an 'on-stage transformation', which would be impossible to achieve in the theatre, at least without technical means that were not at Shakespeare's disposal. Bottom has to go off stage to don the ass's head, and from the neck downwards he remains the actor playing Bottom. At the moment of his reappearance everything depends on visual effect, and although for the audience the effect may be comic, for Quince and his fellows it is one of consternation. A nice balance needs to be struck. If we are to have any sense that Bottom's colleagues have reason to be frightened we must at least momentarily share their fear. In their simplicity, Bottom's friends believe that he truly has been metamorphosed as the result of supernatural agency. 'O monstrous! O strange! We are haunted. Pray, masters; fly, masters: help!' says Quince on first seeing the man-ass, and he and his fellows (possibly but not certainly with Bottom too[5]) run off in a fear which will be all the more genuinely funny if it also seems real. And then Robin exults in his success in words which portray himself as the arch shapechanger; for him, translation is effortless:

> I'll follow you, I'll lead you about a round,
> 　Through bog, through bush, through brake, through brier.
> Sometimes a horse I'll be, sometime a hound,
> 　A hog, a headless bear, sometime a fire,
> And neigh, and bark, and grunt, and roar, and burn,
> Like horse, hound, hog, bear, fire at every turn. (III.i.101–06)

As the bolder of the mechanicals recover their nerve, they lurk back to test the evidence of their eyes. First is Snout:

> O Bottom, thou art changed. What do I see on thee?

And then Quince:

> Bless thee, Bottom, bless thee. Thou art translated.

There is an element of potential paradox in the wording of this reaction. Quince does not say, 'Bless me, here's a donkey, where has Bottom gone?', but unequivocally addresses what he sees as 'Bottom'. Bottom may be 'translated', but he is not transmuted. Just as a passage of prose or verse translated into a different language both is and is not what it originally was, so, to Quince, Bottom is still recognizably Bottom; similarly, the volumes of Ovid's *Metamorphoses*, both in the original Latin and in Golding's English version which no doubt lay open on Shakespeare's desk as he wrote, were recognizable to him as things that both are and are not the same.

The word 'translated' would have had a range of possible meanings for Shakespeare's early audiences. Of course it could mean 'rendered from one language into another', as on Golding's title page—'translated oute of / *Latin into English meeter*, by *A-r*/thur Golding Gentleman', but that is only metaphorically appropriate here. It could signify simply 'changed' in one way or another, but the fact that Snout has already used that word suggests an element of intensification in Quince's usage. The word could also have more elevated senses, including 'transformed' or 'transmuted', and even 'carried or conveyed to heaven without death', and the hint of the supernatural would have been supported by Quince's exhortation to his companions to pray, and by his words 'Bless thee, bless thee', which might well have been heard as more than a conventional expression of good wishes, and might indeed have been emphasized by Quince's making the sign of the cross and/or falling to his knees. The brief episode may then have been given—may still be given—a quality of awe and wonder as the result of the verbal and gestural reactions of those who witness it.

The fact is that more than one sense of the word 'translated' is felt simultaneously here. To Bottom's fellows, he is changed yet remains Bottom, rather as the story of Pyramus and Thisbe is still the same story whether it is told in Latin or in English, or in narrative or dramatic form. On one level Bottom is, we might say, a simile rather than a metaphor. To himself, he is a bilingual edition, with the original at the foot of the page and the translation at the head: he is Bottom to the extent that he has recognized his friends and can apparently speak to them in their own language (though there may be some question about this, since Shakespeare cannot avoid using this language if he is to remain in communication with his audience, and Bottom's fellows do not respond directly to what he says); but he is an ass to the extent that on his next appearance he has a longing for 'good dry oats' and a 'bottle of hay'. And out of this incongruity much mirth comes.

For Titania, however, Bottom is translated in the most elevated sense of the word: roused from her drugged sleep by his singing, she asks what angel has woken her from her flowery bed, while acknowledging that he has enough dregs of mortality in him for her to need to 'purge' his 'mortal grossness' so that he may 'like an airy spirit go'. For her, his translation resembles that of a literary work which so far transcends the original as to constitute an entirely new creation, like, perhaps, *The Rubáiyát of Omar Khayyám*. And Bottom, too, readily accepts a sense of new identity, very much as does Christopher Sly in the Induction to *The Taming of the Shrew*, just as Sly is ministered by the Lord's servants, so Bottom yields to the pleasurable attentions of Titania's attendant fairies, Peaseblossom, Cobweb, Mote and Mustardseed. But Titania belongs to the world of spirits, not of mortal beings, and Bottom, thus translated, enters her exalted sphere. Though Titania and her fairies address him still as a mortal he enjoys immortal privileges. Paul Hardwick beautifully conveyed this in Peter Hall's 1962 Stratford production, of which *The Times* wrote that he was 'quietly discovering unexpected truths about life, as when he accepts modestly but with respectful rapture the embraces of Titania and the homage of her fairy attendants'.[6]

Whether Bottom's privileges include physical union with the fairy queen has been a debating point among critics. David Young thought not,[7] but Carroll, citing Titania's words 'Tie up my lover's tongue, bring him silently', remarks 'I find this last line explicit: Titania is tired of Bottom's voice, and wants him now to perform.'[8] Directors of recent productions—some taking their cue from Jan Kott's well-known assessment of the sexual equipment of the ass: 'Since antiquity and up to the Renaissance the ass was credited with the strongest sexual potency and among all the quadrupeds is supposed to have the longest and hardest phallus'[9]—have been only too ready to agree. Perhaps the best-known image of Peter Brook's famous production is the photograph of David Waller as Bottom with another actor's forearm, fist clenched, rampant between his legs, a moment which in the theatre brought the first part of the play to an exultant conclusion as confetti fluttered down and the band played a snatch of Mendelssohn's wedding march.

Later directors have been even more explicit, representing before the tiring-house wall action which Shakespeare's audience was at the most expected to imagine happening behind it. In Adrian Noble's Stratford version of 1994, for example, Titania beckoned Bottom into the large upturned umbrella that represented her bower, and as it ascended we were treated to the sight of Desmond Barrit's ample posterior lunging energetically up and down in a manner that left the relationship unequivocally sexual. Critics have taken the same tack, to such an extent that 1994 saw the publication of an article by T. B. Boecher entitled 'Bestial Buggery in *A Midsummer Night's Dream*' and beginning with the words 'Although no one has paid much sustained attention to the fact, *A Midsummer Night's Dream* is patently about bestiality.'[10] This substantial, well written and scholarly piece is supported by an Appendix, 'Bestiality and the Law in Renaissance England', providing statistical tables on 'Indictments for bestial buggery in the reigns of Elizabeth I and James I' and 'Animals abused in English Renaissance bestiality indictments'. (The author manfully suppresses any disappointment he may have felt that the list includes no asses.)

The emphasis upon sexuality has no doubt occurred as the result of a reaction against sentimentalizing interpretations, but perhaps it is not unreasonable to suggest that the winsome phrase 'Bestial buggery' affords, to say the least, an imprecise response to the text's tonal register. Even critics heavily committed to a post-Freudian approach have demurred. Though there is truth in Boecher's claim that 'the spectacle of Titania and Bottom embracing and sleeping together comes as close to enacted sexual intercourse as any scene in Shakespearean comedy', intercourse is at most to be inferred; we should perhaps remember that Bottom is not really an ass and that Titania is a fairy, and that she has declared her intention to turn Bottom into the likeness of 'an airy spirit' by purging his 'mortal grossness'—words not quoted by Boecher. And, whatever Titania's fantasies may be, Bottom gives no signs of actively sharing them. He may acquiesce in her embraces, but even Jan Kott has dissociated himself from Brook's emphasis upon sexuality, remarking that 'in the spectacle staged by Peter Brook and many of his followers which emphasizes Titania's sexual fascination with a monstrous phallus (*mea culpa!*), the carnival ritual of Bottom's adventure is altogether lost'. Bottom, says Kott, 'appreciates being treated as a very important person, but is more interested in the frugal pleasure of eating than in the bodily charms of Titania'.[11] And James L. Calderwood has written 'Surely a good part of Oberon's punishment of Titania centres in the physical and metaphysical impossibility of a fairy Queen to couple with an ass.'[12] To which it is worth adding that if the coupling does occur, Oberon has connived in his own cuckolding. If Bottom and Titania do make love, they do it as fairies—or, to quote another of Titania's epithets for Bottom—as angels do. However that may be.

It is also relevant that the relationship is presented as occurring in a dream—or, to use the word that both Titania and Bottom deploy, in a vision. The actor has the opportunity to convey something of this by a shift in consciousness during Bottom's scenes in the fairy court. More, I suppose, than any other character in Shakespeare, Bottom has often been played by performers associated with music hall and popular theatre—Stanley Holloway and James Cagney, Frankie Howerd and Tommy Steele among them. There is no reason why the comic skills of such performers should not be harnessed to the role, and some of them, such as Frankie Howerd, appear to have revealed new sides to their talent in doing so. But the potential range of the role fits it also for the talents of great actors of the 'legitimate' theatre, as Ralph Richardson appears to have demonstrated particularly in these scenes in an Old Vic production of 1931. According to James Agate,

> In the fairy scenes he abandoned clowning in favour of a dim consciousness of a rarer world and of being at court there. This was new to me, and if Mr Richardson had not the ripeness of some of the old actors, his acting here was an agreeable change from the familiar refusal to alternate fruitiness with anything else. Most of the old players seem to have thought that Bottom, with the ass's head on, was the same Bottom only funnier. Shakespeare says he was 'translated', and Mr Richardson translated him.[13]

'Twenty years later', as Griffiths notes, Richardson's 'performance was still being invoked as a benchmark':

> no one before Richardson, and no one after him either, guessed that there was in this weaver so deep a well of abused poetry, such an ineradicable vision of uncomprehended wonder.[14]

For Titania, Bottom's presence at her court is a fantasy induced by Oberon's love potion, and when Oberon has achieved his aim of subduing her and persuading her to return the Indian boy, he reverses the potion's effect. Bottom, still in his (possibly postcoital) sleep, has to be translated back from ass to man, and this translation takes place on stage, as Robin removes the ass-head at Oberon's behest. For the audience the effect is instantaneous, but Bottom, like the lovers, sleeps on, receding from our consciousness through Oberon and Titania's dance of reconciliation, the formal entry of Theseus with Hippolyta and 'all his train', the awakening of the lovers, Theseus's overriding of Egeus's objections to the marriage of Hermia and Lysander, and the lovers' reflections on their dream.

When Bottom wakes it seems at first that no time has elapsed since his translation: 'When my cue comes, call me, and I will answer.' But then he remembers he has had a dream, and starts to try to recall it. He fails, as we all fail when we try to translate our dreams into language. But he knows he has had an experience 'past the wit of man' to translate. He alone among the mortals of the play has had direct communion with the inhabitants of fairyland. He alone has been translated into a higher sphere, if only temporarily.

But the lovers, if they have not actually seen inhabitants of the fairy world, have been unknowingly touched by it and, like Bottom, undergo a

form of translation. Roused by Theseus's hunting horns, they have given classic poetic expression to the sensation of being suspended between sleep and
waking, between the unconscious world of dreams and earthly reality, in lines
that figure Quince's state of mind on beholding the translated Bottom—and
which, we might also suggest, portray the state of mind of a translator struggling to formulate, in a new language, thoughts that have already reached
poetic form in the language from which he is translating:

> *Demetrius*: These things seem small and undistinguishable,
> Like far-off mountains turned into clouds.
> *Hermia*: Methinks I see these things with parted eye,
> When everything seems double.
> *Helena*: So methinks, And I have found Demetrius like a jewel,
> Mine own and not mine own.
> *Demetrius*: It seems to me
> That yet we sleep, we dream. (IV.i.186–92)

To the lover, the beloved is both a possession and something that can never
be possessed, just as a poem is something that can be translated yet never
loses its own perfection of identity. It is a paradox that lies at the heart of
artistic creation; no wonder Benjamin Britten makes a vocal quartet based
on this dialogue a highspot of his opera, dwelling repeatedly and lovingly
on the phrase 'mine own, and not mine own'. Here a great composer was
translating Shakespeare's portrayal of translation in an act of what Inga-
Stina Ewbank has called 'collusive re-creation' which, characteristically of
good translation, adds a new dimension to the original.[15]

Bottom's struggle to dredge from the ooze of his subconscious mind the
jewels that lie there embedded is more effortful but no less genuine. At first
he thinks no time has passed, then simply that he has slept:

> When my cue comes, call me, and I will answer . . . God's my life,
> stolen hence, and left me asleep?

But then the wisp of a memory supervenes:

> I have had a most rare vision. I have had a dream past the wit of
> man to say what dream it was. Man is but an ass if he go about to
> expound this dream.

Bottom's metaphorical use of the word 'ass' appears to trigger his residual
memory of the state of being in which he believed himself truly to be an ass.

Methought I was—there is no man can tell what. Methought I was, and methought I had—but man is but a patched fool if he will offer to say what methought I had.

(IV.i.205–06)

The effort at translation is too great, and he abandons it. But the effort has been made, and it is the sense this gives us that Bottom, for all his asininity, is—like Caliban—capable of having, and of trying to put into words, a vision which lifts the role from clownishness to greatness. At least it does if the actor lets it. It did in 1853, when Samuel Phelps played Bottom:

He was still a man subdued, but subdued by the sudden plunge into a state of unfathomable wonder. His dream clings about him, he cannot sever the real from the unreal, and still we are made to feel that his reality itself is but a fiction.[16]

In some productions, Bottom has discovered about his person a tangible reminder of his dream life—a wisp of hay or a flower, for example.[17] I remember a production in Victorian style at Nottingham when Bottom's departure after his 'dream' was most touchingly marked with that phrase from Mendelssohn's incidental music which has a dying fall symbolizing the power of dream.

But not all actors approach the speech in so romantic a fashion. Everything rests on the nuance given to the words 'methought I had' and the pause that follows. The innocent, and once traditional, interpretation is that Bottom is simply recalling his ass's ears. But directors keen to demonstrate explicit sexual awareness allow their actor, by facial expression or gesture, a leer, a wiggle, or a movement of the hand, to imply that Bottom is coyly avoiding saying 'methought I "had" Titania', or 'methought I had a penis of the proportions ascribed by Jan Kott to the ass'; Desmond Barrit's peering down the front of his pants at this point in Adrian Noble's production meant even more to members of the audience who remembered Jan Kott's remark than to those who did not. One cannot say that this is wrong; but one can say that by narrowing the focus on to the physical it denies the spirituality of Bottom's translation—renders it, so to speak, with a four-letter word.

Bottom's last speech before vanishing into the hawthorn brake is given in the character of Pyramus; his translation comes as an involuntary interruption to a willed attempt at another kind of translation on which he and his fellows were engaged at the moment of his ascent into asininity. When we first see them they are embarking on the task of translating into stage action the preexisting script of *The Most Lamentable Comedy and Most Cruel Death of Pyramus and Thisbe*, and we are left in no doubt that they find the task difficult. The first stage is the assignment of the roles into which each of the performers will endeavour to translate himself, and this introduces the need for deliberate physical transformation. Flute as Thisbe may, Quince tells him, hide his incipient beard—if it truly exists—with a mask; and Bottom boasts of a virtuosic capacity to modulate his voice according to the varied demands of the roles, from Thisbe to Lion, that he aspires to undertake. He appears, too, to have access to a rich collection of false beards (which in some productions he has brought with him).[18]

Once rehearsals get under way, the actors discover that before the text of the play can be translated into stage action certain modifications must be made in order to fit it for performance 'before the Duke' and his ladies. There are episodes, such as Pyramus's drawing a sword to kill himself, 'that will never please'. Starveling fears that the problem can be solved only by cutting the text: 'I believe we must leave the killing out, when all is done.' But Bottom proposes instead to make an addition to the text: 'Write me a prologue, and let the prologue seem to say we will do no harm with our swords, and that Pyramus is not killed indeed.' Additional lines must be written, too, to mitigate the terror of Lion's appearance, and as the rehearsal proceeds the need becomes apparent even to write in two additional characters, Moonshine and Wall, each of them to be represented by an actor who will make adjustments to his personal appearance in the attempt to 'disfigure, or present' the character.

The rehearsal scenes in *A Midsummer Night's Dream* offer a copybook demonstration by Shakespeare himself of the instability of the dramatic text. As the Folio text of the play shows (in its changes of word and stage directions from the Quarto text, in its substitution of one character—Egeus—for another—Philostrate—in the last act, and in its re-allocation of certain lines of dialogue), in the course of its translation from authorial manuscript to promptbook Shakespeare's own text underwent exactly the same kinds of changes, if on a smaller scale, as the play within the play. This makes it all the more surprising that scholars were so long resistant to the notion that variant texts of Shakespeare's plays demonstrate theatrical revision; and the fact that we cannot be sure whether Peter Quince, who makes himself responsible for the additions to the text of *Pyramus and Thisbe*, is the original author of the play, or merely its director with a talent, like some modern directors—John Barton is the most distinguished example—for literary pastiche, reflects our uncertainty whether changes in the texts of Shakespeare's own plays were made by Shakespeare himself, by members of his company, or collectively.

The actors' attempts to translate their text into action are hampered in part by their literalism, and by their expectations of a similar literalism in their audience. The ladies, they fear, will be so totally illuded by what they see that they will take it for reality, so a prologue must assure them, not only that 'Pyramus is not killed indeed', but that Pyramus is not Pyramus 'but Bottom the weaver'; similarly Snug must tell the ladies that he is 'a man, as other men are', and 'indeed name his name, and tell them plainly he is Snug the joiner'. And their audience cannot be relied upon to imagine the moonlight by which Pyramus and Thisbe meet, and the wall through which they talk—as Shakespeare's own audience was required to imagine the moonlight by which Oberon has met Titania, and, so far as we can tell, the 'orchard wall' that Romeo is said to have overleapt in *Romeo and Juliet* (II.i.5)—but must be confronted with an actor in the person of Moonshine and Wall. This literalism is akin to that of a literary translator who, in an over-zealous effort to render a text's substance, fails to convey its spirit. It can be amended only by imagination, and Shakespeare is careful to preface Theseus's wedding entertainment with the discussion between the Duke and Hippolyta about the power of imagination. This is offered as a reaction to the lovers' account of their enchanted night, and Theseus's view—perhaps surprisingly in view of attitudes he will later express—is sceptical; it is Hippolyta who acknowledges that the transformation in the lovers bears witness, not simply to fancy, but to the transmuting power of imagination:

> all the story of the night told over,
> And all their minds transfigured so together,
> More witnesseth than fancy's images,
> And grows to something of great constancy. (V.i.23–26)

In the play's terms, then, a real-life translation has been successfully effected. We are about to see whether the fictional translation of text into performance will similarly succeed; and the omens are not good.

The potentially damaging effects of unskilful theatrical translation are made apparent even in advance of the performance in the reported reactions of Philostrate (or Egeus) to the rehearsal which he has attended as part of the auditioning procedure for the wedding festivities. The ineptitude of the writing and the unfitness of the players have resulted in an involuntary change of genre, the transformation of a tragedy into a comedy:

> in all the play
> There is not one word apt, one player fitted.
> And 'tragical', my noble lord, it is,
> For Pyramus therein doth kill himself,
> Which when I saw rehearsed, I must confess,
> Made mine eyes water; but more merry tears
> The passion of loud laughter never shed. (V.i.64–70)

In spite of this warning Theseus persists in asking for the play to be performed, and does so in lines anticipative of audience response theory in their suggestion that the spectator has a part to play in the success of the performance. Egeus warns him that the mechanicals' play is

> nothing, nothing in the world,
> Unless you can find sport in their intents
> Extremely stretched, and conned with cruel pain
> To do you service. (V.i.78–81)

But Theseus rejects the warning, with a courtly expression of charity:

> never anything can be amiss
> When simpleness and duty tender it. (V.i.82–83)

Theseus's readiness to exercise imagination may seem surprising after the long speech in which he has spoken dismissively of its powers, but the theme is insistently developed in response to Hippolyta's complaint that she loves 'not to see wretchedness o'er charged, / And duty in his service perishing'. Theseus proclaims himself as the ideal member of an audience, comparing the efforts of amateur actors to those of 'great clerks'—people, presumably, such as rectors of Elizabethan universities delivering addresses of welcome to their sovereign—who, overwhelmed by the occasion, 'Make periods in the midst of sentences', exactly as Quince is about to do in his delivery of his Prologue. Theseus can, he claims, 'read as much' 'in the modesty of fearful duty' 'as from the rattling tongue / Of saucy and audacious eloquence'. He rams home the moral with almost priggish ostentation, as if to shame the theatre audience into comparable charity. Shakespeare is preparing us for both the comic incompetence of Bottom and his fellows and the paradoxical skill of the real-life actors who will be required to impersonate incompetence. The audience, like Theseus, has its part to play in the translation process, and Shakespeare not merely tells us but demonstrates that meaning can be apprehended even in a translation so bad that on the surface it means the opposite of what is intended. Although the 'periods' that Quince, shivering and pale, makes in the midst of *his* 'premeditated' sentences cause him to say the opposite of what he means—'All for your delight / We are not here'—both Theseus and we are able to 'take' what he 'mistake[s]'. His lines simultaneously convey opposed meanings, rather as the translated Bottom both is and is not Bottom, with the result that his audience may both laugh at his ineptitude yet appreciate the good will that lies behind it.

The rehearsal scenes have revealed to us only a few lines of the text of the tragedy. As the performance progresses, it becomes clear that this text is comically inadequate as a translation into dramatic terms of the story of Pyramus and Thisbe. Layers of translation here are complex. The story is a preexisting one both for the mechanicals and for Shakespeare. Many members of the original audience, too, would have known it. Shakespeare had certainly read it both in the original Latin and in Golding's translation. We are given no clue whether Bottom and his fellows are supposed to have created the script themselves (except for the interpolated lines) or to have purchased a script from the Athenian equivalent of Samuel French. They cannot certainly be held responsible for its ineptitudes. Nevertheless, they are responsible for using it. Part of the comedy, that is, derives from their unawareness of the bathetic inadequacies of the translation into verse drama of the tragic tale they enact—and a director may make something of this unawareness.

Shakespeare, on the other hand, *is* responsible for the badness of the script, and is indeed to be congratulated on it. This is good bad writing—in other words, excellent parody both of Golding's translation (which Shakespeare seems to have regarded with amused admiration, or admiring amusement) and of the literary and dramatic conventions of the interlude writers.[19] In part, the criticisms of the onstage audience are directed at the inadequacies of the script: 'This is the silliest stuff that ever I heard', says Hippolyta. But the spectators are highly conscious, too, of the performers' failure to translate this script convincingly: 'he hath played on this prologue like a child on a recorder—a sound, but not in government.' Indeed they seem to make little distinction between script and performance, in this perhaps reflecting the Elizabethan theatrical scene, where an audience probably considered a play as a company event in which the writer was simply one member of the company, and may have been performing in his own play. Frequently, that is to say, playgoers went, not to see a group of players interpret a script with which they were already familiar, but to enjoy an entirely new event, an experience that was simultaneously literary, dramatic and theatrical.

As the play scene progresses, the mechanicals' efforts at translation sink to ever deeper levels of ineptitude which can be salvaged only by massive doses of good humour, tolerance, and imagination from its onlookers. Primarily, it represents the mechanicals' efforts at active translation, but it climaxes in a representation of passive translation which takes us back to the point earlier in the play at which we saw Bottom turned into an ass. At that point he was rehearsing the role of Pyramus. Now, enacting that role in a manner that, Theseus is to say, might well prove *him* an ass (V.i.306), he finds himself required to represent the character in the process of a translation from the corporeal to the spiritual state, such as he had himself undergone, at least in the eyes of his fellows and of Titania, within the hawthorn brake. After stabbing himself, he describes his elevation:

> Now am I dead,
> Now am I fled,
> My soul is in the sky.
> Tongue, lose thy light,
> Moon, take thy flight,
> Now die, die, die, die, die. (V.i.296–301)

But even here the translation is not complete; before long Bottom arises from the dead to offer an epilogue or a bergomask dance.

* * *

One of Shakespeare's most striking uses of the concept of translation occurs in *As You Like It*, when Amiens congratulates Duke Senior on his capacity to 'translate the stubbornness of fortune / Into so quiet and so sweet a style' (II.i.19–20). It is striking because it encapsulates the very process of comedy itself, a process that is often, as in *A Midsummer Night's Dream*, symbolized by the overcoming of obstacles to marriage. It is a process that can be accomplished only through the exercise of imagination. The last act of *A Midsummer Night's Dream* recapitulates in comic form the turmoils that the lovers have experienced in their efforts at translation, reminds us that fortune can be stubborn; but as bedtime approaches, Oberon and his train, in their blessing on the house, invoke for us the quietness and sweetness that can come with the translation to the married state. And at the very end Robin Goodfellow, calling for our active imaginative collaboration, invites us to think that we 'have but slumbered here, / While these visions did appear'. Like Bottom, we have been granted a vision; and also like him, we shall be asses if we try to expound it. Men cannot translate dreams into language; but in this play Shakespeare comes pretty close to doing so.

NOTES

1. Quotations and references are to the Oxford *Complete Works*, General Editors, Stanley Wells and Gary Taylor (Oxford: Oxford University Press, 1986, etc).

2. So David E Young, *Something of Great Constancy: The An of 'A Midsummer Night's Dream'* (New Haven and London: Yale University Press, 1966), p. 157: 'Bottom changed to an ass is but a short step, a revelation of inner qualities already familiar to us.' Bottom resembles Dogberry in his good qualities, too; both are men of good will.

3. *A Midsummer Night's Dream*, ed. Trevor R. Griffiths (Cambridge: Cambridge University Press, 1996).

4. William C. Carroll, *The Metamorphoses of Shakespearean Comedy* (Princeton, NJ: Princeton University Press), p. 148.

5. See the note to III.i.100 in Peter Holland's Oxford Shakespeare edition (Oxford: Oxford University Press, 1994).

6. *The Times*, 18 April 1962. I owe this reference, and helpful comments, to Roger Warren.

7. Young, *Something of Great Constancy*, p. 157: 'just as the "marriage" is probably never consummated, so is the transformation incomplete'.

8. Carroll, *Metamorphoses*, p. 152.

9. Jan Kott, *The Bottom Translation*, trans. Daniel Miedzyrzecka and Lillian Vallee (Evanston, IL: Northwestern University Press, 1987).

10. T. B. Boecher, 'Bestial Buggery in *A Midsummer Night's Dream*', in *The Production of English Renaissance Culture*, eds D. L. Miller *et al.* (Ithaca and London: Cornell University Press, 1994), pp. 123–50.

11. Kott, *The Bottom Translation*, p. 52.

12. James L. Calderwood, *A Midsummer Night's Dream*, Twayne's New Critical Introductions to Shakespeare (Hemel Hempstead: Harvester Wheatsheaf, 1992), p. 63.

13. *The Sunday Times*, 8 November 1931, quoted by Griffiths, *A Midsummer Night's Dream*, p. 53.

14. Griffiths, *A Midsummer Night's Dream*, p. 60.

15. Inga-Stina Ewbank, 'Shakespeare Translation as Cultural Exchange', *Shakespeare Survey*, 48 (1995), 1–12.

16. Henry Morley, *The Journal of a London Playgoer, 1851–1866* (London: George Routledge, 1866, repr. 1891), pp. 60–61.

17. Various treatments are discussed in Griffiths's note to IV.i.197–211.

18. Griffiths, *A Midsummer Night's Dream*, note to I.ii.71–78.

19. The burlesque elements of the play are discussed in J. W. Robinson, 'Palpable Hot Ice: Dramatic Burlesque in *A Midsummer Night's Dream*', *Studies in Philology*, 61 (1964), 192–204.

W. H. AUDEN

A Midsummer Night's Dream

A Midsummer Night's Dream is a very familiar work. It is the first play
to show Shakespeare's unique contribution as a dramatist, presenting not
only the sense of the relations of human characters to each other but also
to objects, to nature. Ibsen is the only dramatist who can approach Shakespeare in this respect. Shakespeare's depiction of the relation of social classes
to each other is better than that of other dramatists, but it is not unique.
The subplot in Elizabethan drama generally dealt with lower class characters, and when the use of the subplot ended, English drama itself declined.
Shakespeare is also better than his contemporaries at relating the subplot to
the main plot.

It is very hard in drama to represent the relation of characters to the
earth, though the absence of realistic sets on the Elizabethan stage facilitates
it. It's easier in movies, but settings in movies are at the same time too specific and unsuggestive. We must distinguish the different senses of the term
nature.

(1) as that which is distinctively and characteristically human—as
opposed to the affected or unusual, and
(2) as that which is in contrast to man, the physical frame to which
men must adapt themselves.

From *Lectures on Shakespeare*, reconstructed and edited by Arthur Kirsch, pp. 53–62, 371–72.
© 2000 by Arthur Kirsch for the notes and © 2000 by the estate of W. H. Auden for lectures
and writings by Auden.

115

Classical and Chinese writers use the term *nature* in the first and traditional sense. Under the sanction of biology, the modern West uses the term *nature* in the second sense. The second sense can in turn be divided into four subcategories:

(2a) includes all influences to which the mind is subject from without.

(2b) consists of images and things which, through our imaginative perception of (2a), we see as the world outside—our construction of the music of the wind, for example.

(2c) is an abstraction from (2b), the world of practical experience, as perceived by all men alike. The stone Dr. Johnson kicked to refute Berkeley's assertion of the nonexistence of matter is an example of this sense.

(2d) consists of the laws and theorems used by physics to describe (2a).

We confuse (2c) and (2a) and get panicky over (2b) because it includes emotion. (2d) involves elaborate abstraction and the removal of human emotion. Alfred North Whitehead, in *Modes of Thought*, criticizes the tendency of modern scientific thinking to rely exclusively on (2d), to make catalogues of forms of sense perception that are related only spatio-temporally and that are divorced from emotion. The result, he argues, is a conception of nature that is devoid of impulse and process.

Most artists treat man as totally unrelated to nature, focusing simply on the choices people make, not on how they work, how they eat, etc. As a result, people appear freer than they in fact are, and seem to be composed of pure spirit without the bodies that relate them to animals and stones. Those who make the wrong choice are thus seen as more guilty than they really are. Alternately, during the late nineteenth and twentieth centuries, a school of writers has developed that sees man as a helpless prey of nature, nature as (2d). In their view man has no will, no emotions that are relevant to action, and no responsibility for action. This view is false. It is plausible when you look at other people to say that they couldn't help doing what they did, but if that reasoning is applied to choices that we ourselves make, we get angry. Everyone is angry to hear it of themselves.

In *A Midsummer Night's Dream* Shakespeare uses a different technique to relate man and nature. He mythologically anthropomorphizes nature, making nature like man, and reducing the figurants of nature in size in comic situations. In the tragedies, however, Shakespeare does not anthropomorphize nature. Storms and shipwrecks in the tragedies are represented as the will of God, and they either reflect or contrast with human emotion.

Modern people are skeptical of mythology. They think you're being asked to believe in fairies in *A Midsummer Night's Dream*, which is not true. A minority school on the subject of myth writes serious, solemn, and insufferably boring articles that do not believe in myths but use them as a substitute for religion, Plato's "noble lie." The implication is that *we* don't need to believe in this, but for those incapable of rational thinking, it's all right. There is a difference between religious dogma and myth. Jungian myth addicts say you don't have to believe in anything. But dogma is a presupposition that has to be believed, even though it can't be proved. *Credo ut intellegam*: I believe in order that I may understand. Its confirmation is in the future, in that it changes one's life and becomes a measuring rod by which one evaluates the experience one is given. "God is love," for example, is not a statement derived from experience but a presupposition. Myth, on the other hand, is a proposition about experience, and its truth must be tested by experiment. The story of Adam and Eve in the garden, for example, is a myth, a story of general experience. It is not a question of believing the myth actually happened. The question is, does it adequately describe certain experiences that we have? St. Paul says, "For that which I do I allow not: for what I would, that do I not; but what I hate, that do I." You can say, "I don't have guilt." I say, "I think you're a liar." We may say that Freud's myth of the killing of the father is the better explanation of guilt, by an aesthetic criterion.

Freud discusses the genesis of religious belief in *Totem and Taboo*. In animism, every individual object has, like me, a will that one must either propitiate or appropriate. In polytheism, there is a finite number of universal forces, each autonomous, which must be propitiated or controlled. In monotheism, there is one God who creates the world or is imitated by it, and whose will does not change. You must either establish a relation with God that has previously been lacking, moving from ignorance to knowledge, or put a distorted relation right. Then the autonomous gods of polytheism become subsidiary and become myths. They are no longer the grounds of our own existence. In Milton's "Nativity Ode" the birth of Christ makes the gods dumb:

> The oracles are dumb,
> No voice or hideous hum
>   Runs through the arch'd roof in words deceiving.
> Apollo from his shrine
> Can no more divine,
>   With hollow shriek the steep of Delphos leaving.
> No nightly trance, or breathed spell,
> Inspires the pale-eyed priest from the prophetic cell.

Gods become accidents in substance. Dante, in the *Paradiso*, so describes the apprehension of divine love in Paradise:

> O grace abounding, wherein I presumed to fix my look on the eternal light so long that I consumed my sight thereon!
> Within its depths I saw ingathered, bound by love in one volume, the scattered leaves of all the universe;
> substance and accidents and their relations, as though together fused, after such fashion that what I tell of is one simple flame.

Myths present an analogous fusion of accident and substance.

The use of myths. A myth must have universal applicability, otherwise it becomes a private symbol, and the universal experience must be one to which the individual is related in a unique way—either intermittently, or happily or unhappily. There is no need for a myth on the law of gravity, since we all behave under its influence in the same way, but there is a need for a myth on the experience of falling in love, because its effects are unique. Elaborate polytheism enables one to learn certain laws of nature that you can change. But despite our knowledge, we can't control the weather, we can't control heredity or the distribution of natural gifts to people, and we can't arrange for suitable people to fall in love with each other. In our ordinary experience there is a great deal of accident. When everything falls under natural laws that are subject to control, there is no need for myth. Neither myth nor religion alter *natural* law. But if you can change the conduct of God by magic, as in polytheism, or you can alter your relation to God in yourself, as in monotheism, you have religion. Euripides' *Hippolytus* can be described without benefit of Aphrodite's anger. Its moral, in nonmythical form, is that sex is something you can't afford to make mistakes about.

In *A Midsummer Night's Dream*, mythological characters are used to describe certain universal experiences that we cannot control. You use Puck for a day when you get up and it's raining, you cut yourself shaving, you hurry over breakfast, you miss your train, your boss is sarcastic, your favorite lunch seat is taken, a bar drunk bores you with his life story, the potatoes are undercooked at dinner, and you quarrel with your wife. Or all vice versa. On a bad day, your feeling is, "Things are against me." It isn't just temperament, circumstances must also conspire. That's Puck. The role of pure mathematical chance is not as important as we suppose. We help make our luck. If we are angry with ourselves when we are shaving, we are more likely to be careless. One of my aunts, the younger one, Aunt Mildred, waited on her selfish older sister, who set up for an invalid, was pious, and distrusted pleasure. Just before they were to go on a holiday, her older sister sprained her ankle. Will is an element in such an accident. Even insurance companies take note of such things. The fairies show that these things are important, but the importance lies in how we take them. Good fortune taken too seriously leads to conceit, bad fortune taken too seriously leads to despair. There is no one-to-one relation between character and fortune: fairies are not seriously concerned with humanity. We must be grateful to good fortune and learn to accept bad fortune.

Our duties are to have (1) a right relation to God, (2) a right relation to our neighbor, and (3) a right relation to nature. You must treat your neighbor as a free agent—don't idolize or restrain him. You must help nature—don't idolize it either positively or negatively. One must accept responsibility for making nature what it should be. It is easier for me to say this, coming from Europe, an area where nature can be seen as friendly and domesticated, unlike the USA, where nature is seen as either to be exploited or to be fled to as a relief from civilization. I am continually shocked by the unhumanized nature in this country, no parks, no formal gardens. Nature never intended human beings to live in the USA—only in just a little bit of Europe and in New Zealand. Everywhere else it is either too hot or too cold. The climate in New York is savagely hot. I am happy in New York only from mid-November to March, when it's cold. One mustn't treat nature as morally responsible, or we become superstitious. But we must not regard nature as having no rights and existing solely for our convenience, because nature will revenge itself. You must not exploit nature—exploitation breeds soil erosion. But nature must be tamed.

A Midsummer Night's Dream is like a series of Chinese boxes. It was written for the occasion of someone's wedding. On the outside of the play are the bride and bridegroom and the Elizabethan audience, inside the play are the couples Theseus and Hippolyta, Titania and Oberon, the young lovers, and in the play within the play, Pyramus and Thisbe. We have festivities to mark the pauses between one form of life and another: christening, circumcision, wedding, etc. For Theseus and Hippolyta, as for any bride and bridegroom, the wedding represents the successful completion of a stage of life. Note Oberon's reference to past seductions by Theseus, and Titania's reference to the time Hippolyta was an Amazonian. The past is over, and a new life, with new failures and triumphs, begins.

The second theme of the play deals with the four lovers who have to go through what Theseus and Hippolyta have already experienced. They enter Dante's Wood of Error or Alice's world in *Through the Looking Glass*, which initiates an era of conquest of themselves or others. The quarrel between Oberon and Titania represents a disorder in nature that man is called upon to reconcile:

> The spring, the summer,
> The childing autumn, angry winter change
> Their wonted liveries; and the mazed world,

By their increase, now knows not which is which.
And this same progeny of evils comes
From our debate, from our dissension;
We are their parents and original.
    (II.i.111–17)

Theseus and Hippolyta make it possible for Titania and Oberon to meet, and
through human agency they are reconciled. The tragic figures, Pyramus and
Thisbe, do not get out of the wood. The hunting passage (IV.i.106ff) shows
that the old aggressive life has been modulated to sport, not done away with.
    Theseus gives Hermia the choice of death or life in a nunnery if she
doesn't obey her father, and he says of virginity,

Thrice blest they that master so their blood
To undergo such maiden pilgrimage;
But earthlier happy is the rose distill'd
Than that which, withering on the virgin thorn,
Grows, lives, and dies in single blessedness.
    (1.1.74–78)

Matters of love in *A Midsummer Night's Dream* are surrounded by imagery
of the moon and moisture and Diana, all of which militate against the fire
of love. The original row of Oberon and Titania is not sexual jealousy, but
the punishment for it is involvement in sex. Lysander and Hermia talk like
Romeo and Juliet:

Ay, me! For aught that I could ever read,
Could ever hear by tale or history,
The course of true love never did run smooth.
    (I.i.132–34)

    The story of Pyramus and Thisbe suggests what might have happened to
the people in *A Midsummer Night's Dream* as well as the frivolity of the whole
business of falling in love. It says that tragic things can be due to taking the
frivolous too seriously. Demetrius and Lysander, when they are not in love, are
too weak to control their feelings. Hermia and Lysander at the beginning think
themselves morally superior, and they are conceited over the return of their
love, which is a gift of fortune only. Demetrius thinks himself stronger than
Helena because he's loved while he himself is unloving—it's embarrassing but
delightful. Helena's misfortune makes her spiteful, she betrays Hermia to make
everyone as unhappy as she is. Lysander is equalized with Demetrius through

being unfaithful and not having his love returned. Hermia is equalized with Helena because her love is not returned. Helena learns not to envy others, and she learns also that being loved isn't so grand. There is a complete reversal. Helena is punished for her spite because she doesn't believe the love offered to her is true, and Demetrius realizes what it is not to be loved. All four now, through similar experiences, have grown up, and it is now possible for them to marry.

Oberon accuses Puck, through his mistake with the potion, of confounding true and false love: "Of thy misprision must perforce ensue / Some true-love turn'd, and not a false turn'd true." Puck assumes that romantic love is accidental, however, not true, and justifies his error by an appeal to universal infidelity: "The fate o'errules, that, one man holding troth, / A million fail, confounding oath on oath" (III.ii.90–93). Puck defends himself again, shortly afterwards, by saying that he had, after all, anointed the eyes of a man wearing "Athenian garments," just as Oberon had instructed. The mix-up means that, standing on the outside, one man's like another. As Dr. Johnson remarked, "I believe marriages would in general be as happy, and often more so, if they were all made by the Lord Chancellor, upon a due consideration of characters and circumstances, without the parties having any choice in the matter."

The herb represents ambiguity. Everyone wishes to will other people to will what one wills. It can be done through (1) the exercise of power, as in rape, (2) the influence of one's essential worth: riches, etc., and (3) by sophisticated means, by making people do what you want while thinking *they* want it. Puck's use of the herb shows how dangerous the general fulfillment of such daydreams would be. In the myth of Tristan and Isolde, a love potion becomes the excuse for giving way to illicit love.

The general confusion of persons and the disharmony of nature represented in the Titania-Oberon theme can be tragic, as in *Timon of Athens*, where Timon comes to see the earth itself as a thief (IV.iii.438–45). In *A Midsummer Night's Dream* the quarrel of Oberon and Titania is comic, but it still makes the seas flood and causes a bad harvest (II.i.88–111). Oberon can be seen as Hippolyta's animus, Titania as Theseus' anima. All of their difficulties arise because of possessiveness over a trifle, a changeling boy. Titania in love with Bottom is contrasted with the confused loves of the four young Athenians, but with Titania and Bottom we have a real *mésalliance*. We like to believe that our love is due to the innate value of the object of it. We must beware: (1) for the object's sake—Bottom needs steak, not moonbeams, and (2) for the subject's sake—it is not good for Titania and no sympathy is shown for her. Bottom's relation with the fairies reveals that most unimaginative, prosaic people have aspects we wouldn't dream of. Bottom sees himself as a tough all-doer, and appears in much that way to his fellow workmen. To the audience he is seen as an ass, to Titania as a lovable, gentle, untough ass. Bottom also appears as Pyramus—and maybe he is that too.

The play that Bottom and company put on raises the problem of the metaphysical distinction between existence and essence. Granted talent, etc., I could play another person so as to deceive everyone, but I can't *become* another existence. When we say it would be nice to be another person, we are imagining being ourselves with certain qualities of that other person added to our own essence. There is a difference between the theater and a bull fight. We identify ourselves with the essential suffering of actors in the theater, we can't identify with the existential suffering of the bull and gladiator. We identify with a hero taking a fall, or with a little man getting the princess and a million dollars. Or we take a play as a reversal of real life and say it is "only a play." Neither attitude is right. If we want to be heroes, we must want also to deserve disgrace, and if we don't want to be comic, we don't want to be blessed in all circumstances, but only to be rewarded as we deserve. We should be actors, not madmen who act what they are not, like the man, to take an extreme case, who believes he is Napoleon or a poached egg. Or like a pimply adolescent on the BMT looking at himself in the glass, who says, "How can I tell you how wonderful you are."

Take what you do as a game. There are two mistakes one can make in this, however: a failure to devote oneself, which is bad, and devoting oneself only when one thinks it's important, which is worse. The plays Theseus rejects include the battle of the Centaurs, because it is too personal, the riot of the Bacchanals, because he has seen it before, and the nine muses, because he feels it is too sharp for the occasion. The one he chooses is a "A tedious brief scene of young Pyramus / And his love Thisby; very tragical mirth" (V.i.56–57) and he chooses it for aesthetic reasons:

> Merry and tragical? tedious and brief?
> This is hot ice and wondrous strange snow.
> How shall we find the concord of this discord?
>   (V.i.58–60)

The work Theseus wants must have all the elements, and it must form a pattern. It is in the nature of art that what we like is often dictated by private, not aesthetic reasons. And don't take art too seriously—the game depends on both skill and sincerity. Gifts and talents, as Theseus points out, can be overpraised:

> I will hear that play;
> For never anything can be amiss
> When simpleness and duty tender it.
>   (V.i.81–83)

He says also,

> Our sport shall be to take what they mistake;
> And what poor duty cannot do, noble respect
> Takes it in might, not merit.
> Where I have come, great clerks have purposed
> To greet me with premeditated welcomes;
> Where I have seen them shiver and look pale,
> Make periods in the midst of sentences,
> Throttle their practis'd accent in their fears,
> And, in conclusion, dumbly have broke off,
> Not paying me a welcome. Trust me, sweet,
> Out of this silence yet I pick'd a welcome;
> And in the modesty of fearful duty
> I read as much as from the rattling tongue
> Of saucy and audacious eloquence.
> Love, therefore, and tongue-tied simplicity
> In least speak most, to my capacity.
>   (V.i.90–105)

Theseus suggests the same imaginative generosity in his later exchange with Hippolyta:

> *Hip.* This is the silliest stuff that ever I heard.
> *The.* The best in this kind are but shadows; and the worst are
> no worse, if imagination amend them.
> *Hip.* It must be your imagination then, and not theirs.
> *The.* If we imagine no worse of them than they of themselves,
> they may pass for excellent men.
>   (V.i.213–20)

But there are differences between good and bad art, and Theseus can be perfectly ruthless in his criticism, as he shows in his amused remarks during the performance of what he calls "this palpable, gross play" (V.i.374).

In her last novel, *Between the Acts*, Virginia Woolf describes a pageant presented outdoors by the people of a town at an English country house on the eve of World War II. Like Shakespeare, she interweaves the pageant and its actors and actresses, the reactions of the audience to them and to each other, and the fields, cows, and weather of the natural setting in which the pageant is played. And she also, writing on the eve of World War II, includes airplanes overhead. At the end of the performance, one person says, "Thank

the actors, not the author. . . . Or ourselves, the audience." After the audience
and players disperse and return to their individual lives, Woolf turns, in her
final scene, to the husband and wife, Giles and Isa, at whose house the pageant was presented:

> The old people had gone up to bed. Giles crumpled the news-
> paper and turned out the light. Left alone together for the first
> time that day, they were silent. Alone, enmity was bared; also
> love. Before they slept, they must fight; after they fought, they
> would embrace. From that embrace another life might be born.
> But first they must fight, as the dog fights with the vixen, in the
> heart of darkness, in the fields of night.
>
> Isa let her sewing drop. The great hooded chairs had become
> enormous. And Giles too. And Isa too against the window. The
> window was all sky without colour. The house had lost its shel-
> ter. It was night before roads were made, or houses. It was night
> that dwellers in caves had watched from some high place among
> rocks.
>
> Then the curtain rose. They spoke.

Notes

This lecture has been reconstructed from notes by Arisen and Griffin. In the upper
margin of one of his pages of notes on this lecture, Ansen writes: "WHA's trick of
beginning negative part of antithesis (which comes 1st) with 'No!' or 'No,' and posi-
tive part by 'Yes!'"

Page
115   "subplot . . . English drama itself declined.": Auden, as he told Ansen in
       conversation, was indebted for this observation to William Empson's dis-
       cussion of "Double Plots," in *Some Versions of Pastoral* (London: Chatto &
       Windus, 1935), 27.
116   "stone Dr. Johnson kicked": In *Boswell's Life of Johnson*, eds. George
       Birkbeck Hill and L. F. Powell, 4 vols. (Oxford: Clarendon Press, 1934),
       1:471.
116   Alfred North Whitehead, Lecture VII, "Nature Lifeless," in *Modes of
       Thought* (New York: Macmillan, 1938), 173–201. All four of Auden's sub-
       categories of nature are indebted to Whitehead.
117   "Plato's 'noble lie'": *The Republic*, III.414, in *Dialogues of Plato*, ed. Jowett,
       1:679. Jowett's translation is "royal lie."
117   "*Credo ut intellegam*": Cf. Auden, "New Year Letter," 1.422, and *ACW*, p.
       34. The phrase is Anselm's, quoted by Charles Williams, *The Descent of the
       Dove* (New York: Oxford University Press, 1939), 109.
117   "St. Paul": Romans 7.15.
117   Sigmund Freud, *Totem and Taboo* (1913, tr. 1918).
117   "animism . . . polytheism . . . myths": Cf. *Auden as Didymus*, 25–28.

117 "'Nativity Ode'": John Milton, "On the Morning of Christ's Nativity," XIX.

118 "Gods become accidents in substance.": Following Aristotle, medieval philosophers defined an accident as an entity whose essential nature it is to inhere in another subject. It is thus to be contrasted with substance. Accidents and substance are fused, however, in Scholastic explanations of the Eucharistic Presence, and it is apparently such fusion that Auden sees in polytheistic gods and myths and that he calls attention to in Dante's description of love in the *Paradiso*. Ansen's notes here read: "Gods become accidents in substance. (Dante so says on love), myths."

118 Dante, *Paradiso, The Divine Comedy*, trans. Carlyle-Wicksteed, Canto XXXIII, p. 599.

119 "Nature never intended . . . in the USA": Cf. *DH*, 317 note.

120 "taking the frivolous too seriously": See *DH*, 429–32.

121 "Dr. Johnson remarked": *Boswell's Life of Johnson*, 2:461.

121 "myth of Tristan and Isolde": Cf. *DH*, 119–23, and FA, 23–24.

122 "BMT": A subway line in New York City.

124 Virginia Woolf, *Between the Acts* (New York: Harcourt, Brace, 1941), 218–19. Auden considered the novel Woolf's "masterpiece," *FA*, 414.

KENNETH BURKE

Why A Midsummer Night's Dream?

Lest you expect the wrong things of this talk, please let me say at the start that I shall not be speaking impressionistically. It is not my aim (indeed, it is not within my capacity) to give you, in my own words, on a lecture platform, the kind of experience that you can get somewhat by a sympathetic reading of the work we are to discuss, or still better, by seeing it expertly performed. Though we shall throughout be concerned with one work in particular, the discussion also involves considerations of critical method in general. Some may disagree with this very method. For them the best I can do is try to make it as cogent as possible so that, if anyone cares to raise objections afterwards, we can help make it more certain that the objections are to what I shall have actually said. Objections are all the more to be welcomed because, at least in one notable respect, I ran into some notions that I did not have when beginning my analysis.

I

In his book on Greek tragedy, Aristotle states that it is better to read such plays than to see them performed.[1] This notion is probably due in part to the fact that Aristotle was so thoroughly a bookman, but also to the fact that, at that stage in the development of technology, many visual aspects of a performance must have been quite crude. Consider, for example, the tragedies which involve the appearance of a god in a machine, the *deus ex machina*.

From *Shakespeare Quarterly* 57, no. 3 (Fall 2006): 297–308. © 2006 by Kenneth Burke Literary Trust.

Doubtless the very awkwardness made it good fun to have such a figure in Aristophanic comedy, somewhat as with the farcical performance of *Pyramus and Thisbe* in *A Midsummer Night's Dream*. And though the traditional dance-steps in a tragedy may have had much to recommend them, the masks must have at least made impossible such mobility of bodily expression that we take for granted as an important aspect of the actor's art. By the same token, among what he called the six qualitative parts of tragedy (plot, character, thought, diction, melody, and spectacle),[2] he rated spectacle (*opsis*) lowest[3]— whereas the high development of technology today readily allows for kinds of "spectacular" in which the visual show is the major source of the attraction. The fact that, except for pageantry, the Shakespearean theater also had meager resources as spectacle accounts for one major problem, particularly in the modern filming of a Shakespeare play. Where the playwright is trying to produce, by sheerly verbal means, the sense of a visual experience like dawn or dusk or moonlight (which can now readily be imitated by sheerly technical means but, in the original conditions of performance, were to be imagined in broad daylight), such lines tend to become redundant, since they are aiming to produce a kind of effect that is already being produced by other means. As early as 1816, there was a performance that, to Hazlitt's disgruntlement, stressed spectacle and incidental music, at the expense of the poetry.[4] And the battle has been variously waged since then.

Over the years many things have been done with the play. Sometimes the text has been greatly cut, and music featured—Mendelssohn's, for instance—or folk tunes. There was even a performance that wholly eliminated the courtly figures, and was all buffoonery, by greatly expanding the role of Bottom. I shall work from the text as we have it, in the book—and shall not concern myself with directors' twists (as, for instance, having the same actor play the roles of Theseus and Oberon, or the same actress play Hippolyta and Titania). For regardless of the innovative effects that may be got by such resources, in the last analysis the roles themselves are quite distinct. And in particular I must lay great emphasis upon the standard *distinction* between the two queens.

How quickly things get set up. First there is Theseus saying "Now, fair Hippolyta, our nuptial hour / Draws on apace" (1.1.1–2).[5] He would wed "With pomp, with triumph, and with revelling" (l. 19). Immediately thereafter, an outraged father, Egeus, introduces a first useful complication, in complaining of the young courtier, Lysander, "This man hath bewitched the bosom of my child" (l. 27), whom Egeus, against her wishes, would marry to a different courtier, Demetrius. Even thus early, the theme of bewitchment that will infuse the scenes in the wood is introduced, though perhaps unnoticeably until we give the text a close look. Next we see further evidence of tangles among the lovers, with regard to the two girls, Hermia and Helena.

Then we see the simple workmen, the "mechanicals" (3.2.9), planning the play that will bring the plot back to the court in the last act. Then, in "a wood near Athens" (2.1 sd), we are in the realm of fancy that gives the play its name, with Puck (or Robin Goodfellow), King Oberon, and Queen Titania, variously appointed to help get the plot entangled.

Above all, in this connection, observe that the woodsy atmosphere is charmingly established before we learn of the "little western flower," to be found "where the bolt of Cupid fell" (2.1.166, 165). It had been "milk-white," now it is "purple with love's wound—/ And maidens call it love-in-idleness" (ll. 167–168). It is an "herb," the juice of which "on sleeping eyelids laid / Will make or man or woman madly dote / Upon the next live creature that it sees" (ll. 169, 170–72). And at the same time we are told that this "charm" can be taken from the sight by "another herb" (ll. 183, 184). And so, what with mistakes, and Puckishness, and the dramaturgic convenience of such a magic juice, conditions are set for as many tanglings and untanglings of the plot as the playwright considers advisable. It is Puck who helps Shakespeare help the plot along by mistakenly squeezing the magic juice in the eyes of the wrong courtier, and who deliberately "translates" Bottom (3.1.109) by giving him an ass's head (thus making Queen Titania's infatuation particularly "spectacular").

But the remarkable thing is that, by first establishing the woodsy dimension before introducing talk of this magic juice, and by surrounding it with such lovely connotations when he does introduce it, the combination of Shakespeare's timing and his astonishing stylistic grace shifts our attention away from the rudimentary nature of the device itself, as a way of keeping his plot on the move. And instead, we feel it as infused with the spirit of the same fancifulness with which the imagery as a whole levitates. But in this general account of what is going on in the play, we should also stress the fact that the opening remarks by Theseus clearly establish the *point of view* in terms of which this play is to be received. Except for one notable feature (and my speculations on that matter involve a notion which you might not agree with), I take it that, being in all likelihood written for a wealthy patron who was by implication honored (or, if you will, flattered) in the figure of Theseus, the play is presented from such a noble patron's point of view. Though Shakespeare was as suave in honoring his patron as his "rude mechanicals" were not, both his play, and the handicrafts men's efforts to perform the play-within-a-play, implicitly approached the nature of the social gap "from the top down"—except . . . but on that point, more anon.

II

In the strictest sense, the "Dream" is confined to the sequence of entanglements and disentanglements that take place in the woods. Here we might, for contrast, recall the dark and savage (*oscura, selvaggia*) woods in which Dante was lost at the beginning of his journey into Hell.[6] Morally, it there stands for a region of Error which one first enters at adolescence. Politically, it stands for the "troubled state of Italy in Dante's time." Both works touch upon the kind of attitude that proverbially equates "being in the wood" with "being at a loss." And the expression is even used reflexively when Demetrius refers to the young lovers' confusions as a "wood within this wood" (2.1.192). Yet here the whole notion of confusion is reduced to the antics of a mere comic imbroglio. Maybe I am being over-thorough, but in meditating on this range of meanings (between the fearsome and the playful) I like to think that such a prettifying of the problematical could even be related ultimately to such transformations as are implicit in the thought that the body's powers of *pleasurable* awareness may be attenuated modifications of what began as sensitivity to *pain*. True, as judged sheerly by the resources of stagecraft, the complications of the play can be said to center in the fiction of a magical juice that, when squirted into a sleeper's eyes, "Will make or man or woman madly dote / Upon the next live creature that it sees" (ll. 171–72), plus the availability of another device that will undo this fascination. But we soon run into complications considerably much subtler and more exacting than that.

If we dig deeper, how is the whole work seen to shape up? I shall try to show why much stress should be placed upon the fact that the *dramatis personae* comprise three quite distinct classes of characters. First, there are the figures who are "courtly" in two senses, both as regards their privileged *social* status and as regards their varied involvements in the theme of *sexual* courtship. At the other end of the social scale are the "handicraft" men, the crude "mechanicals" whose ingenuous earnestness makes them the butts of the comedy's fond derision. (I am puzzled as to why Granville-Barker refers to them as "rustics."[7] If they were rustics rather than low-bred townsmen, some of my notions about the underpinnings of the play would have to be considerably altered.)

Between these two contrasted social orders (or perhaps we might better say, alongside them), there are the wood sprites, the fairy people who appear only in the forest scenes, at night, by moonlight. These are the figures whom Shakespeare entrusts with the function of giving the play its miraculously rare dreamlike quality. With them in mind, it does us good to recall what Francis Fergusson, in his charming epitomizing of the play, has summed up thus:

> It is the strange events of Acts II and III, in woodland and summer moonlight, that give *A Midsummer Night's Dream* its name and its magical quality. In creating that sequence Shakespeare drew upon his memories of two age-old festivals of the summer season which must have been familiar, since childhood, to him and his audience:

May Day and Midsummer Eve. The May Day games, when the young people ran through the woods all night to gather boughs and flowers for the maypole (a custom that scandalized the Puritans), suggest the nocturnal hide-and-seek of Hermia, Lysander, Helena, and Demetrius. Midsummer Eve, the summer solstice, was the time of "midsummer madness," and maidens were supposed to dream, that night, of their true loves—as Shakespeare's young people, and even his Bottom and Titania [about whom further anon], do in their odd ways.[8]

Probably commissioned as a kind of masque, to celebrate a wedding among persons of nobility, the "Dream" simply exports the aesthetic and social values of the court to a series of fanciful scenes in the woods, which are the court all over again, but in an idealized form.[9] Here the susceptibility to shifts of allegiance, so "natural" to courtship as so conceived, is treated with the help of contrivances whereby the vagaries of infatuation can be acceptably exaggerated, in both their nature and their instability. Dreams are always a kind of caricature, over-simplifying motives in one way or another. And the machinery of this Dream is designed to provide a masque-like entertainment by the use of such conventions, and the establishing of such expectations, as readily allow for sudden reversals whereby, for instance, a character can at one moment be vowing eternal loyalty to another, and at the next moment is headed in a quite different direction, paying equally zestful court to someone else. Then, to round things out, back at court where the play began, all can end on the assumption that henceforth the time of such confusions is over, all but the wood-sprites have come out of the woods, and for the humans everything ends in perfect order, climaxed by the closing stable relationship between the courtly figures and the laborers, the prime one among whom is Bottom, the weaver, who during the period of confusion had been "translated" into an ass. But no, that isn't quite the case. There is a further scene in which Puck, Oberon, and Titania also speak to undo their association with the intermediate time of turmoil, and to establish it that their attitude, too, is one of total benevolence towards the courtly figures (there is no reference to the "mechanicals").

III

Now that everything has been brought to a state of perfect rest, let us, alas! unloose *our* problems. I have felt that a handy way to bring out the nature of the comic motive in this work would be to contrast it with such a grotesque tragedy as Shakespeare's *Coriolanus*. And as a corollary to that emphasis, I want to discuss some implications of the play's "Puckishness," including its diplomatic tie-in with the famous set-speech of Theseus, the Duke whose impending marriage is the occasion of the events that lead to the incidents in the woods and to the play-within-a-play that comes in the last act, and that the dramaturgic skill of Shakespeare leads us to receive as a kind of long-awaited fulfillment. I refer to the often-quoted lines: "The lunatic, the lover, and the poet, / Are of imagination all compact" (5.1.7–8). It is a formulary that felicitously merges both felicitous and sinister connotations in the concept of the creative. And it is often taken, I think mistakenly, not just as a speech given to Theseus for handling a dimension of this particular play, but as Shakespeare's summarizing of his own skills. To take up these two points in succession:

The tragedy of *Coriolanus* well serves our present purposes because it centers in a character who despises the populace, and takes every opportunity to say so. Thus the drama brings to maximum intensity the conflict between patricians and plebeians, a conflict that the heroic victim's combination of bravery and arrogance constantly accentuates. On the other hand, in the comedy of *A Midsummer Night's Dream*, whereas there is an equally wide social gap between the courtly characters and the "handicraft men" who are so seriously concerned with their plans to perform a play in the Duke's honor, the mood is one of total *relaxation*. Perhaps, in the last analysis, the Duke's friendly condescension towards the self-serious mutts whose bungling he affectionately enjoys is but a variant of the same social ratings as Coriolanus so turbulently swore by. However, the social gap is here presented in an attitude of almost benign amusement, towards the social underlings, on the part of the Duke in whose honor they perform a play in *farcical* earnest.

Maybe I could best make my point this way: While agreeing that we should, first of all, consider a work of art in terms of its internal relationships and transformations, I submit that we can meet such tests without sacrificing a reference to what I might call a kind of "social psychosis" prevailing outside the work. In the case of *Coriolanus*, the point is obvious. In actual life, an intense conflict between social classes can be a cause of much distress. But a tragedy built around the use of such a topic can imitate the actual social problem in such a way that, in its aesthetic analogue, it becomes transformed into a source of *entertainment*. The poetic imitation of a situation that would be tragic in actual life can so transcend the conditions of life that it allows us to experience what Aristotle would call the "tragic pleasure."[10] I have such thoughts in mind when I ask what "social psychosis" a tragedy might be exploiting, for the delectation of an audience. And I have said that the "social psychosis" involved in the tragedy of *Coriolanus* is in the conflict between the nobles and the populace.[11]

But just where are we, when we turn to comedy? And particularly just where are we, when we have such comedy as this, which takes it easy, even when we watch the characters (who don't know of their plight as we do) being temporarily agitated? We *just know* that the "Dream's" entanglements are going to get untangled. Such expectations are built into the form. In fact, the various shifts of allegiance, without any corresponding depths of transformation in the comic characters themselves, are all that is needed to tell us in a general way that this play is under the sign of relaxation.

Though I think that Elder Olson's excellent book on comedy[12] misleads us somewhat by placing too great stress upon the *trivial* as an aspect of comedy's appeal in general, I think he is quite correct in stressing a somewhat related motive, the state of total *relaxation* in which at least a comedy such as *A Midsummer Night's Dream* helps the audience to participate. Where I differ from Olson is in wanting to consider underlying motivational elements which are decidedly *not* trivial. Thus, in reviewing Olson's book, I used the example of some folk-humor that turned up in the old days that doubtless antedated many of you, during the Middle Western dust storms of the Thirties. The comic line ran thus: "I guess Uncle Ebenezer will soon be along. I just saw his farm go by." In contrast with an outcry that might tragically intensify the great gravity of the situation, the joke was "trivial." But it was not "much ado about nothing." Rather, the motive underlying its comic appeal (what I would call the "psychosis" of the situation) was in dead earnest. And I have such considerations in mind when, in asking about a possible "social psychosis" that underlies this masque-like comedy, doubtless written originally for appreciation "from the top down," I would contrast its way of dealing with the distinction between upper and lower classes with comedy's way of treating much the same issue.

We shall return to this point later. Meanwhile, let us consider for a while the other strand, the romantic "Puckishness" with which Shakespeare inspirits the play, by his use of the woodland imagery. (Meanwhile, if my use of the term "psychosis" bothers you, please let it hang for now—and we'll return to it later.)

As regards the *dramatis personae*, obviously there are three dimensions in this play. So far, we have touched upon the contrast between the courtly characters and the beloved low-born mutts (in the stage directions they are called "clowns" [3.1 sd]), whose performance of the play-within-a-play will be considered by the stage-audience farcical, a judgment shared by audiences other than the one for which the original wedding-masque was presumably written. The more they bumbled, the more lovable they were; and all the more so because (as regards the standpoint of the courtly psychosis), in all their bumbling they took for granted the respect that they paid to their patron and his actual bride (doubtless represented in the original performance by Theseus and Hippolyta).

But what of the third dimension among the characters? There is a sense in which we could class the courtly characters and the respectfully subservient "mechanicals" together, in contrast with this woodsy lot, headed in poetic Puck (the self-proclaimed lover of the "preposterous"[13]), King Oberon, and Queen Titania. In considering this third dimension, I ran across an unexpected likelihood. If you won't go along with it, I doubt whether I could prove the point, but I bring it up because it bears upon my distinction between a tragic and a comic use of *extra*-poetic tensions. As regards the crossing of the social gap between upper and lower classes, it is conceivable how the tensions of a courtly psychosis might provide the poetic conditions for the appeal of an intense *tragedy* in which a queen becomes madly in love with a low-bred commoner. But what of a *comedy* that, while written for such an audience, is under the sign of *total relaxation*? I submit that, by an act of highly inventive dramaturgic diplomacy, the dramatist solved the problem by so peopling the woodsy dimension of his cast that he had *two* queens, only one of which, Hippolyta, would have alluded to the bride of the *actual* wedding for which this wedding-masque had been designed. Within these conditions, Shakespeare is able to cross this social gap (and, in that sense, is able to build lightly atop the tension that would be most basic to the courtly psychosis). I would assume that the ultimate dramaturgic grounds for attempting to cross such a gap would be not necessarily social (in the sense that the dramatist wanted to "sneak something across"). The effort would be grounded, rather, in a technical fact; namely: (for all their differences) both comedy and tragedy profit by kinds of imitation that are built atop tense issues as their explicit or implicit subject-matter.

No one can say how much the text may have been modified, if at all, when transformed from a masque for private performance before a select audience to a play designed for appeal to the public at large. In any case, as we now have it, if we consider it from the standpoint of the courtly psychosis (which all dramatists of the time necessarily, or even "naturally," took into account), do we not find, lurking within the work, a delightful twist that is almost an obscenity? For Bottom fails to see any glamour at all in being attended so assiduously by an infatuated queen. He is interested in oats, and in getting his ears scratched (4.1.7, 21–24, 29–30)—and he doesn't want his attendants to be so courteous. While all the courtiers, when lost in the wood, were continually shifting, Bottom was as firm and stable as a rump. Along with his unconscious references to even the sheerly visible nature of his asininity (and Shakespeare works them for all the traffic will bear), there is also, in his "translated" state, this blunt unresponsiveness. And however asininely inappropriate it may seem, within the terms of the courtly psychosis, I can understand the nature of its appeal to lower-class members of the audience, like I'm.

IV

But all that I have been saying has been but leading to a kind of problem which has not been so much as vaguely indicated. Dear friends, though Dante got us out of the woods, and though the play we have been considering never even got us into Dante's woods, we have now brought things to the point where I must break down and admit that, with regard to this play, I am still in the woods.

Let's face the matter thus:

In considering both drama and the dramatizing resources of journalism, and the ways of life itself, I have been much affected by the important role of *victimage*, in either dramatic imitations of life, or journalistic documentary reports of life, or life itself. When, years ago, I first began thinking of this play, I told myself that one ultimate source of the loveliness in it is its total absence of a victim. (And that's a possibility particularly worth considering in these times, when so many enterprisers of so many sorts are doing all within their power to play up victimage.)

But on this score I was cheating somewhat. For although things turn out pleasantly for everyone, and though the audience never has reason to expect that the incidental discordancies along the way will end in victimage, there is a constant succession of such turbulencies, however prettified. And although "*The Most Lamentable Comedy and Most Cruel Death of Pyramus and Thisbe*" (1.2.9–10) with its "very tragical mirth" (5.1.57), but imitates victimage in ways that are not felt as such by either the audience of the play or the audience of the play-within-a-play, the unconscious burlesque of themselves provided by the "rude mechanicals" does in effect class them as victims of a sort. For they are butts of derision, albeit kindly derision, and quite beyond their range of awareness as implied within the terms of the fiction. Yet it all adds up not to the absence of victimage, but to the imitation of attenuated or qualified victimage.

But now where are we? It is a fact that, after several revisions of this piece, I end on what I originally began with. In connection with a seminar I was planning some several months ago, for the final assignment I suggested two topics. For members of the class who would be most at home in the close analysis of one particular text, I suggested *A Midsummer Night's Dream*.

For those who would prefer a general topic, I suggested "Humanism." Was it on the way out? Or was it due for some sort of revival? I had been invited to attend a conference abroad on this subject. But when circumstances prevented my attending, I "sublimated" by proposing that some members of the class take this subject as their point of departure. On the assumption that, throughout our history, various "isms" are defined with relation to other "isms," I had in the back of my mind the thought that a New Humanism now would be defined antithetically to "Technologism," which would be distinguished from mere technology in the sense that, while accepting a large measure of technology as necessary and even desirable, this particular brand of Humanism, local to our time, would programatically condemn (in what it called "Technologism") the assumption, explicit or implicit, that the remedy for technologically caused problems should be sought, not in the attempt to *moderate* such modes of livelihood, but rather in schemes making for still more and more of such technologic clutter.

In this connection I thought of the "Dream" as exemplifying a quite different dimension. Even when it was first performed, I assumed, its scenes of Puckish bewitchment in the woods appealed somewhat by the romanticizing of a fictive realm that, even then, was felt as romantically antithetic to men's ways of life in town. Hence, why not all the more so these days, when a sizable stand of timber marks but an uncomfortably problematic region of overlap between raw material for pulp mills and the environmentalists' view of it as a possible protection against the ravages of progress, population explosion, and pollution.

"Wouldn't it be lovely," I told myself, "to view the relation between town and non-town in terms of Puckish woodsiness?" At that time, I hadn't specifically concerned myself with the problems of accountancy involved in the relation between a courtly psychosis then and what I would want to call a technological psychosis now, though recognizing that the very presence of the play's mechanicals (a carpenter, a joiner, a bellows-mender, a tinker, a tailor, and above all, our ass-bottom weaver) testified already to a fairly advanced technology.

As regards the town's ways of matching its current psychosis in terms of non-town, I think at least of three: (1) fantasies of life technologically made possible beneath the sea; (2) fantasies of life that technology makes possible in outer realms of space and/or time; (3) tourism, with the constant and necessary aid of all the technical and financial and organizational resources that are the very essence of the town. Here are three ways of projecting the town into non-towns that are imaginary counterparts. But *A Midsummer Night's Dream*, I have suggested, is of a different order, dialectically on a different plane entirely, its dream being built by the fragmentary use of old legends that (at the time when the play was written) still did have some living expression, in country customs, still vigorous enough for the Puritans to feel the need of reproving them severely.

Humanism now, as I see the issue, would necessarily confront the Technological Psychosis head on. Thus, it would in some notable respects be *antithetical* to Technologism. As I see the Dream, it is not, in its origins, anti-technologistic. For its embodiment of town-thinking even included, pleasantly, without connotations of resistance, the role of the "mechanicals" in contributing to the ways of the Courtly Psychosis (the tensions implicit in the social situation there being smoothed over so gently, you'd hardly suspect that Shakespeare ever even thought of them, were it not for a grotesque tragedy like *Coriolanus*, in which the same underlying "socio-psychotic" situation is so stridently insisted upon).

Just what, in sum, is my position? This masque-like comedy, at the time of its original production, was clearly infused with the extra-poetic influence of the courtly psychosis. This comes to focus in the farcical performance of *Pyramus and Thisbe* and Titania's infatuation with Bottom. At the same time, the play also had, for the town, an element of medicinal, nostalgic fantasy, in its vision of a romanticized non-town. The sense of its courtly reference is not for us now a *major* aspect of its appeal. But in the meantime, a theory of Humanism that would be defined as antithetical to Technologism brings to the fore a sense of the work's relation to what, as seen from the standpoint of Humanism so defined, would be called a Technological Psychosis.[14]

But maybe you might now see why I would want to speak of a "courtly psychosis" rather than using the orthodox Marxist term for class "consciousness." For Humanism, as I see it now, must square itself against a kind of Technologism that we confront today in capitalist, fascist, socialist, communist, tribalist, or anti-colonialist modes of expectation and exhortation. Regardless of politics, both the Volga and U.S. rivers can now catch fire— have caught fire.[15] Though I strongly doubt whether a Humanism, as so defined, has much of a chance, I see nowhere else to turn. But be that as it may, I see *A Midsummer Night's Dream* as a fanciful embodiment of the Humanistic attitude.

Meanwhile, for a happy ending that befits the tenor of the play, let us revert to those famous lines of Theseus' we mentioned earlier:

> The lunatic, the lover, and the poet
> Are of imagination all compact.
> One sees more devils than vast hell can hold:
> That is the madman. The lover, all as frantic,
> Sees Helen's beauty in a brow of Egypt.
> The poet's eye, in a fine frenzy rolling,
> Doth glance from heaven to earth, from earth to heaven,
> And as imagination bodies forth
> The forms of things unknown, the poet's pen
> Turns them to shapes, and gives to airy nothing
> A local habitation and a name.
> Such tricks hath strong imagination

That if it would but apprehend some joy
It comprehends some bringer of that joy;
Or in the night, imagining some fear,
How easy is a bush supposed a bear!
   (5.1.7–22)

Grand lines, but they are Theseus' lines, not Shakespeare's. For they contain no mention of the astounding rationality he brought to his trade as a playwright. They are not the recipe for Shakespeare. Shakespeare was all that, and more. Also recall, at least, that grand set-piece by Ulysses, on degree, in *Troilus and Cressida* (1.3.101–34). Learn how to discount for shrewd attitudinizing, and there you see him saying, with a whole panoply of pleasantries, what Marx said with his modes of armament, in talking as he did of what, in our terms, might be called the "hierarchical psychosis." Or, returning to our play, let us end with meditations on that much-quoted line of Puck's, "what fools these mortals be!" (3.2.115). Think of the great tribute he paid to us mortal fools, in the astonishing rationality with which he put together his things of the imagination. I do believe he was the sort of craftsman who, if we believed such-and-such, could make a great play out of such beliefs, and could as easily have made a great play out of the opposite beliefs, if those others were what moved us. For what he believed in above all was the glory of his trade itself, which is to say, the great humaneness of the word, and the corresponding search throughout the range of all its aptitudes. True, the miraculous resources of the word have led us into a technologic clutter that threatens to turn both town and anti-town inexorably into modes of horror. But still being born anew, there is the wondrous constructive *rationality* of the word, so masterfully embodied in Shakespeare's blithe dramaturgic schemings.

Notes

   1. Aristotle, *Poetics*, 1462a11–14, 18.
   2. Aristotle, *Poetics*, 1450a10.
   3. Aristotle, *Poetics*, 1450b15–20.

4. William Hazlitt reviewed an adaptation by Frederic Reynolds at Covent Garden, with music by Sir Henry Bishop, in the *Examiner* (London) of 21 January 1816, repr., Stanley Wells, comp. and ed., *Shakespeare in the Theatre: An Anthology of Criticism* (Oxford: Oxford UP, 1997), 43–46.

5. Quotations from Shakespeare have been edited to match the text and line numbers from *The Norton Shakespeare*, Stephen Greenblatt, gen. ed. (New York: W. W. Norton, 1997), since Burke cited various (unknown) editions over the years, often with silent, minor modifications of punctuation, spelling, and sometimes speech prefixes for minor characters. However, *The Norton Shakespeare* was not followed when Burke referred to stage directions; he cited conventional mid-twentieth-century stage directions, usually those established by the British scholar William Aldis Wright (1831–1914), whose work formed the basis of the nineteenth-century Clarendon, Cambridge, and Globe editions.

6. Dante Alighieri, *The Divine Comedy: Inferno*, 2 vols., trans. and comm., Charles Singleton (Princeton: Princeton UP, 1970), 1:2; canto 1, ll. 2, 5.

7. Reprinted in Harley Granville-Barker, *More Prefaces to Shakespeare*, ed. Edward M. Moore (Princeton: Princeton UP, 1974), 94, 125, 127.

8. Francis Fergusson, *Shakespeare: The Pattern in His Carpet* (New York: Delacorte P, 1970), 125. In a deleted passage, Burke continued, "I quote this passage for two reasons. First, it admirably sums up the point about the possible 'archetypal' elements of folklore that, in all likelihood, the dramatist did draw upon, when helping his audience to imagine the magic of moonlight in the woods. But, second, Fergusson is so alive to poetics in the Aristotelian sense, unlike the myth-men he would never propose to derive the structure of the play thus 'archetypically.' Archetypes be damned. In the passage I quoted, he takes care of that angle, and shrewdly, since it often now happens to be in. He indicates how one should make allowances for the 'archetype' way of defining and lining up literary modes. Incidentally, for many purposes, it proves itself to be an exceptionally civilized way of lining things up. But first of all, I submit, if you *must* build the whole set-up around 'archetypes,' then, when you get to one particular text, ask not what *static* 'archetypes' (as mythic background) it exemplifies. Ask, rather, what are the ARCHETYPAL DEVELOPMENTS?"

9. Burke's inference that *A Midsummer Night's Dream* had its origin in private performance, with later revision for public performance, was at the time arguable, but no longer reflects a consensus of opinion among Shakespeare scholars.

10. Aristotle, *Poetics*, 1453b11–13.

11. Burke refers to his essay "*Coriolanus*—and the Delights of Faction," *Hudson Review* 19 (1966): 185–202.

12. Burke reviewed Elder Olson's *The Theory of Comedy* (Bloomington, Indiana UP, 1968); see Kenneth Burke, "The Serious Business of Comedy," *New Republic* 160.11 (1969): 23–24, 27.

13. "Those things do best please me / That befall prepost'rously" (3.2.120–21).

14. In a deleted passage, Burke went on: "Thus, my embarrassment resides in the fact that my ideal play, to represent in fantasy a realm outside a 'technological psychosis' is in its very essence bound to 'courtly psychosis,' though I do think that I have shown how, and why, for us at least, it can outreach those limitations."

15. Burke refers to spontaneous combustion of polluted materials on the Volga River in Europe in 1970 and, likely, to the 22 June 1969 fire on the Cuyahoga River, in Cleveland, Ohio.

REGINA BUCCOLA

"The Story Shall Be Changed":
The Fairy Feminism of
A Midsummer Night's Dream

In early November 1576, Bessie Dunlop of Lyne in Ayrshire was "'conuict, and byrnt'" for witchcraft. The introduction to her testimony charges, "Dilatit of the vsing of Sorcerie, Witchcraft, and Incantatioune, with Inovcatioun of spretis of the devill . . . deling with charmes, and abusing the peple with devillisch craft of sorcerie forsaid."[1] One of the principal spirits of the devil with whom Dunlop associated was the Fairy Queen, or "Queen of Elfame," as Dunlop refers to her. As were most of the other women whose cases I will discuss over the course of this book, Dunlop was married—to one "Andro Jak," according to Pitcairn's record of her deposition, a character curiously absent from her story.

In her testimony, Dunlop claims to have made the acquaintance of the Queen of Elfame[2] shortly before befriending the ghost of Thom Reid, a soldier who had been killed in battle at the Field of Pinkie twenty-nine years before. Living out the narrative of liminality that was popularly believed to govern supernatural interactions, Dunlop reports that she first encountered Reid "as sche was gangand betuix hir awin hous and the yard of Monkcastell" when she herself was "new rissine out of gissane [childbed]."[3] Christian doctrine held that new mothers were vulnerable to spiritual assault from the time they gave birth until they had been ritually purified. Katherine Briggs notes, "Nursing mothers who had not yet been churched were in the greatest

---

From *Fairies, Fractious Women, and the Old Faith: Fairy Lore in Early Modern British Drama and Culture*, pp. 58–82, 211–20. © 2006 by Rosemont Publishing and Printing Corporation.

danger" of being abducted by fairies.[4] According to her own account, Dunlop first met the Queen of Elfame when actually confined to childbed.

Asked, "Gif sche neuir askit the questioun at him, Quhairfoir he com to hir mair (than) to ane vthir bodye?"[5] Dunlop replies: "Remembring hir, quhen sche was lyand in chyld-bed-lair . . . ane stout woman com in to hir, and sat doun on the forme besyde hir, and askit ane drink at hir, and sche gaif hir; quha alsua tauld hir, that that barne wald de, and that hir husband suld mend of his seiknes. The said Bessie ansuerit, that sche remembrit wele thairof; and Thom said, That was the Quene of Elfame his mistres, quha had commandit him to wait vpoun hir, and to do hir gude."[6] So, the Queen of Elfame not only visited Dunlop while she was in childbed, but also appointed Thom Reid as her "guardian."

Reid apparently took his duties as Dunlop's spiritual guardian as seriously as he took his devotion to his mistress, the Queen of Elfame. He greets Dunlop with a devout "Sancta Marie"[7] and by Bessie's own admission he shared his politicoreligious views with her. These views are consistent with the tendency, increasingly common over the period of Protestant religious reform, to link the fairies with "the auld ffayth." At the end of Dunlop's testimony, she is "interrogat, Quhat sche thocht of the new law? Ansuerit, That sche had spokin with Thom about that mater; bot Thom ansuerit, That this new law was nocht gude; and that the auld ffayth suld sum hame agane, but nocht sic as it was befoir."[8] In a footnote, Pitcairn identifies the "new law" as "The Reformed Religion."[9] As Sir Walter Scott notes in his account of the Dunlop case, "In his theological opinions, Mr. Reid appeared to lean to the Church of Rome, which, indeed, was most indulgent to the fairy folk."[10] Keeping the faith for fairies and their followers meant clinging to tenets Dunlop's interrogators had ceased to find compatible with "true" religious devotion.

It is from Reid rather than from the Queen of Elfame herself that Dunlop acquires the information and remedies she uses to help people. Early in the deposition, Dunlop is asked, "Gif sche had socht ony thing at Thom to help hir self, or ony vthir with?" She "Ansuerit, That quhen sundrie persounes cam to hir to seik help . . . Thom gaif her, out of his awin hand, ane thing lyke the rute of ane beit, and baid hir . . . dry it, and mak pulder of it, and gif it to seik persounes, and thai suld mend."[11] Although it may seem to be hair-splitting, in subsequent cases that I will discuss in which the accused parties were acquitted, healing powders such as those that Dunlop describes are received directly from the fairies, and not an intermediary "ghost" such as Tom Reid. His role as remedy-bearing shuttlecock betwixt and between Dunlop and Reid's fairy mistress seems to be one of the damning factors in the Dunlop case. Reid's role also raises both class and gender issues that, as we will see, constitute persistent aspects of fairy narratives: Reid, a male and a soldier (albeit the ghost of one), serves Dunlop, a poor peasant woman, superseding normative class and gender boundaries. The advice that he gives facilitates the improvement of the financial situation of Dunlop and her invalid husband, but it also makes her a mouthpiece for reactionary religious views in a period of contested reform.[12]

There is one other significant aspect to Dunlop's deposition that recurs consistently in the extant testimony of those who professed to gain knowledge and healing powers from the fairies, and that is the parade of nobility who, she reports, sought out her aid. Ratting out the social superiors on whose behalf she has asked Tom Reid's advice, Dunlop testifies that "The Ladye Thridpairt, in the barronye of Renfrew," sent to her to know who had stolen money from her purse. Within ten days, Dunlop had an answer for her "eftir sche had spokin with Thom." Then, "James Cwinghame, chalmerlane of Kilwinning, come to hir about sum beir that was stollin furth of the barne," and "The Ladye Blaire sundrie tymes had spokin with her" about a virtual bridal registry of household linens, plate, and clothing that had disappeared from the house. She had taxed her servants with accusations and punishments to no avail, only to discover that "Margaret Symple, hir awin friend," had stolen them once Dunlop asked Reid to look into the matter.[13] Although Scottish law identified both the practice of witchcraft and private recourse to the practitioners of it as capital crimes, there is no evidence that the Lady Thridpairt, James Cunningham, or the Lady Blair joined Bessie Dunlop when she was burned at the stake.

Fairy beliefs were part of an oral tradition largely attributed to and preserved by women, whether in witchcraft depositions or in fireside tales. In early modern Britain, women especially were considered vulnerable to the possibly benevolent, possibly pernicious influence of the fairies at transitional points in their life, such as birth, death, or periods of life alteration, such as marriage. So, for example, the tradition of carrying the bride across the threshold on her wedding day was related to fairy superstition. This association of the fairies with the threshold of the house and the threshold of a woman's life as girl/daughter and woman/wife points to a central characteristic of the fairies: they are liminal figures.[14] Not only do they exist on the border between the human realm and that of the supernatural, but they are also alternately figured as protecting or attacking those who enter liminal zones, whether it be the "literal" liminal zone of the fairy wood outside Athens in *A Midsummer Night's Dream* or the symbolic liminal zone of the birthing chamber. Bessie Dunlop's tale is in many ways the inverse of the lyrical narrative Titania relates about the death of her Indian votaress and the fairy queen's acquisition of her beautiful son.[15] As I will demonstrate, *A Midsummer Night's Dream* would likely have played very differently before an early modern audience familiar with an omnipotent fairy queen who held mortal men as sexual hostages, abducted human babies, and sometimes graced her mortal devotees with healing arts or powers of divination.[16] Although Titania is drugged for the duration of the play's action, woman's power pervades the play. As soon as he has dispensed with his utterly ungovernable wife, after all, Oberon places himself at the disposal of the desperately lovelorn Helena, chasing the object of her desire through the fairy wood with no mortal guardian in sight. As we shall see, fairies, unruly women, and open confrontation with reformed religious practice form a consistent triad in early modern British drama.

The women who are aligned with the fairies in early modern plays are linked with them in liminality: they engage in socially aberrant behavior but are not subject to the harsh reprisals that might otherwise result from their conduct. Fairy lore and the liberties accorded its airy subjects opened a "free zone" for women who rebelled against social norms for dutiful daughters and properly reticent maidens. Lore regarding fairy guardianship over true love matches, for example, provided a sociocultural safety net for women who successfully defied patriarchal laws governing whom they married and how the marital arrangements were made. Characters such as Helena and Hermia in *A Midsummer Night's Dream* are thwarted in their bold attempts to secure the spouse of their choice in defiance of the men socially positioned to deny the matches until they enter the fairy wood on the margins of their community. Meanwhile, Shakespeare is able to present sociocultural and politicoreligious scenarios that pose direct challenges to British social convention and state mandate in *A Midsummer Night's Dream* largely by virtue of the fairy lore he invokes in conjunction with the subversive aspects of the play's plot, along with its ostensible setting in pre-Christian Athens.

The play begins with two disputes: Hermia's argument with both her father, Egeus, and her ruler, Duke Theseus, over whom she should marry; and the Queen of Fairyland, Titania's, stormy feud with her consort and fairy king, Oberon, over custody of a beautiful young changeling boy. The first of these quarrels has an important offshoot—Hermia's dearest friend, Helena, is in love with Demetrius, the man whom Egeus and Theseus are trying to force Hermia to marry. Hermia and her true love, Lysander, run away into the woods outside Athens with plans to elope; Helena sends Demetrius after them so that she can, in turn, pursue him. All four of the lovers have their mésalliances sorted out in the fairy wood with the assistance of a magical herb that Oberon uses for the cross purposes of assisting the Athenian women (after a few false starts caused by Oberon's lightheartedly wicked lackey, Puck) and stymieing Titania's opposition to his appropriation of the changeling boy.

There are several important connections between women and fairies in *A Midsummer Night's Dream*:

1. Central among the "actual" fairy characters in the play is the fairy queen. Popular belief almost universally construed fairyland to be under the sway of a female monarch, not always paired with a male consort as is Shakespeare's Titania.[17]
2. *A Midsummer Night's Dream* relies on the topos of inversion, particularly with respect to gender roles. If one focuses on the women characters as the axes on which these inversions turn, alternatives to the play's surface texts of patriarchal rule emerge.
3. The play features contrasting depictions of female characters who are linked in their violations of socially prescribed gender norms. It is a particular character's status as a fairy or her alignment with the fairy realm that serves to sanction her socially aberrant conduct.[18]

Though early modern accounts of fairy doings often assigned gender identities to the key figures in the stories, such gender identification did not necessarily cohere with gender-role assignments in the human sphere. The connections forged in this play between women who violate social expectations regarding gender roles and gender-ambiguous fairy characters remove the gender-linked potential for condemnation for scandalous acts such as following one's love unwanted and unchaperoned into the woods. Fairyland is a space free from sociocultural strictures, which were most confining for women and the servant classes. Fairyland is a fanciful space, but it was dreamed up for a reason. To bowdlerize W. B. Yeats, In dreams begin possibilities.

Fairy Lore

Many critics[19] attribute to Shakespeare alone the compression of fairies with moral attributes ranging from the benevolent pastels of rainbows to the malignant shades of charcoal dust and charnel-house ash common in the popular beliefs of his age into monochrome, good-natured sprites able to nap in nutshells. There are also, however, a vocal minority of critics who share my view that Shakespeare rendered the fairies of *A Midsummer Night's Dream* perhaps more good-natured than the devil's kin, but still something less than kind. David P. Young, for example, asserts of the fairies that "Their benevolent presence in this play serves to emphasize the comic context only if they are recognized as potentially dangerous."[20] David Bevington makes a similar claim about Puck and Oberon in particular, noting that "their chief power to do good lies in withholding the mischief of which they are capable."[21]

The confusion about the precise moral nature of the fairies among critics stems from a similar uncertainty conveyed even by Shakespeare's sprites. Puck seems to think that they need to conduct themselves as their demonic counterparts, the "damnèd spirits" (III.ii.382), do, while Oberon insists that they need not do so (III.ii.388ff.) only to contradict himself in conversation with Titania on this same point later (IV.i.94–95).[22] The dispute among the fairies about which set of guidelines for "spirit conduct" applies to them serves as an index of the general ambiguity in which their spiritual status was held.[23] Such ambiguity makes them the ideal overseers of an unknown and unknowable realm such as the fairy wood outside Athens—a region on the margins of a patriarchal society in which the rules of that society no longer apply and experiment and exploration are the order of the day—or night.

It is their ability to veer from the beaten path and yet still reach safe haven that renders liminal figures such as fairies and the characters associated with them pointers toward new ways of ordering personal and social relationships, responsibilities, and institutions. Speaking specifically of *A Midsummer Night's Dream*, Marjorie Garber highlights the potential transformative power of fairy liminality: "It is perhaps not too fanciful to compare such spirits with the impulse to creation, working in the half-light of the subconscious, shadows in place of and in some ways greater than the substance they portend."[24] Since they are the products of the human imagination in the first place, fairies "embody" (in their lack of body) the impulse to imagine life lived differently, social roles cast in other ways.

Fairies offer a number of alternatives to the human social order since there are so many types of fairies who behave in unique ways. Ernest Schanzer quite rightly points out that Shakespeare presents us with no less than "three wholly distinct kinds of fairies": ethereal, acorn-nesting sprites; the apparently human-sized Oberon and Titania (since they reputedly have sexual liaisons with mortals); and Puck, who was not considered a fairy at all until Shakespeare's depiction of him.[25] Minor White Latham discusses Puck's outsider status, noting: "That Robin Goodfellow was not a native of fairyland, Shakespeare seems to have been well aware, since he takes pains to show that he is unknown to the fairies of *A Midsummer Night's Dream*, and to identify him to them and to the audience in the traditional way by which Robin Goodfellow was identified—by his figure and appearance and by a recital of his exploits and characteristics."[26] Robin Goodfellow was typically depicted with a huge phallus and a broom. It takes little present-day imagination to come up with reasons why early modern women might have sat around the fire over their darning sharing tales about a figure with such attributes—or why he was such a popular character in ballads and tales. The Fairy who meets Puck at the beginning of act II identifies him as "that shrewd and knavish sprite ... That frights the maidens of the villagery. ... Mislead[s] night wanderers, laughing at their harm" (II.i.33, 35, 39). These are all activities in which Puck engages during the play, misleading the squabbling Lysander and Demetrius, terrifying Hermia and Helena, jeering all the while, "Lord, what fools these mortals be!" (III.ii.115).[27]

Yet it is vital to recognize the ambiguity of all of the fairy characters in this play. Jan Kott, for instance, points out that the lullaby that the fairies sing to Titania in II.ii is rather more alarming than soothing, with its catalog of snakes, newts, and so forth, signaling to the audience that the wood is "inhabited by devils and lamias, in which witches and sorceresses can easily find everything required for their practices."[28] Though Kott tips the balance rather far toward the demonic end of the scale in his discussion of the fairies, he is quite right to point out the way in which they can alternately appear as magnanimous with a veneer of menace, or vice versa.

Titania warns her ass-headed lover, Bottom, not to try to leave the woods because "I am a spirit of no common rate" (III.i.154). This is an interesting line to set off against Oberon's "We are spirits of another sort" (III.ii.388). Oberon's claim is a collective reference, whereas Titania focuses on herself and sets herself apart from—and above—other spirits. The action of the play bears this out, since Oberon is unable to "control" his wife (or get her changeling boy) until he drugs her. The stage directions in the 1600 quarto of the play trace out this power dynamic. While all stage directions refer to Oberon and Titania as the King and Queen of Fairies, his speech prefixes throughout are "Ob." whereas hers undergo a metamorphosis tied directly to her drugging. So, in their first scene, her speech prefixes shift among "Queene," "Queen," and "Qu.," while his are always "Ob." Significantly, once Oberon anoints Titania's eyes, she undergoes a demotion in speech prefixes. While she is still referred to as the "Queene of Fairies" in stage directions, her speech prefixes from this point onward shift to "Tytania" or "Tyta." or "Tita.," rather than her title.[29] Popular lore about fairies almost universally imagined the realm under the sway of a fairy queen, specifically. The presence of such beliefs in the background of *A Midsummer Night's Dream* adds resonance to the fact that the main plot concerns two rebellious young Athenian women who successfully defy the express commands of father, duke, and—in Helena's case—future spouse by foraying into the fairy kingdom.

Fairy Feminism

Given the play's interrogation of sociopolitical structures, it is significant that the realm to which Helena and Hermia fly is a matriarchy, albeit one in the throes of a temporary period of Saturnalian misrule by its king. For her part, Hermia finds her voice before she ever leaves Athens, publicly defying father and duke in boldly expressing her desire to marry Lysander.[30] She and Helena only fully realize their own visions, however, once they have passed a night in the fairy wood.

Situated on the margin of the patriarchal Athenian city-state, the fairy wood is a place where these defiant young women are free to explore not only another world and mode of life, but the gender-role inversions that Helena invokes as she soliloquizes about her plan to flee Athens and its oppressions. The fairies and the women who are aligned with them, their ambiguous natures, and their subversive activities serve as presentations of alternatives that are not dismissed or appropriated by the existing patriarchal system in the last act simply because that system still exists. This is particularly clear when characters such as Oberon (whose love juice has helped Hermia and Helena to the spouses they fought patriarchal order to obtain), Titania, and Puck have the last words in the play. The audience has not entirely left the fairy realm for Athens at the play's close, since Puck—an interloper into even the fairy world—has found his way into the city-state to deliver the play's final word, and Demetrius is blissfully married to Helena only because he is still suffering the effects of a fairy drug.[31]

Puck and Oberon collude in both hindering and promoting the romantic action in *A Midsummer Night's Dream* (hereafter cited as *MND*), driving the play toward its comic climax. However, the plot into which they intervene has already been planned out and set in motion by Hermia and Helena.[32] Hermia deceives her father to secure Lysander as her spouse, and Helena deceives both her friends (Hermia and Lysander) and the object of her affections (Demetrius) in the hope of winning what seems a lost love cause. Both women play the matchmaker for themselves. Their boldness in this regard is seconded—significantly, not *initiated*—by Oberon. Thus, Hermia and Helena's conduct links them to the roles typically undertaken by fairies in mortals' love lives[33] and receives the explicit sanction of the fairy king, who assists in actualizing their desires.

The critical debate over the status of the "conquered" queens in *MND* and the relationship that they bear to the play's paradoxically paired yet polarized women can be sorted out if one imagines all four of the play's central female characters on a continuous power loop. At the outset, Hermia may not know by what power she is made bold to speak, but she is so emboldened. She also starts out in a stronger position than Helena with respect to her love life, because she has the love of the man she wants to marry, Lysander. However, as Hippolyta has, Hermia has won the heart of a man, Demetrius, who is willing to coerce her into an unwanted union. Hippolyta may be a queen, but she is a conquered and captured one when the play opens, regardless of how one interprets her attitude toward Theseus and the notion of marrying him. Even though Hermia is much lower on the social hierarchy than Hippolyta, she initially has more power on the marriage market than the captive queen because she manages to escape Athens and its restrictive marital code.

Titania, as supernatural monarch, holds sway in the fairy kingdom when she enters the scene, but she becomes linked to the lovelorn Helena after Oberon uses the same drug to interfere in both of their affairs. Both Titania and Helena have a fierce devotion to a loved one that they will risk everything to preserve: in Titania's case, it is the changeling boy, and in Helena's case it is Demetrius. When the play opens, Titania is in possession of her love object, while Helena is deprived of hers but determined to do what it takes to get him. Until the last act of the play, no one woman's fortune rises without causing a consequent fall in that of another. For instance, the same bit of fairy magic—the pansy juice—is used to wrest Titania's treasured changeling from her and catapult Helena into the power position held by Hermia in Athens: pursued by two men, one of whom she deeply loves.

The catfight between Helena and Hermia is significant with respect to this cycle: with so little legitimate power at their disposal in a patriarchal culture, they are reduced to attacking one another to gain any ground. The culture in which Shakespeare wrote *MND* was marked by intragender power struggles, such as the tendency of women to deflect responsibility for legal and moral crises in their communities from themselves by accusing one another of witchcraft. However, in this play the sorcerer and his apprentice are male and, by act V all four of the central female characters have broken out of the endless oscillation of the power loop. Titania is restored to her rightful role as queen if not as surrogate mother (a question that I think the play leaves ambiguous), both Hermia and Helena are comfortably settled into the relationships they want, and even the forcibly married Hippolyta has her day in the Sun since she realizes the import of the lovers' "dream." As Jean Howard and Phyllis Rackin put it, "In accepting the lovers' consensus as a kind of authority for their story, she is willing to entertain the possibility of a realm of experience that Theseus neither dominates nor acknowledges."[34] Christy Desmet goes further still, arguing that the play's poetic structure and language are feminized and stand in contradiction to Theseus's patriarchal construction of his own authority: "Through the art of rhetorical ornament, *A Midsummer Night's Dream* counters Theseus's rationalist ethics with a feminized fairy poetics."[35] The spokesperson for this poetics, Hippolyta, is a powerful queen among the Amazons, but a prisoner in Athens—a woman on the verge of the life-altering event of marriage brought low by circumstance, comparable to Bessie Dunlop or Helena, and, therefore, uniquely open to fairy influence. Little wonder, then, that she can make allowance for a narrative that her fiancé, that paragon of patriarchy, cannot countenance. Though she is still marrying her captor, her powers of insight and interpretation in the final scene are demonstrably superior to his, since the fairies whose power she is willing to acknowledge whereas her husband is not remain present to the omniscient audience, cavorting around the stage.

Fairy Sexuality

David Marshall suggests reading *MND* through the lens of the story of the Bacchae to find the calm within the fairy-precipitated chaos, contending that if one considers that tale of female sexual power unleashed as "a hidden model for Shakespeare's play," one discovers *"A Midsummer Night's Dream* as a conflict between 'masculine' principles of rationality and order and 'female' principles of sexuality and passion."[36] Sexuality pervades the play, from Hermia's demure plea that Lysander "lie further off" (II. ii.50) to Titania's luxurious bestial interlude with the ass-headed Bottom, to Demetrius's threatening acknowledgment of the ways that he might take advantage of Helena's unchaperoned presence in the fairy wood. Since Hermia has also willingly entered the fairy wood with no escort save a man whom she has been forbidden to marry, both heroines engage in inappropriate female conduct according to the gender conventions of the day. The rapacious sexuality invoked by Demetrius in the wood is in keeping with fairy belief, in which tales of fairy abduction tinged with sexual tension figure prominently. After first threatening to leave Helena to the mercy of the wood's wild beasts, Demetrius swears, "If thou follow me, do not believe / But I shall do thee some mischief in the wood" (II. i.236–37).[37] In response, Helena first laments the Athenian social order, which mandates that women "cannot fight for love, as men may do" (II. i.241). However, the as yet uncoupled couple are no longer in Athens, but in fairyland, a fact at which Helena unwittingly glances when she swears to "follow thee and make a heaven of hell" (II.i.243). Fairyland is a convenient space in which to undertake such a daunting task since, in popular lore, it was either associated directly with the liminal spiritual zone of purgatory or construed as an ambiguous intermediary space between heaven and hell. In the convoluted fairy love-drug fest that ensues, all of the lovers sample both bliss and torment.

Helena's speech on inversion launches the play's exploration of the topos of the world "upside-down"[38] and sets the stage for a consideration of gender relations in the physical realm specifically since she invokes mythological rape narratives even as she promises to alter the standard power dynamic. Helena does not intend to rape Demetrius in the sexual sense, but, rather, in the sense of making him captive to the marital union she so fiercely desires and he resists. Watching Demetrius run away from her (in pursuit of Lysander and Hermia), Helena vows:

> The story shall be changed:
> Apollo flies and Daphne holds the chase,
> The dove pursues the griffin, the mild hind

Makes speed to catch the tiger—bootless speed,
When cowardice pursues and valor flies!
     (II.i.230–34)

It is intriguing, given the way that matters fall out, that Helena invokes the example of an aborted rape. Rather than being transformed into a laurel tree by sympathetic divine forces (as Daphne is, fleeing her would-be rapist, Apollo), Demetrius is transformed into precisely what Helena wants him to be: her doting paramour. The supernatural sympathies in this case are aligned with the pursuer, rather than her victim. Helena's speech thus presents a vision of a woman successfully pursuing and capturing a man.

"The Problem of Helena"

Kott focuses on Helena's act I soliloquy[39] as "really the author's monologue . . . in which, for the first time, the philosophical theme of the *Dream* is stated (love and death)."[40] Although she has the most stage time of any of the mortal characters in the play,[41] Helena typically gets short shrift in the critical attention paid to *Dream*. Literary critics pass her by as a pathetic example of passivity in subordination. We ought all, however, to pay the attention to Helena that Oberon does within the play. "You, mistress, all this coil is 'long of you'" (III.ii.339), Hermia hisses in the play's cat fight. That is true: Helena is, in fact, the somewhat unwitting dea ex machina of much of the plot. Demetrius follows Hermia and Lysander into the woods because Helena pushes him in that direction. And it is because Oberon overhears Helena's pathetic exchange with Demetrius that he sends Puck on his series of misdirected love-drug errands. Furthermore, Helena is the woman in the play who ultimately gets the man she wants against seemingly insurmountable odds: the opposition of the duke (who intends him for her friend, Hermia) and the opposition of the man himself (who has sworn her off in favor of Hermia). Hermia, at least, has Lysander on her side. In the end, Hermia is, in essence, a side-car beneficiary of Oberon's stated goal of helping Helena get her man.

Oberon forges a connection with Helena as soon as he finds her in the wood. Significantly, at precisely the moment when he decides to take pity on her, Oberon calls Helena a "nymph": "Fare thee well, nymph. Ere he do leave this grove / Thou shalt fly him, and he shall seek thy love" (II.i.245–46). Noel Williams notes that the etymological roots for *fairy* include the Latin *nympha*.[42] Thus, Oberon aligns Helena by name with the fairy realm he inhabits as he echoes her promise to change not just myth but her own story to its diametrical opposite. It is indicative of the liberating spirit of fairyland that Oberon's initial impulse when confronted with Helena's lamentation about and promised fight against the social strictures that limit her ability to pursue the man she wants is to help her get what she wants, on her terms. As Diane Purkiss notes, "Very often in fairy stories, the fairies are the only allies a woman has."[43]

"Ill met by moonlight, proud Titania" (II.I.60)

The majority of theatrical and popular representations of fairyland in early modern England depicted a queen who had either sole sovereign authority or dominance over her partner. The Welsh fairy queen's name was Mab, a fact of which Shakespeare seems to have been cognizant when writing Mercutio's fanciful speech on the origin of dreams in *Romeo and Juliet* (I.iv.53–95). Mab is not given a consort, and neither is the fairy queen of Shakespeare's *Merry Wives of Windsor* (though Sir Hugh is available to play him). Neither Thomas Dekker nor Ben Jonson pairs his fairy queen with a partner, coequal or otherwise, in *The Whore of Babylon* and *The Alchemist*, respectively.[44] Spenser implies that his Gloriana is single in anticipation of her union with Arthur, but *The Faerie Queene* does not depict this relationship. Yet more examples from early modern fairy plays by Michael Drayton and John Lyly, among others, could be offered. English and Welsh lore identified fairyland's queen as the center of power.[45] In the context of that belief, Shakespeare's depiction of Oberon as lording it over the drugged Titania serves as another of the play's many inversions. In Titania's case, this inversion involves both class (i.e., queen doting on a laborer; queen doting on a creature part man, part animal) and gender inversion (when not under the influence of drugs, she clearly has no problem denying Oberon's requests).[46]

The first encounter between Titania and Oberon highlights another of the fairy queen's standard attributes in popular lore: her sexual taste for mortal men. According to Oberon, Titania has disrupted several of Theseus's dalliances in order to seduce him herself (II.i.74–80). As Diane Purkiss notes, "The queen's sexual unruliness is a signifier both of her otherness and her power,"[47] hence the significance of the fact that Oberon uses the pansy juice not only to overpower Titania's otherwise indomitable will where the changeling child is concerned, but also to place her in a compromising position with a dim-witted peasant wearing an ass head.

Titania's conduct poses a direct challenge to the early modern rubric for the good wife, "chaste, silent and obedient."[48] She neither obeys nor prioritizes her spouse—her friendship with the votaress and the associated devotion that she has to the votaress's child, the changeling boy, are higher priorities for Titania. Discussing the "counterdiscourse" active within and activated by *MND*, Louis Montrose writes: "*A Midsummer Night's Dream* pinpoints some of the joints and stresses in the ideological structures that shaped the culture of which it is an instance; and it discloses—perhaps, in a sense, despite itself—that patriarchal norms are compensatory for men's perception that they are vulnerable to the powers of women."[49] Titania is an interesting figure to examine in the light of this logic, since she is a fantasy construct of a female figure with "real" power.[50]

Though we see Titania's world turned upside down during the period of misrule that constitutes most of the play's action, Titania is still the fairy queen. She is the wellspring of the alternative feminine power that the play explores since that exploration takes place in her realm—even if she has been incapacitated for the duration. Titania's status as fairy queen is an important aspect of Oberon's role as the lord of misrule. Oberon as fairy king "adopts" Helena, as it were, from the moment she enters the wood, linking her to the liminal zone he inhabits both by the interest he takes in her and by his identification of her as a kindred spirit—a nymph. As a male monarch in a realm ruled by a queen, Oberon is something between ruler and ruled. He is, therefore, sympathetic to the cause of a woman bold enough to pursue her love indecorously into the woods, but sufficiently insecure to whimper, "I am your spaniel; and, Demetrius, / The more you beat me I will fawn on you" (II.i.203–4).[51] Although Titania has not ordered him to take up the task, Oberon stands in a relation to Helena similar to that of Tom Reid with respect to Bessie Dunlop—he is her spirit world guardian. As lord of misrule, Oberon, and his miscreant messenger, Puck, are only too pleased to help Helena realize her unruly goal of reversing the age-old story of man chasing woman since, as Puck gleefully notes, "Those things do best please me / That befall preposterously" (III.ii.120–21).

Yet many critics read Oberon as subversive of Athenian patriarchal structures only, neglecting the matriarchal aura of fairyland. Mary Ellen Lamb, for example, asserts that "patriarchy is restored as Oberon overcomes Titania's brief rebellion against his wishes"[52] while Leonard Tennenhouse figures Oberon as "the traditional alternative to patriarchal law. . . . He is the figure of carnival."[53] This reading is only half right: Oberon is not merely the figure of misrule because he embodies alternatives to Theseus's patriarchal rigidity in act I, as Tennenhouse suggests here, but because he undermines the power of the fairy queen, who has apparently been able to deny him the changeling child he wants on her own strength prior to her incapacitation under the influence of Oberon's drug. Caroline Bicks goes even further, identifying Oberon as the "parallel ruler" to Theseus, who is plotting over the course of the play Titania's "*re*-appropriation into his bed and polity."[54] The problem with this logic is that to an early modern audience Titania would be the parallel ruler to Theseus. Oberon is merely appropriating her power—temporarily. Read through the lens of popular lore about fairies and the eminence of their queen, the act of defiance in the fairy realm of *A Midsummer Night's Dream* is not Titania's refusal to relinquish the Indian boy to Oberon, but Oberon's seizure of the boy from a furtively drugged Titania.

Changelings

The eye of the storm swirling around Oberon and Titania, wreaking havoc on the Athenian landscape, is the treasured Indian boy. A number of critics have discussed the absent presence of this child rendered charming through description alone.[55] In a sense, Oberon gains custody of a whole group of changelings—the four Athenian lovers as well as the Indian boy—once he decides to drug Titania.[56] *Changeling* was a rather elastic term in early modern England and could refer to any substitute for another person or to general fickleness in addition to the literal fairy brat substituted for a healthy human infant.[57] Given the virtual interchangeability of Helena and Hermia as far as Demetrius and Lysander are concerned once they are drugged, any and all of the four lovers could be construed as changelings. Despite his insistence on securing the Indian boy for his henchman, Oberon seems to lose interest in him once he has secured the child in his bower to focus instead on his *chère* apparent, Helena.

As does the fairy king who helps her, Helena gains the relationship she has so craved with a "changeling boy" of her own. Fickle Demetrius, who once professed to love her but then switched his allegiance to Hermia, has been sent ricocheting back to Helena again by virtue of Oberon's love drug. When Oberon directs Puck to release Lysander from his pansy-induced attachment to Helena to restore him to his rightful mistress, Hermia, he offers an herb "whose liquor hath this virtuous property, / To take from thence all error with his might" (III.ii.367–68). Later, when he applies this same herb himself to the eyes of the sleeping Titania to release her from the love juice spell, Oberon does so with these words: "Be as thou wast wont to be / See as thou wast wont to see" (IV i.70–71). She was wont to deny him the changeling boy—to exactly which manifestation of her former self, therefore, is Oberon restoring her? For an early modern audience familiar with the lore surrounding the fairy queen and the unquestioned centrality of her authority, the drug-induced free love antics of Titania would have been amusing in large part because of their anticipation of her return to her senses—and her return to control.

Titania stands in contrast to the lovers, whose transformations, G. K. Hunter argues, have to be preserved "to complete the pattern."[58] As do many other critics, Hunter here lumps together the experiences had by the lovers in the fairy wood although they are actually quite distinct. The one character in the text whose transformation is preserved in the final act is Demetrius.

Lysander's "transformation" does not count as such since it was a mistake—he is turned away from Hermia by accident, only to be turned right back again. Demetrius is the one character who has not been released from the influence of Oberon's pansy-juice drug in the final scene. At the play's conclusion, he is still Helena's drug-addled love slave. Demetrius is the only person who does not get what he wants from his sojourn in the fairy wood and he is deprived of success so that Helena may be accorded it.[59]

The chaos in the lovers' lives is sustained rather than alleviated in the woods to which they flee in hopes of succor by Puck; Oberon, who issues the orders for the use of the pansy drug, has no intention of causing Helena more heartache—he seeks only to solve her romantic problems. The confusion reaches its zenith, of course, in act III, when all four lovers are reunited and Helena's status as a changeling for Hermia—as the recipient of both Lysander's and Demetrius's affections—becomes apparent. Helena launches the name calling in the play's climactic catfight, addressing Hermia as "You counterfeit, you puppet, you!" (III.ii.288). The reference to Hermia as a "puppet" has fairy significance.[60] Robert Greene's play *The Scottish History of James IV*, for example, opens with a scene in which Oberon treats Bohan, a Scottish misanthrope, to a fairy dance "to gratulate" him for his hatred of the world. The testy Bohan scares the dancing sprites away and then asks, "What where those Puppits that hopt and skipt about me year whayle?" to which Oberon replies, "My subjects." Bohan scoffs, "Ha, ha, ha, thinkest thou those puppits can please me?"[61] Having been identified as puppet and nymph, respectively, both Hermia and Helena have been linked by label to the fairies by the middle of the play.

The language of fairydom (puppet and dwarf) coexists with that of May Day in Hermia's response. Her reference to Helena as a "painted maypole" returns the fairy compliment Helena paid her with "puppet" and simultaneously glances at the fact that Helena has gained the upper hand of her, since one of the figures of folklore popularly imagined as presiding over May Day's saturnalia was the Fairy Queen.[62] Hermia's enraged reply to Helena's taunt also reinforces the connection between her and the fairies suggested by Helena, since she identifies herself as "dwarfish":

"Puppet?" Why, so! Ay, that way goes the game. . . .
And are you grown so high in his esteem
Because I am so dwarfish and so low?
How low am I, thou painted maypole? Speak!
How low am I? I am not yet so low
But that my nails can reach unto thine eyes.
    (III.ii.289, 293–97)

Actually, it is not because Hermia is "dwarfish" that the tables have been turned at all, but because a dwarf's near kin, Puck, has exerted his influence over the situation.

Even Lysander gets in on the fairy insults eventually, piling up epithets that link Hermia to the fairies: "Get you gone, you dwarf! / You minimus, of hindering knotgrass made! / You bead, you acorn!" (III.ii.328–30). Though not, strictly speaking, fairies, dwarfs were considered inhabitants of fairyland. Referring to Hermia as an acorn looks back to the first fairy exchange staged in the play, in which Titania and Oberon's elves are depicted as hiding from the wrath of their mistress and master by creeping into acorn cups (II. i.30–31). By the end of the catfight, therefore, both Hermia and Helena have been firmly linked to the fairy realm, a connection that will prove to have a salvific effect on their romantic lives. In a certain sense, Oberon underscores the bankruptcy of his own behavior toward Titania in his stern chastisement of Puck for using the love juice to set up a love triangle contrary to the desires of a woman—Helena.[63] That is precisely the manner in which Oberon himself is employing the love juice—to override the desires of not only a woman, but his queen.[64]

As her husband has a penchant for Helena, Titania, too, has a history of great sympathy for a mortal woman, her deceased friend, the Indian votaress. The passage about her passionate devotion to the changeling boy for his mother's sake in the first fairy scene is crucial to understanding her refusal to hand him over to Oberon:

> The fairyland buys not the child of me.
> His mother was a vot'ress of my order,
> And in the spicèd Indian air by night
> Full often hath she gossiped by my side
> And sat with me on Neptune's yellow sands,
> Marking th'embarkèd traders on the flood,
> When we have laughed to see the sails conceive
> And grow big-bellied with the wanton wind;
> Which she, with pretty and with swimming gait,
> Following—her womb rich with my young squire—
> Would imitate.
>   (II.i.122–32)

Titania pours out her heart to her husband, exposing the full depth of her grief when her friend, "being mortal, of that boy did die" (II.i.135), emphasizing how close they were while she lived. Indeed, Caroline Bicks suggests, "In addition to evoking the relationship of mother and gossip, then, the two women appear to share a sexual past through their parentage of the child, a bond that erases the father altogether."[65] Seemingly hopeful that her explanation will suffice, Titania goes on graciously to invite Oberon to accompany her and her fairies in the "moonlight revels" being hosted for Theseus's wedding. In his reply, Oberon seems rather self-absorbed and petulant: "Give me that boy, and I will go with thee" (II.i.141, 143). The potence of emotional attachment and the pain that it can cause are not ideas that Oberon seems capable of comprehending when Titania describes them to him. This makes his immediate sympathy with Helena's plight all the more unlooked-for and ironic.

Stevie Davies argues that Oberon's jealousy over Titania's possession of the Indian boy

> seems invalidated by the power of the poetry in which Titania evokes her dead friend. The baby's mother was herself a "votaress" like Hermia and like Diana, and, like them, a point of mediation between mortal and immortal worlds. Titania dramatises a moment in a friendship which, natural, human and playful as it was, was also impossible. It was amity between a mortal and an immortal, on equal terms—gossiping, laughing, playing—upon the narrow margin between sea and land, experienced late in that transition between states of being which is the nine-month period of human pregnancy.[66]

The liminality that Davies identifies in this passage (the seashore, a pregnant woman about to deliver, a votaress who is mortal but spends her days in devotion to and contemplation of the immortal) serves as a reminder of the liminality of the fairies themselves.

Both Davies and Montrose contrast Titania's speech about her Indian votaress with Oberon's speech about the Imperial Votaress who just missed being struck by Cupid's shaft, which lighted instead on the pansy that produces Oberon's love-inducing herb.[67] Montrose notes: "The evocative monologues of Titania and Oberon are carefully matched and contrasted: The Faery Queen speaks of a mortal mother from the east; the Faery King speaks of an invulnerable virgin from the west. Their memories express two myths of origin: Titania provides a genealogy for the changeling and an explanation of why she will not part with him; Oberon provides an aetiology of the metamorphoses flower that he will use to make her part with him."[68] In Montrose's analysis it is Titania, the fairy queen, who is grounded in the life-and-death realities of the mortal realm and Oberon—who ultimately interferes in the mortal realm more over the course of the play's action who is associated with immortal invulnerability and magic. Such an approach belies the common critical division of the play's motifs into male and female principles. Typically, the male is construed to be the rational, ordering principle—Theseus dismisses the lovers' account of their evening as "these fairy toys" (V.i.3). In such dichotomous critical approaches the female thread in the play is the passionate, the fanciful—Hippolyta finds the lovers' tale savors of "something of great constancy" (V.i.26).[69] Yet this essentialist interpretation of the play's gender-divided visions ignores the examples offered by those figures of fancy the fairies themselves. Titania's friendship with a mortal woman and her unflinching acceptance of its consequences—"she, being mortal, of that boy did die" (II.i.134)—smacks of the grim refusal of hope-against-hope flights of fancy attributed in essentializing analysis to the masculine principle (i.e., Theseus rejects the lovers' "fairy" tale). On the other hand, Oberon's reality-defying insistence that Helena will have the man who spurns her and his reliance on magical herbs align him more with the fantastic faith attributed to the feminine principle (i.e., Hippolyta is willing to entertain the possibility of the lovers' tales of the fairy wood). This serves as yet another instance in which the fairies slip out of essentialist gender-based frames, suggesting that their mortal counterparts might do the same and, as Helena does, succeed.[70]

Irene Dash contends, "Although some critics consider Oberon's potion a symbol of love, as it applies to Titania it appears to be more a symbol of power, or at least of revenge for her failure to release the child."[71] However, one can also see its use on Demetrius as vengeful, too, since Oberon anoints his eyes not only because he wants to help Helena, but because he resents the way that Demetrius treats her. It is ironic that Oberon takes such umbrage at Demetrius' cruelty to Helena since he is not treating his own partner particularly well. It is also interesting that Oberon corrupts the purity of the pansy juice (given its myth of origin: a shaft deflected from Cupid by a vestal virgin) in using it to entangle Titania in an adulterous, animalistic union. What is really important, however, about Oberon's dependency on the pansy's power is the fact that he can only get the upper hand of Titania temporarily, by drugging her. Apparently, when her mind and her will are her own, she is an indomitable woman, wife, and queen.

Fairy Catechism

Despite its pagan setting, *MND* is book-ended with references to Christian teachings of ambiguous institutional affiliation, and its title savors suspiciously of throwback Catholicism. Among the dates that the reformers attempted to purge, but that hung on with a vengeance among the populace, was Midsummer Day, June 24. Although the Athenian pagan Theseus opines that the four sleeping lovers have been out to observe "the rite of

May" (IV.i.132), the specific titular reference to Midsummer is interesting, particularly in light of the "bonfires and floral garlands ... pageants and parades featuring artificial giants, dragons and hobby horses that barely coexisted with Christian tradition" used to celebrate it as late as the 1590s.[72] Even if the lovers were celebrating only the rite of May, as we have already seen in the discussion of the play's catfight, May Day had pagan (and fairy) associations as well. Despite its pagan setting, *MND* addresses some key Christian tenets: the obedience owed to fathers by their daughters, chastity, and the rejection of all gods save the one, true God.

In the first scene, Theseus threatens the intractable Hermia with a life of chastity that sounds remarkably like the Catholic sisterhood (although the play's setting is pre-Christian Athens) if she continues to defy her father's decision that she marry Demetrius. He cautions her to consider well:

> Whether, if you yield not to your father's choice,
> You can endure the livery of a nun,
> For aye in shady cloister mewed,
> To live a barren sister all your life,
> Chanting hymns to the cold fruitless moon.
> (I.1.69–73)

As Titania's memories of the changeling boy's mother and their relationship remind us, pagan goddesses had devotees who lived out their life in worship just as priests, monks, and nuns did in the Christian tradition. However, the terminology that Theseus uses has anachronistically pointed Christian reference.

Theseus says that Hermia will be held hostage in a "cloister" as a "barren sister." The earliest cloisters date from medieval times, and the female attendants of pagan shrines are referred to as votaresses or priestesses, but not typically addressed as "sister." Protestants did away with convents and did not ordain nuns.[73] While Catholic devotional practice is glanced at, it appears as a threat: "Either to die the death or to abjure / Forever the society of men" (I.i.65–66). Living as a "barren sister" is presented as at least equal to immediate death. This scene, therefore, offers no particular indication of Shakespeare's religious biases but does encapsulate some key doctrinal distinctions at issue during the Reformation. However, Hermia is saved from the barren sisterhood by her own boldness and daring, seconded by the fairies.[74]

The religious issues surging through the play reach their zenith in Bottom's garbled rendition of St. Paul's "Eye hath not seen" text after he is released from Puck's ass-head spell. Given Bottom's inspiration for his exegetical affront—a carnal relationship with the Queen of the Fairies—this foray into Christian spirituality also bears directly on the play's gender issues. Bottom has, in a sense, violated both the Pauline doctrine of chastity and the Mosaic injunction against false gods. He joins a long line of early modern English-, Scots-, and Welsh (wo)men prepared to swear before judge and jury to having been entertained by that paragon of fairy hospitality, the Fairy Queen.[75] The Fairy Queen is indisputably the most popular figure of fairy lore people claim to have met. She is also a pagan figure, placed firmly outside the bounds of Christian tradition by those concerned to cultivate and protect it. It is curious and in questionable taste for Shakespeare to have the still-dazed lover of the Fairy Queen, moved by his fresh memories of dallying in her bower, spout a woefully bastardized version of Paul's celebration of the boundlessness of God's love.[76]

Recent commentators on this scene have begun to grasp the significance of the bizarre placement of English biblical text in a peasant mouth still smacking with fairy kisses. Gail Kern Paster and Howard Skiles note, "The matter of supernatural belief could not have seemed trivial to Shakespeare's audience, caught up as they were in the ideological warfare between Protestant reformers and the Catholic Church. Bottom's interaction with fairy creatures ... might have seemed like a comic displacement of more urgent matters of faith or it might have seemed somewhat subversive."[77] However, Thomas Stroup claims that Bottom's speech reveals that "Bottom has discovered the bottom of God's secrets," proceeding to identify the fairies as spirits of God—not an interpretation that would be borne out by early modern belief.[78] Such a view would, in fact, be pure blasphemy. Discussing the same textual moment, Chris Hassel points out that Paul was associated by the Protestants with anti-Catholicism, and that, therefore, *MND* ends with a powerful affirmation of reform doctrine.[79]

In fact, Bottom's speech allows Shakespeare to have it both ways.[80] Catholics relied on mystery to hold the attention of the faithful, allowing communion only to the priest who recited the Mass ceremony in Latin. Protestants scoffed at this approach, perceiving it as a manipulative way for a weak institution to maintain control over its members. They advocated vernacular delivery of the church service and public access to biblical texts in addition to lay participation in the communion ritual. So, Latinate Catholics in Shakespeare's audience could blame Bottom's Bible botching on the Protestant provision of access to sacred mysteries beyond his comprehension. As Emma Wilby observes, "For those with a particularly obscure grasp of Christian teaching the cosmos would have been peopled by a medley of supernatural figures, of both Christian and pre-Christian origin, with little or no discrimination made between them, either morally or ontologically."[81] Whatever their grasp of the Scripture they studied, the Protestants in the audience could just as easily feel confident that Bottom makes such a bad job of his catechism because he is stumbling through a maze of Latin with no assistance. Protestants came to equate key Catholic tenets with fairy superstitions as a means of debunking both traditions. The spirit in which Shakespeare depicts Bottom, spouting crisscrossed scriptures with fairy dust fresh in his hair, is not at all clear. As are the fairies themselves, who are often reputed to be visible only out of the corner of one's eye, Shakespeare's religious sensibilities seem impossible to view straight on.

Conclusion

It is significant that the fairies are contained neither by the wood outside Athens nor by the play text itself.[82] In the epilogue they emerge in character from the action of the play proper to ask the audience's thanks for their performance and to send them on their way. As characters who are, by the final act, both no longer characters and still characters, they thus display their liminality even in their very relationship to Shakespeare's text and its representation. Just as they slip into Athens from out of the woods, they likewise slip into the Globe from out of *A Midsummer Night's Dream* in the epilogue. Richard Strier notes that Puck's final salvo "may well manifest a real anxiety that the learned Protestant 'gentles' in the audience will truly be tempted to 'reprehend' a play that at least might be (mistakenly) taken as hearkening back to the bad old days when Robin Goodfellow and Hob Goblin were credible, and before popery was 'sufficiently discovered.' . . . Being on the side of the fairies might not put us on the side of the angels."[83] It may well, however, put us on the side of the women.

The lovers in *A Midsummer Night's Dream* are ultimately united by a fairy force aligned with the female desires of both Helena and Hermia. I am not concerned with whether or not the play asserts the existence of fairies but, rather, the conditions of possibility for the things depicted as occurring under fairy influence. The play depicts not what *does* happen in marriage, but what *could* happen. Daphne could pursue Apollo. She could catch him, even. Daughters could step out of or—better still—refuse ever to enter the mold their father makes for them.[84] Wives and female rulers could have such puissance that they need to be incapacitated with drugs before their will can successfully be defied. The story, as Helena says, could be changed; acting in concert with the fairies, the women of *A Midsummer Night's Dream* show us how.

Notes

1. See R. Pitcairn, *Ancient Criminal Trials in Scotland* (Edinburgh, 1833), 49 fn. 4 and 51. My account relies primarily on the transcription of Bessie Dunlop's testimony in Pitcairn, but see also Alec Derwent Hope, *A Midsummer Eve's Dream: Variations on a Theme by William Dunbar* (New York: The Viking Press, 1970), esp.

90–93, and Lizanne Henderson and Edward J. Cowan, *Scottish Fairy Belief* (East Linton, Scotland: Tuckwell Press, 2001), esp. 84–85. For a complete list and synopsis of the 133 Scottish witchcraft depositions that involve fairy beliefs, see Julian Goodare and others, The Survey of Scottish Witchcraft, University of Edinburgh http://www.arts.ed.ac.uk/witches.

2. In Scottish dialect elves are analogous to fairies, the Scottish Elfame synonymous with fairyland. See Katherine Briggs, *The Vanishing People: Fairy Lore and Legends* (New York: Pantheon Books, 1978), glossary, and also Maureen Duffy's *The Erotic World of Faery* (London: Hodder, 1972), 35 fn. 18, where she observes that, even in England, the term *elf* was applied to figures now more popularly identified as fairies as late as 1300. Diane Purkiss helpfully precedes me in providing a rationale for using Scottish witchcraft testimony about fairies to explore their presence in early modern English drama. See *At the Bottom of the Garden: A Dark History of Fairies, Hobgoblins, and Other Troublesome Things* (New York: New York University Press, 2000), 87–88, and "Old Wives' Tales Retold: The Mutations of the Fairy Queen," *"This Double Voice": Gendered Writing in Early Modern England*, chap. 5, ed. Danielle Clarke and Elizabeth Clarke, 119, fn. 5 (New York: St. Martin's, 2000). See also Emma Wilby, who argues that "fairy beliefs played a more significant role in the creation and promulgation of beliefs concerning the witch's familiar than has been hitherto acknowledged." "The Witch's Familiar and the Fairy in Early Modern England and Scotland," *Folklore* 111 (2000): 283.

3. That is, "as she was going between her own house and the yard of Monk-castle" when "new risen out of childbed." Pitcairn, *Ancient Criminal Trials*, 51.

4. Katharine Briggs, *Fairies in Tradition and Literature* (London: Routledge and Kegan Paul, 1967), 119.

5. Dunlop is asked, "If she never asked him, Wherefore he came to her more than to anyone else?" Pitcairn, *Ancient Criminal Trials*, 56.

6. Reid helps Dunlop recall: "When she was lying in child-bed, a stout woman came in to her and sat down beside her and asked a drink of her, which she gave her; who also told her that her newborn child would die, and that her husband would mend of his sickness. The said Bessie answered that she remembered well thereof, and Tom said That was the Queen of Elfame his mistress, who had commanded him to wait upon her and do her good." Pitcairn, *Ancient Criminal Trials*, 56–57. Sir Walter Scott commiserates with the reader whose fairy fancies might be stifled at the thought of the Queen of Fairies as "a mere earthly gossip" and "be a little hurt at imagining the elegant Titania in the disguise of a *stout* woman, a heavy burden for a clumsy bench, drinking what Christopher Sly would have called very sufficient small-beer with a peasant's wife." See *Letters on Demonology and Witchcraft*, 2nd ed. (New York: The Citadel Press, 1970), emph. orig., 127–28.

7. Pitcairn goes on to note the singularity of this spirit's "use of the most pious salutations. . . . No doubt these were the common salutations of the Catholics of the Church of Rome of this period, but assuredly not lightly to be pronounced by such questionable characters as Thom." See *Ancient Criminal Trials*, 52. Lizanne Henderson and Edward J. Cowan also discuss the nostalgia for Catholicism inherent in Dunlop's testimony in *Scottish Fairy Belief*, 130.

8. Pitcairn, *Ancient Criminal Trials*, 56. The question posed to Dunlop is "What she thought of the new law? Answered, That she has spoken with Tom about that matter; but Tom answered, That this new law was not good; and that the old faith should come home again, but not such as it was before."

9. Ibid., 56 fn. 8.

10. Scott, *Letters*, 127.

11. Pitcairn, *Ancient Criminal Trials*, 53. Asked "If she had sought anything from Tom to help herself or any other?" Dunlop replies, "That when sundrie persons came to her to seek help . . . Tom gave her, out of his own hand, a thing like the root of a beet and bade her dry it and make powder of it and give it to sick persons and they should mend."

12. As Diane Purkiss puts it, "The fairy stories [in Scottish witchcraft testimony] I am going to be discussing are the sounds of silence in two senses. Firstly, they represent a moment when a normally silent group—women of the lower orders—makes an appearance as storytellers on the historical stage. Secondly, they represent the things those women could not ordinarily say." See "Sounds of Silence: Fairies and Incest in Scottish Witchcraft Stories," chap. 4, *Languages of Witchcraft: Narrative, Ideology and Meaning in Early Modern Culture*, ed. Susan Clark, 81 (London: Macmillan, 2001).

13. Pitcairn, *Ancient Criminal Trials*, 55.

14. As Diane Purkiss notes of Elspeth Reoch's testimony about fairy fraternization, "Elspeth's encounters occur at the two most common life moments for such encounters: the threshold of womanhood and the aftermath of childbirth." See "Sounds of Silence," 87.

15. Diane Purkiss compellingly asks of Titania's beautiful speech about her deceased Indian votaress: "what if Bessie Dunlop were to tell this story? What if this is Bessie's story, as seen by the queen of the fairies?" See *At the Bottom of the Garden*, 178. Purkiss discusses *A Midsummer Night's Dream* on pages 166–82.

16. *A Midsummer Night's Dream* was published in quarto in 1600, but it is listed in Francis Meres's *Palladis Tamia*, which was published in 1598, so the play was presumably written in the mid- to late 1590s. Floris Delattre argues that, in this era, "Just as most of the play-goers, the most thoroughly educated as well as the most ignorant, believed, when they saw the ghost of Hamlet's father striding across the stage, that such things would happen, thus the fairies of *A Midsummer-Night's Dream* even leaving aside their unparalleled, literary qualities, must have struck Shakespeare's contemporaries as well-known and, in fact, all but natural beings." *English Fairy Poetry from the Origins to the Seventeenth Century* (London: Henri Frowde, 1912), 127.

17. For example, the *Standard Dictionary of Folklore* asserts that fairyland "is ruled over by a king and queen, but generally the queen is dominant." See *Funk & Wagnalls Standard Dictionary of Folklore, Mythology, and Legend*, ed. Maria Leach and Jerome Fried (San Francisco: Harper & Row, 1984), 363. Sir Walter Scott notes of the fairies that "their government was always represented as monarchical. A King, *more frequently* a Queen of Fairies, was acknowledged; and sometimes both held their court together." *Letters*, emph. added, 105. See also Pitcairn's discussion of the court testimony offered by Isobel Gowdie, who professed to have met the Queen of Fairies; Wirt Sikes, *British Goblins: Welsh Folk-Lore, Fairy Mythology, Legends and Traditions* (London: Sampson Low, Marston, Searle, & Rivington, 1880), 14; and Emma Wilby, "The Witch's Familiar and the Fairy in Early Modern England and Scotland," *Folklore* 111 (2000): 283–305. As the seventeenth century wore on, it became more common to focus on the king of fairies in literature; however, this seems to be the result of the shift to a male ruler (James I) and of the fact that men had begun fully to appropriate the traditional beliefs for their own creative purposes. For examples of a dominant fairy

king, see Robert Greene (?), *The Scottish History of James the Fourth*, The Malone Society Reprints, ed. W. W. Greg (1598; reprint Oxford: Oxford University Press, 1921), *A Description of the King and Queene of Fayries, their habit, fare their abode, pompe, and state* (London: Richard Harper, 1635), and Thomas Randolph, *Amyntas or the Impossible Dowry, A Pastoral Acted before the King and Queen at White-hall* (London, 1638), published in *The Poems and Amyntas of Thomas Randolph*, ed. John Jay Parry (New Haven, CT: Yale University Press, 1917). Note that, with the exception of Greene's play, all of these examples date from the Jacobean era.

18. Speaking of Scottish witchcraft testimony regarding fairies, specifically, Diane Purkiss notes that "These stories not only undo our assumption that fairies are small gauzy-wingy thingies; they also undo the assumptions about the true nature of femininity which tend to accompany the gauzy-wingy beings." See "Sounds of Silence," 95.

19. See Dale Blount's "Modifications in Occult Folklore as a Comic Device in Shakespeare's *A Midsummer Night's Dream*," *Fifteenth-Century Studies* 9 (1984): 1–17; G. K. Hunter, "A Midsummer Night's Dream," *Shakespeare: The Late Comedies* (London: Longmans, Green & Co., Ltd., 1962), 7–20; Keith Sagar's "*A Midsummer Night's Dream*: A Marriage of Heaven and Hell," *Critical Survey* 7, no. 1 (1995): 34–43; and Minor White Latham, *The Elizabethan Fairies: The Fairies of Folklore and the Fairies of Shakespeare* (New York: Octagon Books, 1972), 176–218.

20. *Something of Great Constancy: The Art of "A Midsummer Night's Dream"* (New Haven, CT: Yale University Press, 1966), 29.

21. "'But We Are Spirits of Another Sort': The Dark Side of Love and Magic in *A Midsummer Night's Dream*" in *Medieval and Renaissance Studies*, ed. Siegfried Wenzel, 84 (Chapel Hill: University of North Carolina Press, 1978). Jan Kott makes a related argument about the fairies in *A Midsummer Night's Dream*, though he renders them evil incarnate, rather than a complex synthesis of good and evil. See "Titania and the Ass's Head," *Shakespeare, Our Contemporary*, trans. by Boleslaw Taborski, preface by Peter Brook (1965; reprint, New York: Norton, 1974), 207–28; and also Winfried Schleiner, "Imaginative Sources for Shakespeare's Puck," *Shakespeare Quarterly* 36, no. 1 (1985): 65–68; David Young, *Something of Great Constancy*, 26–29 and David Marshall, "Exchanging Visions: Reading *A Midsummer Night's Dream*," *Journal of English Literary History* 49 (1982): 543–75.

22. All textual references to *A Midsummer Night's Dream will* refer to *The Complete Works of Shakespeare*, 4th ed. ed. David Bevington, 147–77 (New York: Harper Collins Publishers, 1992).

23. Stephen Greenblatt discusses the questionable spiritual nature of the fairies with respect to their association with the dead specifically in *Hamlet in Purgatory* (Princeton, NJ: Princeton University Press, 2001), 162–64.

24. *Dream in Shakespeare: From Metaphor to Metamorphosis* (New Haven, CT: Yale University Press, 1974), 69.

25. "The Moon and the Fairies in *A Midsummer Night's Dream*," *University of Toronto Quarterly* 24, no. 3 (April 1955): 234.

26. *The Elizabethan Fairies: The Fairies of Folklore and the Fairies of Shakespeare* (New York: Octagon Books, 1972), 220–21. G. K. Hunter also acknowledges Puck's outsider status in the fairy world: "Shakespeare has indicated the difference between his fairies and the traditional spirits by having one of the latter as a member of his fairy court. . . . Puck supplies the element of mischief and even malice which is lacking in Shakespeare's other fairies." "A Midsummer Night's Dream," *Shakespeare: The*

Late Comedies (London: Longmans, Green & Co., Ltd., 1962), 16. Such an attitude toward Puck fails to acknowledge that although an outsider to fairyland, Puck is doing the bidding of its king, Oberon. One can only see Puck as the sole element of mischief in the play if one fails to see Oberon as malicious in his attitude toward and treatment of Titania.

27. Bevington also notes the manner in which Puck demonstrates his capacity for malicious mischief. See "'But We Are Spirits of Another Sort'" 80–92.

28. "Titania and the Ass's Head," *Shakespeare, Our Contemporary*, trans. by Boleslaw Taborski, preface by Peter Brook, (1965; reprint, New York: Norton, 1974), 218. Dorothea Kehler notes that "Kott now believes that *Dream* is susceptible to *light* as well as dark interpretations." See "*A Midsummer Night's Dream*: A Bibliographic Survey of the Criticism," in *A Midsummer Night's Dream: Critical Essays*, ed. Dorothea Kehler, 15 (New York: Garland Publishing, Inc., 1998).

29. William Shakespeare, *A Midsummer Night's Dream* (London, 1600), BL shelfmark C.34.K.30. See sig. B3 verso, sig. B4 recto, sig. D3 recto, and sig. F2 verso. The Newberry Library also owns a copy of the 1600 quarto, shelfmark Case 3A 894. The signatures of the two texts correspond in these passages.

30. Keith Sagar asserts, "Hermia says that she does not know 'by what power' she is made bold to refuse. The rest of the play defines that power and sets it up in opposition to the sterile and arbitrary legal power which governs Athens." "*A Midsummer Night's Dream*: A Marriage of Heaven and Hell," *Critical Survey* 7, no. 1 (1995): 38. In a powerful formulation of the role that the women play in *Dream*, Christy Desmet asserts: "First, the women of *Dream* usurp masculine rhetoric by speaking in the public sphere, disfiguring the patriarchal fictions that order erotic and social relationships in Shakespearean Athens. Second, they reconfigure that social rhetoric by offering alternative tropes for new ideals of love." See "Disfiguring Women with Masculine Tropes: A Rhetorical Reading of *A Midsummer Night's Dream*," in *A Midsummer Night's Dream: Critical Essays*, ed. Dorothea Kehler, 309 (New York: Garland Publishing, Inc., 1998).

31. Marshall asserts that "plays that end in marriage are not necessarily comedies . . . Is it asking too much of an antique fable and a fairy toy to be skeptical about the 'gentle concord' created by the sudden reconciliation and rearrangement of the lovers at the end of play?" "Exchanging Visions: Reading *A Midsummer Night's Dream*," *Journal of English Literary History* 49 (1982): 547.

32. As R. W. Dent observes, "The eventual pairings, then, are determined by Oberon, although always with the recognition that the heroines' choices are in some mysterious way right, that the pairings, to be 'true loves,' must correspond with their wishes." See "Imagination in *A Midsummer Night's Dream*," in *A Midsummer Night's Dream: Critical Essays*, ed. Dorothea Kehler, 90–91 (New York: Garland Publishing, Inc., 1998).

33. As for the fairies generally, whom Latham describes as committed to chastity, Robin Goodfellow would assist no "sluttish" maids; "nor would he lend his aid to men or women unless they conformed to his standard of morality in regard to love. If they were true lovers, he took a tremendous interest in their affairs, in which he meddled, until he brought about a happy consummation. So well known were his match-making instincts and his devotion to the cause of true love that his endeavors in this regard were recognized as one of his functions." *The Elizabethan Fairies: The Fairies of Folklore and the Fairies of Shakespeare* (New York: Octagon Books, 1972), 249.

34. Jean Howard and Phyllis Rackin, *Engendering a Nation: A Feminist Account of Shakespeare's English Histories*, Feminist Readings of Shakespeare (New York: Routledge, 1997), 36.

35. "Disfiguring Women with Masculine Tropes," 300.

36. David Marshall, "Exchanging Visions: Reading *A Midsummer Night's Dream*," *Journal of English Literary History* 49 (1982): 557.

37. Peter Holland reads this passage as "comic rather than genuinely dangerous." See "Theseus' Shadows in *A Midsummer Night's Dream*," *Shakespeare Survey* 47 (1994): 148. However, it is likely that an early modern audience would have at least entertained the possibility that Helena is in legitimate danger, particularly given Robin Goodfellow's role in her woodland sojourn. In *A Pleasant Comedie Called Wily Beguilde* (1606), for example, Robin oversees a whole variety of sexual indiscretions including a trumped-up rape charge and is credited with the ability to predict "how many Maides would be with childe in the / towne all the yeare after." He also professes the ability to "Effect such wonders in the world / That babes wil curse me, that are yet vnborne. / And honest women rob of their good name." Finally, in lines well suited to his shenanigans with the four lovers in *MND*, Robin asserts, "But the chiefe course of all my life, / Is to set discord betwixt man and wife." See The Malone Society Reprints, ed. W. W. Greg (Oxford: Oxford University Press, 1912), scene xv, lns. 1906–7, and scene xvi, lns. 2054–56 and 2061–62.

38. Rajiva Verma notes that "The liminal phase in seasonal group rites usually takes the form of a period of saturnalian misrule or carnival in which all social relations are turned topsy turvy." See *Myth, Ritual, and Shakespeare: A Study of Critical Theory and Practice* (New Delhi: Spantech Publishers, Pvt. Ltd., 1990), 80–81. Verma's identification of the period of misrule as a liminal phase underscores the way in which the fairies, as overseers of the woodland period of misrule that ultimately leads to the play's comedic conclusion, are liminal figures. It is significant that Helena—a woman—introduces the notion of inversion; as François Laroque puts it, "In the upside-down world of the forest and under the influence of Oberon's night-rule everything works backwards. . . . Midsummer misrule has turned into the rule of mis(s)!" See "Ovidian Transformations and Folk Festivities in *A Midsummer Night's Dream, The Merry Wives of Windsor* and *As You Like It*," *Cahiers Elisabethains* 25 (April 1984): 24.

39. As alluded to in the heading of this section, David Marshall claims that "the problem of Helena" lies in the fact that "she often seems to embody the opposites of the qualities shared by the other women in the play: defiance, self-respect, independence, dignity. Could it be to emphasize by contrast the paths that Hippolyta, Titania, and Hermia have not taken? . . ." "Exchanging Visions: Reading *A Midsummer Night's Dream*," *Journal of English Literary History* 49 (1982): 558. This casts Helena as the antifeminist foil against whom this trio of feminists in the rough shine the brighter. I find that Helena stands in a more complex relation to the other women characters than this, however, as my succeeding points will make clear.

40. "Titania and the Ass's Head," 216.

41. Dash notes that though "Seldom the subject for criticism, Helena has the largest percentage of lines (10.4) and words (11.2) of any woman character in the play although Hermia has more speeches (9.5 percent to Helena's 7.14)." *Women's Worlds in Shakespeare's Plays* (Newark: University of Delaware Press, 1997), 262 fn. 20. Lisa J. Moore, who portrayed Helena in 1994 at the Playhouse Theater in Seattle, adds, "Helena is the only one of the Lovers who soliloquizes." See "Transposing Helena

to Form and Dignity," in *A Midsummer Night's Dream: Critical Essays*, ed. Dorothea Kehler, 463 Garland Reference Library of the Humanities (New York: Garland Publishing, Inc., 1998).

42. Though he offers some suggestions for why this may not be an accurate assessment, Noel Williams notes, "Etymologies for *fairy* have generally been derived from words denoting female supernatural creatures in other languages. Thus it has been derived from the Latin *nympha*, and from Arabic *peri*." See "The Semantics of the Word *Fairy*: Making Meaning Out of Thin Air," in *The Good People: New Fairylore Essays*, ed. Peter Narváez, 462 (New York: Garland Publishing, 1991). This argues for a feminine inflection to the term *fairy* regardless of the gender assigned to the sprites by name. Helena's association with the fairies is reinforced later in the play when Demetrius awakes and his love-juice-streaked eyes light on Helena; one of the first epithets he applies to her is "nymph," He says, "O Helen, goddess, nymph, perfect, divine!" (III.ii.137),

43. "Sounds of Silence," 94.

44. See chapters two and three for a full discussion of the fairy queens in *Merry Wives* and *The Alchemist*.

45. Diane Purkiss observes that "The queen of the fairies is itself a rewriting of a range of stories, probably women's stories or old wives' tales, which survive only in fragmentary form, but which gesture at women's investment in the idea of a powerful and eroticized matriarchy which is not an object of desire but a possible fantasy self." See "Old Wives' Tales Retold: The Mutations of the Fairy Queen," *"This Double Voice": Gendered Writing in Early Modern England*, chap. 5, ed. Danielle Clarke and Elizabeth Clarke, 104 (New York: St. Martin's, 2000).

46. As Wendy Wall puts it, "Fairylore becomes a channel through which Shakespearean drama grapples with the class-specific practices that subtend debates about English community in the late sixteenth and early seventeenth centuries." See *Staging Domesticity: Household Work and English Identity in Early Modern Drama* (New York: Cambridge University Press, 2002), 95.

47. See "Old Wives' Tales Retold: The Mutations of the Fairy Queen," *"This Double Voice*," 110 and 116–17.

48. See the introductory material in *Rewriting the Renaissance: The Discourses of Sexual Difference in Early Modern Europe*, ed. Margaret W. Ferguson, Maureen Quilligan, and Nancy J. Vickers (Chicago: University of Chicago Press, 1986), xv–xxxi.

49. *The Purpose of Playing: Shakespeare and the Cultural Politics of the Elizabethan Theatre* (Chicago: University of Chicago Press, 1996), 151.

50. Irene Dash describes the ass-loving Titania as "the strongest and seemingly freest woman character in *A Midsummer Night's Dream*: Titania, the fairy queen, who so delights us at her first entrance and later raises questions about women's roles. Is she the victim of male power, male irrationality, trickery, or jealousy? Is she merely a fairy? Or does she illuminate the feelings and attitudes of women reacting to dominating male behavior?" *Women's Worlds in Shakespeare's Plays* (Newark: University of Delaware Press, 1997), 83.

51. One could well question the wisdom of Helena's choice of Demetrius since he consistently conducts himself as an abusive ass until he is drugged. However, such considerations are beyond the scope of the present discussion. The point is that regardless of Helena's prudence (or lack thereof), she, gets the man that she wants by the final curtain.

52. "Taken by the Fairies: Fairy Practices and the Production of Popular Culture in *A Midsummer Night's Dream*," *Shakespeare Quarterly* 51, no. 3 (Autumn 2000): 309.

53. "Strategies of State and Political Plays: *A Midsummer Night's Dream, Henry IV, Henry V, Henry VIII*," in *Political Shakespeare: Essays in Cultural Materialism*, 2nd ed. ed. Jonathan Dollimore and Alan Sinfield, 111 (Ithaca, NY: Cornell University Press, 1994).

54. *Midwiving Subjects in Shakespeare's England* (Burlington, VT: Ashgate, 2003), 85, emph. mine.

55. Kate Chedzgoy discusses the fact that the changeling is not represented in the play in *Shakespeare's Queer Children: Sexual Politics and Contemporary Culture* (Manchester: Manchester University Press, 1995). Stevie Davies also notes the conspicuous absence of the changeling boy, but she places any thought of him in act V with the *reading* audience, rather than any of the characters on the stage. See *The Feminine Reclaimed: The Idea of Woman in Spenser, Shakespeare and Milton* (Lexington: University Press of Kentucky, 1986), 128.

56. Marshall notes "The changeling comes to represent all of the characters in the play who are traded or fought over as property . . . the other characters are changelings in the sense that the play's plot revolves around their exchanges: their substitutions and their interchangeability. . . . The changeling boy is mysteriously absent in *A Midsummer Night's Dream*, but in a sense he is everywhere; the play casts its characters as changelings." "Exchanging Visions: Reading *A Midsummer Night's Dream*," *Journal of English Literary History* 49 (1982): 568–69.

57. According to the *OED*, as early as 1555 the term could be applied to "a fickle or inconstant person" or any "person or thing (surreptitiously) put in exchange for another" and not just a fairy-switched infant. Since it is the men who are inconstant in *MND* whereas women are stereotypically associated with flightiness, this suggests yet one more of the play's reversals of popularly conceived gender roles.

58. "A Midsummer Night's Dream," *Shakespeare: The Late Comedies* (London: Longmans, Green & Co., Ltd., 1962), 9.

59. Flabbergasted by the implications of the fairy intervention into human love affairs, David Marshall wonders: "How are we to take Demetrius' recovery from the 'sickness' of abandoning Helena and loving Hermia since it is just as much the product of enchantment as Lysander's abandonment of Hermia and love for Helena? Are we to be pleased by the success of Helena's subjection of herself to Demetrius or Titania's sudden and manipulated surrender to Oberon?" See "Exchanging Visions: Reading *A Midsummer Night's Dream*," *Journal of English Literary History* 49 (1982): 548. These are excellent questions that suggest numerous ways to approach the central plot points from a woman-focused perspective.

60. Scott Cutler Shershow links the etymylogical root of puppet, *pupa*, to the term *nymph* and notes the feminine inflection of both terms:

> The original Latin word *pupa* has also been adopted unchanged into English as a biological term for the intermediate stage in the life cycle of certain insects: the "chrysalis" or "nymph" between the caterpillar and the butterfly. *Nymph* and *nympha* are also recorded in the seventeenth century as scientific (and occasionally poetic) terms for the labia minora. . . . The pervasive, overdetermined etymological link between the performing object and the female body suggests

that conventional philosophic and scientific vision of the latter, consolidated in authoritative medical texts from Aristotle to Galen to the scholastics and beyond, as an inverted, imperfect, or incomplete version of the male body, a puppet-like vessel providing passive material for the active masculine form.

See *Puppets and "Popular" Culture* (Ithaca, NY: Cornell University Press, 1995), 70. Suggesting the questionable spiritual stature of fairies, at the St. Osyth witch trial (1582), in Essex, imps or familiars were identified as "puppets, spirits, or mammettes." A bit further on, *puppet* and *mammet* are used as proper names for familiars. Alice Manfield testifies that she has four imps, the last of which is "Puppet alias Mamet." Puppet seems to be a "she" familiar—the weaker sort, according to Ursula Kemp's testimony. See *The Witchcraft Papers: Contemporary Records of the Witchcraft Hysteria in Essex, 1560–1700*, ed. Peter Haining, 56 and 58 (London: Robert Hale & Company, 1974). Finally, Lewis Spence uses the term *puppet* to describe the "stocks" left in place of women and children abducted by the fairies. See *The Fairy Tradition in Britain* (New York: Rider and Company, 1948), 242.

61. *The Scottish History of James the Fourth*, The Malone Society Reprints, W. W. Greg, ed. (1598; reprint Oxford: Oxford University Press, 1921), lns. 20–21 and 80.

62. C. L. Barber notes that the May Lady's role could be played by "Many pagan goddesses, as well as nymphs," and goes on to note, "On other occasions there is an English name for the goddess, the Fairy Queen; she may come with her maids to dance and sing in the garden." *Shakespeare's Festive Comedy: A Study of Dramatic Form in Relation to Social Custom*, 2nd. ed. (Princeton, NJ: Princeton University Press, 1972), 34. Such an identificatory association, incidentally, aligns Helena once again with the topos of inversion since the maypole is the centerpiece of a public saturnalian celebration.

63. Dash notes Oberon's seemingly contradictory uses of the magic herb: "Ironically, Oberon, who would have the fairy queen exhibit the kind of self-abasement practiced by Helena, expresses great sympathy for the mortal woman." *Women's Worlds*, 94.

64. The uses to which Oberon puts the love juice simultaneously align him with and distinguish him from his demonic spiritual counterparts, witches. Frances Dolan notes that in the witchcraft plays of the early modern era, supernatural influence in love relationships typically affected men negatively while it impacted women positively. With respect to witches, specifically, Dolan contends:

> Playing on conceptions of sexual desire as invading from without, the drama explores the role of such malicious outsiders in instilling, removing or manipulating eros, which was already understood as invasive. This interference focuses on men. Whether they seek the witch's assistance or are the victims of her spells, magic works to frustrate and humiliate them and to support women's integrity and self-determination. Many witch plays focus on the coercion of sexual choice—rape and enforced marriage; but while physical, financial, and parental pressures act to constrain women, witches do not. When male characters turn to witches as a means to secure women's love, the witches consistently refuse to provide this service. They can interfere with intercourse, but they cannot control love, which is depicted

as too deeply rooted in the subject's consciousness to be tampered with. As this works out in the plots, witches can manipulate male characters' sexual responses but cannot interfere in female characters' feelings, desires, or wills.

See *Dangerous Familiars: Representations of Domestic Crime in England, 1550–1700* (Ithaca, NY: Cornell University Press, 1994), 215. While this description fits very well what transpires between Helena and Demetrius, fairy magic seems to differ from witchcraft in its capacity to interfere in female characters' feelings, desires, and wills since Titania develops a healthy lust for an ass-polled weaver and loses the force of her will to oppose Oberon's demand for the changeling boy (at least temporarily) under its influence.

65. See *Midwiving Subjects in Shakespeare's England*, 31. Bicks's reading of the Indian votaress/Titania/Oberon triangle is excellent, with the caveat that she sees Oberon as the center of power.

66. *The Feminine Reclaimed*, 126.

67. In that passage, Oberon tells Puck:

> . . . I saw, but thou couldst not,
> Flying between the cold moon and the earth
> Cupid, all armed. A certain aim he took
> At a fair vestal thronèd by the west,
> And loosed his love shaft smartly from his bow
> As it should pierce a hundred thousand hearts;
> But I might see young Cupid's fiery shaft
> Quenched in the chaste beams of the watery moon,
> And the imperial vot'ress passèd on,
> In maiden meditation, fancy-free.
> Yet marked I where the bolt of Cupid fell:
> It fell upon a little western flower,
> Before milk-white, now purple with love's wound.
> (II.i.156–67)

It is fitting that Oberon, monarch by marriage of the fairy realm, is able to see Cupid in flight between the Earth and the Moon—the same sort of ambiguous region neither in the heavens nor of the earth that the fairies themselves inhabit.

68. *The Purpose of Playing: Shakespeare and the Cultural Politics of the Elizabethan Theatre* (Chicago: University of Chicago Press, 1996), 170.

69. As C. L. Barber and René Girard, among others, do, David P. Young addresses the fact that Hippolyta has a point when she says that the lovers' story is rather persuasive: "In the play's terms, there are such things as fairies, and, by extension, there is truth in antique fables and fairy toys. . . . Theseus has conveniently forgotten what we remember hearing in the first act: that he, like the lovers, like Bottom, was once a fairy victim too, led 'through the glimmering night' by Titania herself, who has followed his fortunes and come to bless his wedding." *Something of Great Constancy*, 139.

70. Thus, I disagree with Barbara Freedman's view that "Oberon's manipulation of vision, however tricky, ultimately affirms a patriarchal ideology that equates men with right perspective and women with an irrational nature that defies orderly

sight." See "Dis/Figuring Power: Censorship and Representation in *A Midsummer Night's Dream*," in *A Midsummer Night's Dream: Critical Essays*, ed. Dorothea Kehler, 206 (New York: Garland Publishing, Inc., 1998).

71. *Women's Worlds*, 96.

72. For these and other details about Midsummer Day, see David Cressy, *Bonfires & Bells: National Memory and the Protestant Calendar in Elizabethan and Stuart England* (Berkeley: University of California Press, 1989), 25–26. The quoted material is from page 26.

73. Henry VIII ordered the dissolution of the monasteries (including convents) in 1536 and 1539. Patricia Crawford, *Women and Religion in England, 1500–1720* (New York: Routledge, 1993), 22.

74. Keith Sagar refers specifically to the punishment that Theseus offers Hermia for refusing to marry Demetrius as "to become a nun." He contends that this barren, unappealing form of spirituality is set off against the vibrant fertility of the play's other sort of spirits, the fairies, who oversee the play's marriages. "*A Midsummer Night's Dream*: A Marriage of Heaven and Hell," *Critical Survey* 7, no. 1 (1995): 38–39.

75. For the original testimony provided by these and other visitors to fairyland, see Pitcairn's *Ancient Criminal Trials*. Diane Purkiss discusses the matriarchal, sexualized world of fairyland with respect to *MND* and the testimony of one Andro Man, professed lover of the fairy queen for thirty-two years. See *At the Bottom of the Garden*, 134–39; see also Henderson and Cowan, *Scottish Fairy Belief*, 58, and Alec Derwent Hope, *A Midsummer Eve's Dream: Variations on a Theme by William Dunbar* (New York: The Viking Press, 1970), 92.

76. Marjorie Garber contends that both Titania's bower and the serpent in Hermia's dream function as in-text allusions to the Genesis account of the Eden myth. See *Dream in Shakespeare: From Metaphor to Metamorphosis* (New Haven, CT: Yale University Press, 1974), 72. See also Marina Warner's *From the Beast to the Blonde: On Fairy Tales and Their Tellers* (New York: Farrar, Straus & Giroux, 1994), 144–45, for a discussion of the associative links between witches and asses, particularly with respect to sexuality.

77. *A Midsummer Night's Dream: Texts and Contexts*, ed. Gail Kern Paster and Skiles Howard (New York: Bedford/St. Martin's, 1999), 307–8.

78. "Bottom's Name and His Epiphany," *Shakespeare Quarterly* 29, no. 1 (Winter 1978): 81.

79. R. Chris Hassel, Jr., "Saint Paul and Shakespeare's Romantic Comedies," *Thought* 46 (1971): 377.

80. Roland Frye also finds Shakespeare's works ambivalent or, at best, enigmatic on questions of religious dogma. *Shakespeare and Christian Doctrine* (Princeton, NJ: Princeton University Press, 1963).

81. "The Witch's Familiar and the Fairy in Early Modern England and Scotland," *Folklore 111* (2000): 301–2.

82. David P. Young emphasizes the importance of the fairies' reappearance in act V of the play, noting that "Theseus unwittingly adds the final twist by announcing that it is 'almost fairy time.' Then, as the mortals leave the stage, Puck replaces them with his superb nocturnal litany and all the fairies troop in to bless the marriages. By coming round to 'fairy time' again, the play asserts the validity and constancy of both its worlds, day and night, reason and imagination." *Something of Great Constancy*, 88–89. The return of the fairies is certainly important, as is the fact that they may oversee the goings on in the wood but are not confined to it.

83. The title of Strier's article makes clear why he would find such a reading of the play's epilogue mistaken: "Shakespeare and the Skeptics," *Religion and Literature* 32, no. 2 (Summer 2000): 180.

84. I am referring here to Theseus's act I injunction to Hermia:

> To you your father should be as a god—
> One that composed your beauties, yea, and one
> To whom you are but as a form in wax
> By him imprinted, and within his power
> To leave the figure or disfigure it.
> (I.i.47–51)

Chronology

1564	William Shakespeare christened at Stratford-on-Avon April 26.
1582	Marries Anne Hathaway in November.
1583	Daughter Susanna born, baptized on May 26.
1585	Twins Hamnet and Judith born, baptized on February 2.
1587	Shakespeare goes to London, without family.
1589–1590	*Henry VI, Part 1* written.
1590–1591	*Henry VI, Part 2* and *Henry VI, Part 3* written.
1592–1593	*Richard III* and *The Two Gentlemen of Verona* written.
1593	Publication of *Venus and Adonis*, dedicated to the Earl of Southampton; the *Sonnets* probably begun.
1593	*The Comedy of Errors* written.
1593–1594	Publication of *The Rape of Lucrece*, also dedicated to the Earl of Southampton. *Titus Andronicus* and *The Taming of the Shrew* written.
1594–1595	*Love's Labour's Lost, King John*, and *Richard II* written.
1595–1596	*Romeo and Juliet* and *A Midsummer Night's Dream* written.
1596	Son Hamnet dies.

1596–1597	*The Merchant of Venice* and *Henry IV, Part 1* written; purchases New Place in Stratford.
1597–1598	*The Merry Wives of Windsor* and *Henry IV, Part 2* written.
1598–1599	*Much Ado About Nothing* written.
1599	*Henry V, Julius Caesar,* and *As You Like It* written.
1600–1601	*Hamlet* written.
1601	*The Phoenix and the Turtle* written; father dies.
1601–1602	*Twelfth Night* and *Troilus and Cressida* written.
1602–1603	*All's Well That Ends Well* written.
1603	Shakespeare's company becomes the King's Men.
1604	*Measure for Measure* and *Othello* written.
1605	*King Lear* written.
1606	*Macbeth* and *Antony and Cleopatra* written.
1607	Marriage of daughter Susanna on June 5.
1607–1608	*Coriolanus, Timon of Athens,* and *Pericles* written.
1608	Mother dies.
1609	Publication, probably unauthorized, of the quarto edition of the *Sonnets*.
1609–1610	*Cymbeline* written.
1610–1611	*The Winter's Tale* written.
1611	*The Tempest* written. Shakespeare returns to Stratford, where he will live until his death.
1612	*A Funeral Elegy* written.
1612–1613	*Henry VIII* written; The Globe Theatre destroyed by fire.
1613	*The Two Noble Kinsmen* written (with John Fletcher).
1616	Daughter Judith marries on February 10; Shakespeare dies April 23.
1623	Publication of the First Folio edition of Shakespeare's plays.

Contributors

HAROLD BLOOM is Sterling Professor of the Humanities at Yale University. He is the author of 30 books, including *Shelley's Mythmaking, The Visionary Company, Blake's Apocalypse, Yeats, A Map of Misreading, Kabbalah and Criticism, Agon: Toward a Theory of Revisionism, The American Religion, The Western Canon,* and *Omens of Millennium: The Gnosis of Angels, Dreams, and Resurrection. The Anxiety of Influence* sets forth Professor Bloom's provocative theory of the literary relationships between the great writers and their predecessors. His most recent books include *Shakespeare: The Invention of the Human,* a 1998 National Book Award finalist, *How to Read and Why, Genius: A Mosaic of One Hundred Exemplary Creative Minds, Hamlet: Poem Unlimited, Where Shall Wisdom Be Found?,* and *Jesus and Yahweh: The Names Divine.* In 1999, Professor Bloom received the prestigious American Academy of Arts and Letters Gold Medal for Criticism. He has also received the International Prize of Catalonia, the Alfonso Reyes Prize of Mexico, and the Hans Christian Andersen Bicentennial Prize of Denmark.

RENÉ GIRARD is professor emeritus at Stanford University. He authored numerous works, including *A Theater of Envy: William Shakespeare* and *Violence and the Sacred.*

WILLIAM W. E. SLIGHTS is professor emeritus at the University of Saskatchewan and the author of *The Heart in the Age of Shakespeare, Managing Readers: Printed Marginalia in English Renaissance Books,* and other titles.

JAY L. HALIO is professor emeritus at the University of Delaware. He edited works of Shakespeare for various publishers, edited collections of

175

essays on various Shakespeare works, and authored books, including *Understanding Shakespeare's Plays in Performance*.

JAMES L. CALDERWOOD is professor emeritus at the University of California, Irvine. He authored *Shakespearean Metadrama*, which covers several plays, including *A Midsummer Night's Dream*. Also among his work is *A Midsummer Night's Dream* for the Twayne's New Critical Introductions to Shakespeare series.

DAVID WILES is a professor of theater at Royal Holloway College, University of London, where he also has been involved with various productions. His publications include *Shakespeare's Clown: Actor and Text in the Elizabethan Playhouse* and *A Short History of Western Performance Space*.

STANLEY WELLS is professor emeritus of the University of Birmingham. He was director of its Shakespeare Institute for several years. He is a general editor of *The Oxford Shakespeare: The Complete Works* and co-editor of *The Oxford Companion to Shakespeare* and *The Cambridge Companion to Shakespeare*. He also edited *A Midsummer Night's Dream* for the New Penguin Shakespeare.

W. H. AUDEN was a poet, essayist, playwright, editor, and librettist. He was Professor of Poetry at the University of Oxford and taught at several universities in the United States. He wrote many volumes of poetry and edited or co-edited many anthologies, including *Poets of the English Language*.

KENNETH BURKE was an independent intellectual whose writings influenced a range of academic fields. He was the author of many books, including *A Grammar of Motives*, *A Rhetoric of Motives*, and *Essays Toward a Symbolic of Motives*.

REGINA BUCCOLA is an associate professor at Roosevelt University in Chicago. She is co-editor of *Marian Moments in Early Modern Drama* and she has published essays, reviews, and poetry as well.

Bibliography

Abraham, F. Murray. *A Midsummer Night's Dream*. London: Faber and Faber, 2005.

Barber, C. L. *The Whole Journey: Shakespeare's Power of Development*. Berkeley: University of California Press, 1986.

Baxter, John. "Growing to a Point: Mimesis in *A Midsummer Night's Dream*." *English Studies in Canada* 22, no. 1 (March 1996): 17–33.

Blits, Jan H. *The Soul of Athens: Shakespeare's* A Midsummer Night's Dream. Lanham, Md.: Lexington Books, 2003.

Calderwood, James L. *A Midsummer Night's Dream*. New York: Twayne Publishers, 1992.

Comtois, M. E. "The Comedy of the Lovers in *A Midsummer Night's Dream*." *Essays in Literature* 12, no. 1 (Spring 1985): 15–25.

Crosman, Robert. "What Is the Dream in *A Midsummer Night's Dream*?" *Annotations: A Journal for Critical Debate* 7, no. 1 (1997–1998): 1–17.

Dutton, Richard, ed. *A Midsummer Night's Dream*. New York: St. Martin's Press, 1996.

Fike, Matthew. *A Jungian Study of Shakespeare: The Visionary Mode*. New York: Palgrave Macmillan, 2009.

Grady, Hugh. "Shakespeare and Impure Aesthetics: The Case of *A Midsummer Night's Dream*." *Shakespeare Quarterly* 59, no. 3 (Fall 2008): 274–302.

Hackett, Helen. *A Midsummer Night's Dream*. Plymouth, U.K.: Northcote House in association with the British Council, 1997.

Halio, Jay L. *A Midsummer Night's Dream*. Manchester [England]; New York: Manchester University Press; New York: distributed exclusively in the USA and Canada by St. Martin's Press, 1994.

————. A Midsummer Night's Dream: *A Guide to the Play*. Westport, Conn.: Greenwood Press, 2003.

Holland, Peter. "Theseus' Shadows in *A Midsummer Night's Dream*." *Shakespeare Survey* 47 (1994): 139–51.

Honigmann, E. A. J. *British Academy Shakespeare Lectures 1980–89*. Oxford: Oxford University Press, 1993.

————. *Myriad-Minded Shakespeare: Essays on the Tragedies, Problem Comedies and Shakespeare the Man*. Basingstoke, England; New York: Macmillan; St. Martin's, 1998.

Huffman, Clifford Chalmers, ed. Love's Labor's Lost, A Midsummer Night's Dream, *and* The Merchant of Venice: *An Annotated Bibliography of Shakespeare Studies, 1888–1994*. Binghamton, N.Y.: Medieval & Renaissance Texts & Studies, 1995.

Hunt, Maurice. "Individuation in *A Midsummer Night's Dream*." *South Central Review* 3, no. 2 (Summer 1986): 1–13.

————. "A Speculative Political Allegory in *A Midsummer Night's Dream*." *Comparative Drama* 34, no. 4 (Winter 2000–2001): 423–53.

————. "The Voices of *A Midsummer Night's Dream*." *Texas Studies in Literature and Language* 34, no. 2 (Summer 1992): 218–38.

Kehler, Dorothea, ed. A Midsummer Night's Dream: *Critical Essays*. New York: Routledge, 2001.

Kennedy, Judith M., and Richard F. Kennedy. *A Midsummer Night's Dream*. London; New Brunswick, N.J.: Athlone Press; Somerset, N.J.: distributed in the United States by Transaction Publishers, 1999.

Knowles, Ronald, ed. *Shakespeare and Carnival: After Bakhtin*. New York: St. Martin's Press, 1998.

Kott, Jan. "Bottom and the Boys." *New Theatre Quarterly* 9, no. 36 (November 1993): 307–15.

McGinn, Colin. *Shakespeare's Philosophy: Discovering the Meaning Behind the Plays*. New York: HarperCollins, 2006.

Montrose, Louis. *The Purpose of Playing: Shakespeare and the Cultural Politics of the Elizabethan Theatre*. Chicago: University of Chicago Press, 1996.

Nostbakken, Faith. *Understanding* A Midsummer Night's Dream: *A Student Casebook to Issues, Sources, and Historical Documents*. Westport, Conn.: Greenwood Press, 2003.

Nuttall, A. D. "*Midsummer Night's Dream*: Comedy as Apotrope of Myth." *Shakespeare Survey* 53 (2000): 49–59.

Paster, Gail Kern, ed. "*A Midsummer Night's Dream*: Texts and Contexts." Boston: Bedford, 1999.

Patterson, Annabel. "Bottom's Up: Festive Theory in *A Midsummer Night's Dream*." *Renaissance Papers* (1988): 25–39.

Pennington, Michael. A Midsummer Night's Dream: *A User's Guide*. London: Nick Hern, 2005.

Rhoads, Diana Akers. *Shakespeare's Defense of Poetry:* A Midsummer Night's Dream *and* The Tempest. Lanham, Md.: University Press of America, 1985.

Shulman, Jeffrey. "Bottom Is Up: The Role of Illusion in *A Midsummer Night's Dream.*" *Essays in Arts and Sciences* 16 (May 1987): 9–21.

Stavig, Mark. *The Forms of Things Unknown: Renaissance Metaphor in* Romeo and Juliet *and* A Midsummer Night's Dream. Pittsburgh: Duquesne University Press, 1995.

Taylor, A. B. "'When Everything Seems Double': Peter Quince, the Other Playwright in *A Midsummer Night's Dream.*" *Shakespeare Survey* 56 (2003): 55–66.

Taylor, Mark. *Shakespeare's Imitations*. Newark: University of Delaware Press; London; Cranbury, N.J.: Associated University Presses, 2002.

Turner, Henry S. *Shakespeare's Double Helix*. London; New York: Continuum, 2007.

Watts, Cedric. "Fundamental Editing: In *A Midsummer's Night Dream*, Does 'Bottom' Mean 'Bum'? And How About 'Arse' and 'Ass'?" *Anglistica Pisana* 3, no. 1 (2006): 215–22.

Wells, Stanley. "*A Midsummer Night's Dream* Revisited." *Critical Survey* 3 (1991): 14–29.

Wells, Stanley, and Lena Cowen Orlin, ed. *Shakespeare: An Oxford Guide*. New York: Oxford University Press, 2003.

White, Martin. *A Midsummer Night's Dream*. Basingstoke, England; New York: Palgrave Macmillan, 2009.

Wilson, Richard. *Secret Shakespeare: Studies in Theatre, Religion, and Resistance*. Manchester, England: Manchester University Press, 2004.

Acknowledgments

René Girard, "Bottom's One-Man Show." From *The Current in Criticism: Essays on the Present and Future of Literary Theory*, edited by Clayton Koelb and Virgil Lokke. © 1987 by Purdue University Press. Unauthorized duplication not permitted.

William W. E. Slights, "The Changeling in *A Dream*." From *Studies in English Literature* 28, no. 2 (Spring 1988): 259–72. Copyright © 1988 by and reprinted with permission of *Studies in English Literature* 1500–1900.

Jay L. Halio, "Nightingales That Roar: The Language of *A Midsummer Night's Dream*." From *Traditions and Innovations: Essays on British Literature of the Middle Ages and the Renaissance*, edited by David G. Allen and Robert A. White. © 1990 by Associated University Presses.

James L. Calderwood, "*A Midsummer Night's Dream*: Anamorphism and Theseus' Dream." From *Shakespeare Quarterly* 42, no. 4 (Winter 1991): 409–30. © 1991 by Folger Shakespeare Library. Reprinted with permission of The Johns Hopkins University Press.

David Wiles, "*A Midsummer Night's Dream* as Epithalamium." From *Shakespeare's Almanac:* A Midsummer Night's Dream, *Marriage and the Elizabethan Calendar.* © 1993 by David Wiles.

Stanley Wells, "Translations in *A Midsummer Night's Dream*." From *Translating Life: Studies in Transpositional Aesthetics,* edited by Shirley Chew and Alistair Stead. © 1999 by Liverpool University Press.

W. H. Auden, "*A Midsummer Night's Dream.*" From *Lectures on Shakespeare*, reconstructed and edited by Arthur Kirsch. © 2000 by the Estate of W. H. Auden. Reprinted by permission of Curtis Brown, Ltd.

Kenneth Burke, "Why *A Midsummer Night's Dream?*" From *Shakespeare Quarterly* 57, no. 3 (Fall 2006): 297–308. © 2006 by and reprinted with permission of the Kenneth Burke Literary Trust.

Regina Buccola, "'The Story Shall Be Changed': The Fairy Feminism of *A Midsummer Night's Dream.*" From *Fairies, Fractious Women, and the Old Faith: Fairy Lore in Early Modern British Drama and Culture.* © 2006 by Rosemont Publishing and Printing Corporation.

Index